Islam in Hong Kong

A series on socio-economic and cultural changes in Hong Kong

Hong Kong Culture and Society

General Editors
Gerard A. Postiglione   Faculty of Education,
                         The University of Hong Kong
Tai-lok Lui   Department of Sociology,
                         The University of Hong Kong

Panel of Advisors
Ambrose King   The Chinese University of Hong Kong
Alvin So   The Hong Kong University of Science and Technology
Siu-lun Wong   The University of Hong Kong

Other titles in the series

The Dynamics of Social Movements in Hong Kong
Edited by Stephen Wing-kai Chiu and Tai-lok Lui

Consuming Hong Kong
Edited by Gordon Mathews and Tai-lok Lui

At Home with Density
Nuala Rooney

Toward Critical Patriotism: Student Resistance to Political Education in Hong Kong and China
Gregory P. Fairbrother

Changing Church and State Relations in Hong Kong, 1950–2000
Beatrice Leung and Shun-hing Chan

Collaborative Colonial Power: The Making of the Hong Kong Chinese
Law Wing Sang

Desiring Hong Kong, Consuming South China: Transborder Cultural Politics, 1970–2010
Eric Kit-wai Ma

Repositioning the Hong Kong Government: Social Foundations and Political Challenges
Edited by Stephen Wing-kai Chiu and Siu-lun Wong

Culture and Society

Islam in Hong Kong

Muslims and Everyday Life in China's World City

Paul O'Connor

香港大學出版社
HONG KONG UNIVERSITY PRESS

Hong Kong University Press
The University of Hong Kong
Pokfulam Road
Hong Kong
www.hkupress.org

© Hong Kong University Press 2012

ISBN 978-988-8139-57-6 (*Hardback*)
ISBN 978-988-8139-58-3 (*Paperback*)

All rights reserved. No portion of this publication may be reproduced or transmitted in any form or by any means, electronic or mechanical, including photocopy, recording, or any information storage or retrieval system, without permission in writing from the publisher.

British Library Cataloguing-in-Publication Data
A catalogue record for this book is available from the British Library.

Digitally printed

With love to Sarah,
Sennen,
Perec, and Liran

Contents

List of illustrations	ix
Series foreword	xi
Acknowledgements	xiii

Section 1 Foundations

1.	Introduction: Oi Kwan Road	3
2.	The history of Islam in Hong Kong	21
3.	Transformations	35
4.	Islam, Chungking Mansions, and otherness	55

Section 2 Religious Practice

5.	Learning to be Muslim	69
6.	Daily practice	85
7.	The ambiguity of halal food in Hong Kong	97

Section 3 Language, Space, and Racism

8.	Muslim youth, language, and education	117
9.	Chinese/not Chinese	139
10.	Racism versus freedom	151
11.	Use of space	171
12.	Conclusion: Thoughts on an anonymous letter	191

Appendix	199
Bibliography	201
Index	213

Illustrations

Figure 1	'Osman Kebab' halal takeaway in Wanchai	7
Figure 2	The Kowloon Mosque in Tsim Sha Tsui	22
Figure 3	Muslims demonstrate in Kowloon over the Danish cartoon depictions of the Prophet Muhammad in 2006	40
Figure 4	A protestor complains about discrimination and the treatment of Iraqi prisoners at Abu Ghraib prison in Iraq	41
Figure 5	Indonesian foreign domestic workers at the Kowloon Mosque	52
Figure 6	Chungking Mansions in Tsim Sha Tsui	57
Figure 7	The halal butcher at Bowrington Road Wet Market	101
Figure 8	Halal and *haracm* on display in a Wanchai takeaway	107
Figure 9	South Asian young men playing cricket in Wanchai	186

Series foreword

Most past research on Hong Kong has been generally aimed to inform a diverse audience about the place and its people. Beginning in the 1950s, the aim of scholars and journalists who came to Hong Kong was to study China, which had not yet opened its doors to fieldwork by outsiders. Accordingly, the relevance of Hong Kong was limited to its status as a society adjacent to mainland China. After the opening of China, research on Hong Kong shifted focus towards colonial legitimacy and the return of sovereignty. Thus, the disciplined study of Hong Kong was hindered for almost half a century, and richness of a society undergoing dramatic economic, social and political change within the contemporary world was not sufficiently emphasized.

The unfolding of culture and society in Hong Kong is no longer confined by the 1997 question. New changes are shaped by local history as much as by the China factor. Rather than being an isolated entity, Hong Kong is an outcome of interaction among local history, national context, and global linkages. An understanding of the future development of Hong Kong requires sensitivity to this contextual complexity.

The volumes in this series are committed to making Hong Kong studies address key issues and debates in the social sciences. Each volume situates Hong Kong culture and society within contemporary theoretical discourse. Behind the descriptions of social and cultural life is a conceptual dialogue between local agenda, regional issues, and global concerns.

This series focuses on changing socio-economic structures, shifting political parameters, institutional restructuring, emerging public cultures and expanding global linkages. It covers a range of issues, including social movements, socialization into a national identity, the effect of new immigrants from the Mainland, social networks of family members in other countries, the impact of the colonial legacy on the identity of forthcoming generations, trade union organization within the shifting political landscape, linkages within Southeast Asian societies, Hong Kong's new role between Taiwan and the Chinese mainland, the transformation of popular culture, the globalization of social life, and the global engagement of Hong Kong's universities in the face of national integration.

Gerard A. Postiglione
Tai-lok Lui

Series General Editors

Acknowledgements

It is with great pleasure that I acknowledge and thank the following individuals and organisations, all of whom have played important roles in supporting this work. Images from the 2006 Danish Cartoon demonstrations are used with the kind permission of Alex Hofford. The doctoral research on which this book is based produced two previous articles. Reworked portions of these articles appear in this book and I thank Taylor and Francis for their permission to use them.

Anita Harris has been a guiding light in this research from its inception. She provided an enduring commitment to the work and its vision and has been an exemplary mentor in her integrity and poise. I thank Zlatko Skrbis for his support and guidance and also Andrew Singleton for his helpful comments and wit. Numerous academics have taken time to give advice and information over the years and I am honoured to have had such excellent input. In particular, I would like to thank Nelida Fuccaro, James Morris, Tariq Modood, Tam Wai Lun, Graeme Lang, Peter Baehr, Chan Kwok Bun, Ho Wai Yip, Scott Poynting, Pam Nilan, Vince Marrota, Fethi Mansouri, Amel Boubekeur, Caroline Plüss, Philip Lewis, Les Back, Annalisa Frisina, and Josh Roose.

This research would have been impossible without the support and co-operation of the Islamic community in Hong Kong. The young people who participated in this study have my utmost respect and gratitude. These young Muslims provided vibrant accounts of their daily lives and experiences. In aiding me in this aspect of the research I extend my thanks to Sithi Hawwa, K.P. Chan, Josephine Chung, Mr. Ma, Bruno Yusuf Ma, Hakima Ma, and Imam Uthman Yang along with other members of the Islamic Union of Hong Kong. I am similarly indebted to the many adult Hong Kong Muslims and Indonesian foreign domestic workers who gave their time to contribute to this work. I must also mention Dixon, Bashir, Stevie, Muhammad, Asad, Sheikh Muhammad, Felecia Sallay, Saqib, Mr.

and Mrs. Ali, and the warm and generous friendship of Mr. and Mrs. Husain.

My deepest thanks go to Gordon Mathews who gave first-class advice and good humour along the way. I must also acknowledge the help of Jo-Anne Dooner, Kirk Troy, Laura and Jimmy Chow, Caroline Chan, and the Hong Kong Anthropological Society. I thank Chris Munn for his kind encouragement and balanced advice. Thanks also to Clara Ho and Michael Duckworth and the team at Hong Kong University Press. Special mentions go to the White family for their support and to Mark Russell, Matt Huddleson, and Marcus Hartopp for their intellectual stimulation. Thanks to you all.

This book is in essence a triumph shared by my wife and three sons. It is they who have lived with every part of this book in its various forms. They have been the most patient, and given the greatest support. My wife, Sarah, has constantly provided a fresh perspective on a text I have worked on for many years. My sons have provided lively distraction and un-paralleled joy and have each inspired and propelled my work; my love and appreciation to you all.

Section 1

Foundations

1
Introduction: Oi Kwan Road

When we think of Hong Kong, Islam is not something that springs to mind. Popular images of Hong Kong portray hyper-modern skyscrapers, Chinese signs in bright neon, a place of commercial and gastronomic delights. The Hong Kong that is popularly imagined evokes an association of dynamic cultural fusion, the exotic yet familiar, a cocktail of tradition and innovation. Islam does not share these associations. More typically Islam is considered a traditional and monolithic religion and ideology. Islam in Hong Kong is therefore an issue and topic that sounds unusual. If you are unfamiliar with Hong Kong, the words simply seem mismatched, a random juxtaposition of un-related terms. If you know Hong Kong well and have lived here all your life you may associate Islam with the Kowloon Mosque on Nathan Road, or the many Indonesian women who populate Causeway Bay on Sunday mornings. Some might think of Chungking Mansions, a place popularly associated with ethnic minorities, or perhaps the Pakistani security guard at their residential complex. But very few would acknowledge Islam as having played an important part in the history of Hong Kong or as having a living vibrant role in the city today.

Over 220,000 Muslims live and work in Hong Kong and as a group they account for 3% of the population (*Hong Kong Yearbook* 2009b). They come from many different backgrounds and are involved in a variety of trades and pastimes in the territory. In my travels beyond Hong Kong I have had an array of curious reactions from Muslims and non-Muslims alike about this topic. Most typically, people wonder, sometimes with worried frowns, who actually are the Muslims of Hong Kong? I have also fielded many questions about Islam in Hong Kong. Are there any terrorists? Are they all Chinese? Surely, there can't be many of them? What these questions have taught me is that people are curious about Muslims in Hong Kong. Even those who do not know Hong Kong are intrigued by the experience of life for minorities in this fascinating city.

The truth is that Islam has long been a part of the Hong Kong story. Indian Muslims and traders were present in the South China Sea during the first Opium Wars, and have lived and worked in the territory in a variety of different roles ever since. Chinese Muslims, or *Hui*, have also come to Hong Kong during various periods of political oppression on the Mainland. Now they number around 30,000 and have their own organisations. In recent years the largest population of Muslims in Hong Kong have been Indonesian, totalling 148,000. These are foreign domestic workers who have come on a short-term basis to provide domestic support for Hong Kong families. South Asian Muslims, the majority of whom are Pakistani, number over 17,000 (*Hong Kong Yearbook* 2009a). It is the *Hui* and Pakistani communities that account for the largest number of locally-born Muslims. Muslims in Hong Kong represent a sizeable minority in the city of 7 million people.

Oi Kwan Road

Hong Kong is a small but densely populated territory in Southern China. It is located in the southeast of the Pearl River Delta in the South China Sea. It is unique, having both a colonial history and special status as a recently re-incorporated region of the People's Republic of China. The northern part of Hong Kong Island and the Kowloon peninsula comprise the urban heart of Hong Kong. The Central District rests on the northern shore of Hong Kong Island opposite the southern tip of the Kowloon peninsula, Tsim Sha Tsui. This district is the financial and commercial heart of the territory. Victoria harbour, which separates Hong Kong Island and Kowloon, provides one of the world's most striking city skylines. Towering skyscrapers are over-shadowed only by the dramatic plush green hills of Hong Kong. East from Central is the Wanchai district, famous for its nightlife and entertainment. It was here that the well-known book and film *The World of Suzie Wong* was set. Wanchai still attracts all manner of tourists across the globe and is one of the most cosmopolitan parts of Hong Kong, with a vast array of different cultural groups and social classes rubbing shoulders with one another in everyday life. Oi Kwan Road is one rather small area of Wanchai and is at first glance quite unremarkable. Yet it is here that I have come to observe, over many years, not simply the comings and goings of Muslims attending prayers in the local mosque, but also their participation in the daily melange of everyday life in Hong Kong.

Oi Kwan Road is opposite the north entrance to the Happy Valley racetrack and is situated near the Sikh Gurdwara. The road houses the Osman Ramju Saddick Islamic Centre and Mosque, the Queen Elizabeth Stadium, Tang Chi Ngong public health clinic, four schools, and a public swimming pool complex. The southeast corner of this road has a public park that includes a children's playground and a skateboard and bicycle track. The road is in many senses representative of Hong Kong, a compressed urban space. It also has a variety of public services, businesses, and private apartments. Most importantly, from our point of view, it houses a significant place for Muslims to meet, pray, eat, and celebrate.

The Islamic centre is home to one of Hong Kong's five main mosques. The building itself is an inconspicuous high rise, unlike the Kowloon mosque in Tsim Sha Tsui which follows a more traditional design and can house 3,500 worshipers. The eight storey building in Wanchai has a library, a kindergarten, a restaurant and prayer halls for men and women that can accommodate up to 1,500 people. The many people that use the facilities here are also commonly found in other parts of Oi Kwan Road. Pakistani women with their infant children attend check-ups at the health clinic, and Muslim men can often be found sitting on the benches of the park.

Like the city of Hong Kong, the park on Oi Kwan Road has multiple lives. It is frequented by young children throughout the day and dominated by a mix of adolescents in the evening when skateboarders of all types of ethnicity and age are a common sight. Other groups of teenagers gravitate to this same space, some huddle around mobile phones or MP3 players, smoke, or flirt with one another. Often, elderly Hong Kong citizens perform evening exercises in their pyjamas. Some visitors come to collect clippings from plants that grow in the garden while, at other times, a swarm of people occupy the park as they attend a Cantopop concert or sports tournament in the adjacent stadium. In the daytime, foreign domestic workers meet each other when they bring the children in their care to play in the playground. Occasionally, an elderly Chinese woman swiftly hunts through the bins to collect drinks cans for recycling earning herself a meagre wage, while a smartly dressed office worker sits on the wall and steals a cigarette break.

I have passed the park and seen visiting American professional skateboarders film a video. On another occasion, a fashion shoot for a magazine took place in which a scantily clad model posed languidly on the back of a motorbike in the bright sunlight and dense humidity. More often though, you can see young Pakistanis running around with school friends playing chase and dodging skateboarders, or practising their bowling in a makeshift game of cricket while their fathers attend Friday prayers at the nearby mosque. The park has a rhythm that is determined not only by the time of the day, but also the day of the week, and by the people who use the surrounding facilities and who live in the area. It is just one small area of Hong Kong, not representative of the territory as a whole, but certainly representative of its compressed space and cultural mix.

Sharif, a 14-year-old Pakistani boy, spends much of his time in the locale of Oi Kwan Road. His family originate from a village in the Attock district of Pakistan's Punjab province. For many years his father has worked in Hong Kong as a night watchman, a job common for many Pakistani men in the territory. At the age of eight, Sharif came to live in Hong Kong permanently along with his mother and elder brother. He has since come to regard Hong Kong as his home and he aspires to live and work here as an adult.

Sharif visits the Wanchai mosque situated on Oi Kwan Road many times each week. Along with the Qur'anic lessons he receives at school, Sharif is also training to be a *hafiz*, a person who has committed the Qur'an to memory. It is a respected title among the Pakistani community and one that has already been attained by Sharif's elder brother. The mosque is the place where this specialised recitation is practised. After these lessons Sharif spends time at the local park where he meets friends and plays games of cricket and chase, sometimes late into the evenings. On Fridays in particular, the Muslim holy day, much of his time is spent around Oi Kwan Road. Nearby the mosque there is a Pakistani takeaway where inexpensive meals and snacks are provided. Sharif occasionally visits this establishment. This takeaway 'Osman Kebab' is also well known to him as it is owned by the father of one of his classmates.

It is on Sundays that Amisha, a 31-year-old Indonesian foreign domestic worker, spends most of her time at Oi Kwan Road at the Islamic Centre. She leaves the home of her employer, a Singaporean Chinese family, by 10 a.m. and makes her way across town. At the Islamic Centre

Introduction: Oi Kwan Road

Figure 1 'Osman Kebab' halal takeaway next to Cantonese street food just off Oi Kwan Road in Wanchai (photo by author)

she meets with friends and prays in the mosque. She also attends lectures on Islam that are frequently given on Sundays and are very popular among Indonesians. She, like many of her friends, turns out weekly in her best clothes, modestly dressed with colourful headscarves. Sunday has become her holy day in Hong Kong and she devotes it to the Islamic Centre on Oi Kwan Road. Here, amidst the eight different floors she can learn Arabic, study books from the library, and even dine at the halal restaurant. More often than not, ever conscious of her budget and wishing also to eat some authentic spicy Indonesian food, she brings her own to share with friends. Climbing the stairs of the Islamic centre on a Sunday you will encounter many Indonesian women like Amisha, eating, phoning home, and reading the Qur'an.

Sometimes on weekday evenings Benny, a 52-year-old *Hui*, makes his way to the Islamic Centre to dine with fellow Chinese Muslims and partake in discussions about community events. He looks indistinguishable from other Hong Kong Chinese. He works as a salesman in a finance group located less than a mile from Oi Kwan Road. He is eager and enthusiastic to talk about how easy it is to obtain halal food in China, unlike Hong Kong. In the Mainland he informs me, many people recognise that halal food is carefully prepared and can be trusted. Many non-Muslims therefore eat it as well as Muslims. His wife is not Muslim and his teenage daughter is largely indifferent to religion. This, however, is fine with him for the time being as he believes that her studies should take priority.

These are just a handful of the different Muslim characters for whom Oi Kwan Road is an important place. These brief vignettes show that religious and ethnic minorities in Hong Kong have daily lives that are entwined with both Hong Kong culture and their religious practices. This overview provides a necessary starting point to this book; one that brings life to the phrase 'Islam in Hong Kong'.

Introducing the participants

Before exploring the history of Islam in Hong Kong, let me explain the origins of this project. I first came to Hong Kong in 1999 with my wife who was born in the territory. At that time I was involved in research for my master's degree on British Muslims and the pilgrimage to Mecca. I was intrigued to stumble upon the Jamia Masjid on Shelley Street while travelling on the escalators in the Mid-Levels. This old and ornate mosque, tucked away inconspicuously, piqued my curiosity about Islam in the territory. Visiting it was the catalyst for what has turned out to be a long and fascinating project. The bulk of this research took place over the last eight years. It includes a variety of interviews, observations, and discussions with numerous Hong Kong Muslims and much of it was undertaken as part of my doctoral research. It has since been expanded and adapted in order to write this book. A total of 37 informants provided interviews. In addition, I conducted numerous informal discussions with a variety of Muslims throughout Hong Kong. I spoke to Imams, businessmen, housewives, retired bank managers, youth workers, domestic helpers, and musicians. The participants included 22 Pakistanis, 7 Indonesians, 1 Sri Lankan, 2 Indians, 2 Somalians, 1 Ghanaian, and 2 Hong Kong Chinese; of these 22 were female and 15 male. The majority of the participants are young Muslims from working-class homes where only one parent works (in all cases the father). Out of the 22 Pakistani respondents, only 4 had fathers who were not engaged in menial labour, and they were salesmen. Many working-class South Asian families in Hong Kong have low incomes and South Asian men in Hong Kong often encounter numerous difficulties in obtaining work. Just before the peak of the global economic downturn in 2008 reports show that 20% of South Asian men in Hong Kong were unemployed compared to just 5.1% of the general population (Ng 2010). Therefore, the family and domestic context of many of these participants varies considerably from the more general Hong Kong Chinese population who have grown up amidst a wealth of employment opportunities, good education and a recreational environment where material consumption is a cornerstone of everyday life.

    The fieldwork involved the recruiting of young participants from a collection of schools throughout the territory with sizeable Muslim student populations. These schools were identified because they cater for Hong Kong's ethnic minorities, providing government-subsidised education in English-medium institutions. Contacts were made with three schools and volunteers were recruited from randomly chosen classes, with the assistance of school teaching staff. In-depth individual interviews were then arranged which focussed on the spectrum of everyday experience of being Muslim in Hong Kong. In two schools, additional focus groups were organised to enable the participants to discuss particular issues together. The bulk of these interviews took place over a two-month period in 2006 and again in 2011. Some additional interviews were arranged through the Wanchai Mosque and their Islamic Youth Association, and through contact with some parents I already knew in the Islamic community. In approaching adult Muslims, more informal interviews were arranged. I spoke with a variety of Muslims at Chungking Mansions and Indonesians around Causeway Bay. In both cases, I spent considerable time in these areas observing social interactions and soaking up the rhythms of everyday life. Along with these core interviews I also spoke extensively to a collection of individuals from Islamic community organisations and those involved in the education and welfare of young Muslims. These interviews enabled me to construct a context for identifying the more general culture of Islam that exists in Hong Kong and recognising distinctions between different Islamic communities in the territory. All of the participants in this work are Sunni Muslims, though I do touch upon some of the different Islamic sects that exist in the territory and have had some indirect contact with one Shia contributor to this project. My fieldwork also included participant observation and the scrutiny of particular urban zones that became part of my own everyday life. I took time to frequent and observe spaces important to everyday scenarios of the Muslim community. In doing so, I was able to recognise particular patterns regarding the use of space, language, and consumption of food as well as gain insight into some of the gendered differences in the lives of young Muslims in Hong Kong.

Out of the 37 core respondents, 10 have lived in Hong Kong their whole lives, a further 12 have lived in the territory for over 10 years, and only 4 participants have been in Hong Kong for less than 3 years. So this work is representative of a permanent Muslim population and is supplemented with insights from new arrivals and those who plan to stay for just a few years. A total of 26 of the participants are in full-time education. There is also a varied spread of ages; 22 are aged between 13 and 17, the rest are aged 18 to 52. This sample provides a basis for insight into young Muslims in Hong Kong, but also balances their responses with feedback from some older Muslims, too. All the names in this book are pseudonyms provided to protect the identities of the respondents.

Hong Kong

Hong Kong became a Special Administrative Region of China in 1997 after 156 years of British colonial rule. The territory has a population of over 7 million people and one of the highest population densities on earth with 53,110 people living per square kilometre in the Kwun Tong district of Kowloon (*Hong Kong Yearbook* 2009a). Nearly 95% of the population are of Chinese descent, and the remaining 5% are ethnic minorities.

The territory is comprised of Hong Kong island, the Kowloon peninsula, the New Territories that extend beyond Kowloon and towards Mainland China, and over 200 outlying islands. The territory totals only 426 square miles and of this land just 25% is developed. Much of Hong Kong is rural while the urban areas consist of tightly nestled high-rise buildings. Urban Hong Kong is thus a compression of residential and commercial space entwined with public amenities.

Politically, Hong Kong enjoys a high degree of autonomy from Beijing. The Basic Law agreed upon by Britain and China in 1984 ensures that the capitalist system on which the territory has thrived remains in place for 50 years following 1997. The Chief Executive of Hong Kong is elected by an electoral committee of Hong Kong people, appointed by the central Mainland authorities. Under the current system it would be virtually impossible for a candidate to become Chief Executive without the approval of the Chinese government. Full democracy, although continually debated, remains to be awarded to the territory. However, a limited form of democracy is in place in the public election of some of the members of the legislative council. This body passes new laws, debates important topics for Hong Kong society, approves government budgets, and appoints some senior judges.

Situating Islam in Hong Kong

In a great many ways Hong Kong is not a multicultural city, especially when we see the territory from the viewpoint of its Hong Kong Chinese majority population. The great bulk of Hong Kong's Cantonese population are either immigrants or the descendants of immigrants from the Mainland. However, Hong Kong has a deeper sense of mix and cosmopolitanism than many may immediately perceive. For instance, 30% of the Hong Kong Chinese population hold foreign passports and English and Putonghua are spoken alongside Cantonese. Unlike other multicultural cities, Hong Kong is not characterised by ghettoisation. As a result, different communities live with one another and simply have to engage in everyday affairs. Combining these factors with the colonial history of the territory, it is easy to understand why words and phrases such as 'cosmopolitan', 'cultural fusion', and 'hybridity' are so often used to describe Hong Kong. It is all of these things and more. Yet, Hong Kong is not typically multicultural, a descriptor that has not been adopted in either the political or popular contexts. Minority rights, fought for and protected in multicultural nations such as the UK, Australia, Canada, and Singapore, carry little political weight in Hong Kong, despite the protestations of concerned non-government organisations (NGOs) and individuals.

Islam is, however, an important part of the Hong Kong story and a visible part of everyday life in the territory. In the next chapter, I provide a history of Islam in Hong Kong and show how Muslims have lived, contributed, and shared in the development of the city. Situating Muslims in Hong Kong involves challenging our ideas about Muslim minorities. The fact that Hong Kong is a place of mixed heritage, a vibrant setting that is able to bridge and suture together disparate people and cultures should not be dismissed. Hong Kong culture is a cocktail of East Asian,

Chinese, and Western values, commodities, social mores, and tradition. Muslim youth in the territory experience this and similarly contribute to it. The Hong Kong environment places the young Muslims in this study in a unique social situation. Sharif, for example, has a very different type of intercultural experience in comparison with his Muslim peers in the West. He is taught in English and yet attends a school where over 80% of the students are Chinese. By a different measure he has freedoms entirely foreign to his life in Pakistan.

No doubt, many who read this book will also be interested in positioning Muslims in Hong Kong in the broader debate of Muslims as minorities in countries like the UK and the United States. It is therefore helpful to provide a brief discussion on the discourse of Muslim minorities. This, to clarify, is simply an overview and does not go into a great deal of depth but it provides a way to contrast the context of this work with what is now a significant and established literature on Muslims as minorities.

The discourse of Muslim minorities

Communities of Muslims in the West are currently pathologised as a deviant group for whom multiculturalism is particularly problematic. From this has emerged an association of Islam being in conflict with the West. Sardar (2009, p. 13) comments that 'in contemporary Britain being a Muslim is a problem no matter what you do as a human being or British citizen'. This is said with good reason because while minority communities in the UK, such as the Chinese or the Jewish, have maintained their ethnic distinctiveness they have not strived to alter British life. The perception of Islam, however, is that it has global political and ideological resources that are 'capable of overtaking and displacing indigenous identity', that Muslims want a 'superior position' in society (Sardar 2009, p. 15).

The political context of work on Muslim communities as minorities is entwined in a variety of issues such as post-colonialism, cultural difference, and notions of ideological extremism. Accordingly, these themes have influenced the way in which young Muslims are discussed and understood. In media, policy, and academic work, Muslim youth are approached in a qualitatively different manner from other minority youths, such as Afro-Caribbeans in Britain, or Koreans and Japanese in the United States. It is clear that terrorism and 11 September 2001 have become the dominating themes articulated in contemporary work on minority Muslim youth (Fekte 2004; Poynting and Mason 2007). This pervasive focus has meant that work on the identity and culture of Muslim youth in the West has been largely replaced by enquiries into terrorism, social justice, nationalism, and racism (Turner 2003, p. 415; Maira 2005). From this is deduced, quite erroneously, that terrorism and 9/11 are the most pressing and immediate issues for Muslims. Consequently, there are concerns that while the culture and identity of other minority youths are still discussed, the topic of Muslim youth is debated using a qualitatively different approach which defines young Muslims in a post-9/11 frame; one which may be of little relevance both to the lives they lead and their self-conceptualisation. It hardly seems likely that every Muslim on the streets of London, Paris, Sydney and New York is animated and occupied by 9/11 and suicide bombings. Yet the intense focus of media, policy and research on precisely these issues has inflated a notion of Islam in the non-Islamic world dominated by these themes. A body of research has identified that media representations of Islam in non-Islamic countries is 'overwhelmingly negative' (Hopkins 2009, p. 35). In light of this information, one important exercise to perform is a revision of the circumstances surrounding these contemporary developments in order to understand their setting and emergence.

Some scholars argue that the origins of the discontent between Islam and the West extend back to medieval Europe and the spread of Islam. Huntington's (1993) widely read essay on the clash of civilisations argues that there is an ingrained cultural conflict between Western and Islamic cultures. In contrast, Ballard (1996) suggests the medieval European understanding of Islam can be viewed as a distorted polarisation of Christianity. This perspective sees Muhammad as the alternate Christ and focuses on the Prophet as a warmongering licentious beast (Ballard 1996, p. 25). Ballard's discussion highlights the legacy of European ignorance of Islam that Said's Orientalism thesis similarly identifies, that the close monotheistic similarities between Christianity and Islam have for a long time gestated a conflict.

Rather than a new era, the aftermath of 9/11 is more accurately an escalation and mutation of a long existing tension between the Western and Muslim communities. Young Muslims have accordingly come to be studied in a dominating context of conflict that permeates all levels of enquiry about them, from national and political discussions to debates on identity and belonging, and inclusion within schools. The fact that Muslim communities are and have been living as minorities in countries throughout the world for centuries indicates that cultural conflict is an inadequate model for such enquiry. However, in many works that look into the experience of being a Muslim minority in a multicultural society there is an enduring binary analysis. While the label of 'between cultures' is increasingly shunned, the conceptual thinking underpinning it endures. There is a paucity of work that acknowledges the cultural mix of Muslims as denizens within urban multiculturalism. Muslims tend to be seen as separate from the 'multiculture', not participating, not mixing, and not being influenced by Western culture. The purpose of looking at accounts of young Muslims in Hong Kong as complex social actors involved in cross-cultural communication and learning is to present a balance to the abundance of works that dismiss these types of issues.

The very simple issue here is to acknowledge that this book, solely because of its topic, is associated with some complicated political baggage that is not immediately relevant to Hong Kong. Particularly when considering media reportage from Britain, the United States, and Australia there is a very discernible negative representation of Muslims. In some cases the politics of the Middle East, and the plight of American and British troops, or the threat of Al Qaida tend to be seen as more relevant and of more immediate concern to the identity of Muslim minorities than their citizenship, the country in which they have been born and raised, and the community to which they belong. The prevalence of contentious representations of Islam in the media assures that this book will be associated with terrorism, 9/11, and religious extremism. On many occasions during my research colleagues and acquaintances have commented on how topical Islam is and how worrying the issue of international terrorism has become, as if the two were synonymous. These geopolitical issues and events are simply those that have come to be associated with Islam; they are not representative of the daily lives of Muslims in Hong Kong, or around the globe. This indicates that within research on Muslim minority communities a powerful discourse of deviance has occluded the more prosaic analysis of Muslims in our societies. It is a point that Hopkins elucidates and urges should be addressed.

> We rarely read accounts or see images associated with the standard everyday practices of Muslim families and communities, such as those associated with the compassion and warmth experienced by Muslims attending the local mosque, Muslim young men who train hard every week as part of their football team, Muslim families who work long hours to make sure their parents and children can live decent lives. Academic research has a role to play here too, as work here tends to focus on the margins ... When Muslims are not being represented through negative images and discourses they tend to be absent. (Hopkins 2009, p. 36)

For Hopkins it is in the domain of the everyday where the necessary renegotiation of the representation of Islam needs to occur. The dynamic is quite clear in his analysis; positive accounts of Muslims exist but are simply not represented in the media, explored by academics, or supported by funding. There is thus an absence of accounts of Muslims being shown in a 'positive light' (2009, p. 28). Therefore, the role that everyday sociology must take is not to aggrandize Muslims and provide alternative accounts which celebrate them, but to be candid and provide a quotidian representation of their lives, pastimes, concerns, and aspirations. The task is quite simply to present a balance to the profusion of work that recycles and arguably reinforces the Islamic social problems of our era. In Section 3 of this book I explore these very simple everyday practices. Considering how Muslim youth use space (Chapter 11) in their recreation is one way in which we can come to understand these youngsters beyond their religious beliefs and practices and learn more about simply 'what they do'. A more contentious topic is that of racism, very much an everyday encounter for ethnic minorities in Hong Kong.

Part of the task of overcoming the powerful stereotypes of Islam is to shed the focus on Islam defining every aspect of a Muslim's life. Lewis (2007, p. xiii) argues that in his previous work on Islamic Britain he was concerned with the lack of consideration placed on religion in academic work on Muslims; now, in the wake of 9/11, he argues that Muslims need to be understood beyond religion. It is therefore key to represent Muslims through a 'democracy of the senses' (Back 2007, p. 8) that engages with referents such as culture, space, linguistics, experiences of prejudice, along with religious practices. Of course, such a focus delivers us into the world that Muslim minorities occupy and, in Hong Kong, one that is a cultural hybrid. Therefore, these 'everyday' representations of Muslims also tell another story, contributing to the broader focus on the diversity of our contemporary communities and lived accounts of cosmopolitanism, multiculturalism, and hybridity. The everyday is thus a focal point of this book. It presents the mundane aspects of the participants' lives, but it also delivers a political message about what the challenges are for young Muslims in Hong Kong.

Everyday hybridity and Hong Kong's Muslim youth

Hong Kong is for many who live beyond the territory, a quaint oddity, a peripheral location notable for its unique history and combination of Eastern and Western cultures. For the residents of the territory, both present and past, these signifiers of Hong Kong are familiar but coexist with an array of others contextualising the complexity of the city and its cultural connections. What is seldom addressed, and what is a concern in this study, is that Hong Kong possesses prized circumstances for doing social research. Particularly in the present world in which the boundaries between the East and West have become increasingly blurred, Hong Kong offers circumstances that are both different and relevant. Post-colonial migration to Britain created these circumstances for much of the Muslim community, including the younger generation of Muslims currently living there. In a similar way, colonial connections brought Muslims to Hong Kong, and continue to influence their status and opportunities in the territory. Research on Muslims in Hong Kong is relevant to work on Muslim minorities throughout the West contributing not only to the debate on Islam, but also multiculturalism, migration, and Asian culture.

The critical perspective of this book is everyday hybridity which traces a path between the social theory of everyday life, as popularised by writers such as Michel de Certeau and Henri Lefebvre; and, on the other side, by the sociology of multicultural politics and identity studies. My conception of everyday hybridity works by taking the cues provided by everyday life theorists, that the everyday is a site of revolution (Lefebvre) and that individuals find a variety of ways to disrupt the order and uniformity imposed on them (de Certeau 1984). But my interests in the politics of everyday life also move in another direction. I would like to see everyday life as a type of prefigurative politics where what people do is the most important analytic issue. Prefiguration encourages change by being directly located in the ethos of personal politics. 'By fully embodying the change, you make change' (Maeckelbergh 2009, p. 66), I therefore wish to read everyday actions as the tokens through which the principles, values and aspirations of these youths can be understood. In analysis this means moving away from identity studies, where we look at what individuals say and their introspective appraisal of culture, ethnicity, and religion. In looking at the everyday we engage with a person in action, what they do and how they live. In this sense, prefigurative politics meet de Certeau's circumvention (1984, pp. 24–36). Rather than everyday tactics and practices being a tool of the weak and the dispossessed, they are actually nascent and progressive political developments. The mundane becomes the radical. What is now mundane was, in many cases, once radical. This is certainly observable when we consider technology, gender relations, race, dress, beliefs, and the behaviour connected with all these things. So in presenting the everyday life of young Muslims in Hong Kong, I am also presenting a politics of hybrid Hong Kong, of minority youth and their values and pastimes.

Occasionally throughout the text, I highlight themes of everyday hybridity that are entwined with a variety of dissimilar topics, sometimes ludic and sometimes sobering. Ultimately, they serve to put a simple conceptual frame around the often complex cultural convergences that occur.

Overview of the book

The scope of this book is broad and it attends to many issues under the rubric of Islam in Hong Kong. I do not, however, discuss the theological components of Islam. At times, I do expand on some specialised religious issues when they are relevant to the story of a particular respondent. Anyone looking for an introduction to Islam, though, should not start here. Fundamentally, this is an ethnographic work and is centred on the experiences of Muslims rather than their core beliefs.

That being said, this work will address the curiosity that people have about Islam in Hong Kong. Historical facts and demographics are included, as is a great deal of social commentary relevant to contemporary Hong Kong. Underlying these themes are hopeful accounts about Muslims, their lifestyles, and their future in Hong Kong. Throughout the writing of this work a great many changes have taken place in Hong Kong society that directly affect Muslims growing up and working in the territory. Examples include the Racial Discrimination Ordinance and very recent moves by the police to open up new levels of recruitment for ethnic minorities. These have an impact on the quality of life for Muslims in Hong Kong. The accounts that are given in this book are also relevant beyond the region and relate to our understanding of religious and ethnic minorities, urban living, and cultural globalisation across the globe.

So, with all of this in mind, let me explain what the rest of the book has in store. For ease the book is divided into three sections; the first looks at foundations regarding the topic of Islam in Hong Kong. This encompasses the history of Hong Kong that is covered in Chapter 2. It is here that I chart the origins of Islam in Hong Kong back to the Opium Wars and look at the development of an Islamic community with organisations, mosques, and cemeteries. This history deals essentially with the roles Muslims played in society, their jobs and status, during the colonial period. Chapter 3 begins by looking at the contemporary history of Islam in Hong Kong and charts the most important transformations that have occurred since the 1997 handover of Hong Kong to China. One key aspect of this discussion is an exploration of the most recent and largest community of Muslims in Hong Kong, that of Indonesian foreign domestic workers. We learn much here about their lifestyles and the challenges they face in their work. Chapter 4 looks at present-day Hong Kong through the imaging of the iconic Chungking Mansions, a place widely associated with ethnic minorities, and by default Muslims. I explore the relevance of this building and discuss the experiences and understanding of Hong Kong with some Pakistani and African individuals who have daily lives connected to this place. I show how, despite the association of Chungking Mansions with Muslims in Hong Kong, it is actually a place that is in many ways cut off from the day-to-day life of the territory. It does, however, work as a metaphor for Hong Kong's flux and hybridity.

From this point on, the book looks exclusively at the experiences of Muslims living their daily lives amidst the broader Hong Kong Chinese culture of the territory. These accounts come mainly from the school-aged respondents and give a very vibrant picture of growing up as a Muslim in Hong Kong. The second section of the book deals with religious practice and its accompanying issues in Hong Kong. Chapter 5 focuses on how young Muslims come to learn about Islam. It asks what are the processes and institutions that form their Islamic knowledge and influence their practice? We see the importance of the home, the mosque, and school in the teaching, learning, and acquiring of religious understanding. Chapter 6 discusses how Muslims engage in their daily religious practices. The respondents discuss how they make their prayers and also detail their experiences of Ramadan and fasting in the Hong Kong setting. Chapter 7 brings an even sharper focus to the discussion of religious practices by looking at the topic of halal food. It is here we come to understand the ambiguity of food choices in Hong Kong and the variety of conflicting decisions young people make about food. This chapter provides an unusual insight into the pastimes of local Muslims and how they integrate these with their Chinese cultural environment.

The final section of the book takes a step beyond religion and examines the fundamentals of everyday life for Muslim youth. It is here that the issue of being an ethnic minority comes into sharper relief. I discuss a series of topics that paint a representative portrait of the social issues that are key to Muslims growing up and working in the territory. Chapter 8 looks at the twin issues of language and education, where I discuss the complications that many Muslims have as ethnic minorities, in accessing suitable education in Hong Kong. The issue of Chinese-language education for these ethnic minorities is of acute concern. This is contrasted with the accounts of the respondents that detail the variety of languages spoken among the sample and their language experiences in the territory. Muslim youth are shown to be engaged in Hong Kong culture and to recognise the importance that learning Chinese holds for them. Chapter 9 engages with the accounts of two respondents: one a Pakistani Muslim, the other a *Hui*. Both of them can be understood as being Chinese, but in quite different ways. This chapter allows us to explore the identities of these individuals and understand the interplay between being Muslim, being Chinese, and being 'other' in Hong Kong. Chapter 10 presents the accounts of the respondents regarding the topic of racism. This chapter explores the ways in which many Muslims shrug off popular racism in Hong Kong. They make little fuss about the issue and explain how Islam is never focussed on as a reason for prejudice. The fact that Muslims in Hong Kong feel their religion is accorded respect, and that the territory delivers some very valuable and unique freedoms, enables them to be ambivalent about much of the racism that occurs. Chapter 11 explores how Muslim youth engage with Hong Kong space. Looking at a number of gender differences, this chapter shows how and where Muslim youth tend to spend much of their recreation time. The home and public parks are key in this discussion, but so are a variety of spatial dynamics involving the accommodation of space, virtual space, and domestic space. In the concluding chapter, I discuss one further contributor to the project who sent me an anonymous letter. This frames my appraisal of the variety of experiences that the book covers and the everyday and tangible hybridity it demonstrates in the lives of those individuals whose accounts have formed it.

2
The history of Islam in Hong Kong

Riding on Hong Kong's crowded but efficient Mass Transit Railway (MTR) underground system is an experience that personifies the modernism of Hong Kong. The trains, despite the estimated 4 million passengers they take every day, are noticeably clean, impressively frequent, and easily accessible. The mix of passengers indicates at once that Hong Kong is a Chinese city but it is also ethnically and socially mixed and is home to both the wealthy and the poor. All sorts of people use the MTR, for all sorts of trips to many different destinations. One very common everyday excursion is the cross-harbour journey from Hong Kong to Kowloon. The train arrives underground at the frenetic hub of activity that is East Tsim Sha Tsui. As passengers make their way up the escalators and through the station concourse there are a multitude of routes available to get you back to the city streets. Exit B1 delivers you on to Cameron Road. As one climbs the stairs and the passengers disperse, the view becomes dominated by the large dome of the Kowloon Mosque. For many visitors this vast ornate building is one of the first sights they will see as they tour around Hong Kong. It is peculiarly placed, amidst so much modern grandeur, so much neon signage, and the ever-present enticement to spend money, consume, and indulge. Yet there it stands as an undeniable affirmation of the historic importance of Muslims to Hong Kong and their continued presence and vitality in the territory. The mosque announces that Hong Kong is neither simply a Chinese city, nor that it is it a binary metropolis of East and West. It is prosaically a living hybrid territory.

This chapter serves as a foundation for the rest of this book because it discusses the historical context of today's Islamic community. It also provides a much-needed account of Muslims as minorities in Hong Kong. The fact that Muslims of different ethnicities have been contributing to the development of Hong Kong indicates the unquestionably longstanding diversity of the territory. Much of what is explored in these pages

Figure 2 The Kowloon Mosque as viewed when exiting the Tsim Sha Tsui MTR (photo by author)

underscores the Islamic institutions that exist today. There are tremendous differences between the early origins and status of Muslims in Hong Kong and the communities that presently exist in the city. However, many of the historic circumstances that are discussed remain relevant, if not crucial, to understanding the current Islamic community. This community is disparate, comprised of quite different ethnicities and cultures, ages and genders. Suggesting that Hong Kong has 'a' Muslim community is a problematic notion in itself. Some Muslims in the territory are here for a very brief time and engage very superficially with both Hong Kong and other Muslims. Representative of such temporary and disconnected engagement are some of the Indonesian domestic helpers, and also South Asian illegal workers in Chungking Mansions. However, as we shall see in the following chapters, there are some distinct concerns and experiences that are particular to Muslims in Hong Kong, despite their differences.

I begin by discussing the first Muslims in the territory, who were sailors and merchants, and then show how the community has expanded as Muslims played a vital role in the defence and security of the colony. The transformations in Hong Kong itself chart the vicissitudes of the Islamic community. This is followed by a comparative analysis of the Islamic institutions in the territory, which provides a deeper insight to the more general history of the community. In previous research these issues have not been covered together and this text therefore represents a valuable overview of the Islamic history of Hong Kong. These dynamics are carried over into Chapter 3 which reviews some of the recent transformations and current issues that have directly involved and affected Muslims since 1997.

Origins

The history of Islam in Hong Kong dates back to the early nineteenth century when Europeans trading in the South China Sea brought South Asian sailors and merchants to Guangzhou, Macau, and Kowloon. The presence of Muslims in the region dates back much further to the eighth century (Weiss 1991, p. 419) when Arabian, Persian, and South Asian traders visiting Guangzhou settled there. Over several generations these Muslims who introduced Islam to China, became the Muslim Chinese, or *Hui* people. Today, they are ethnically and racially indistinguishable from Han Chinese and their Islamic practices have, over the last 1,200 years, developed a number of specific Chinese traits and concerns. *Hui* may have lived in and visited Hong Kong prior to the arrival of the British. However, there are no records to indicate that they did so. While a sizeable *Hui* population lives in Hong Kong today, their presence in the story of the Islamic history of Hong Kong is marginal. Instead, it was the British colonial relationship with India, merchant sailing, and the opium trade that provided the circumstances for Hong Kong's first Islamic community. It is for these reasons that most of the work on Islam in Hong Kong is generally concerned with its Indian, or South Asian, community. However, the history of Islam in Hong Kong, although very much part of the larger Hong Kong story, has often been overlooked or dismissed as merely a footnote. For instance, the *South China Morning Post* (1998) acknowledged that Frank Welsh's well-known history of Hong Kong makes no mention of Islam or local Muslims.

In 1829 the emerging company of Jardine Matheson built their first opium clipper in Calcutta and Muslim men predominated in its crew (White 1994, p. 59). These sailors, or lascars as they were known, settled in an area near the modern Central district of Hong Kong and performed their Friday *Jumu'ah* prayers collectively in the street. One early story of this community resonates with the contemporary experience of being a Muslim in Hong Kong. The story goes that the local Chinese came to learn that these Muslims would not eat pork and the market traders made efforts to avoid carrying the meat through the street so as not to offend them (Weiss 1991, p. 420). This anecdote which is often recounted in written material on Hong Kong's Muslims (Bouma and Singleton 2004, p. 13; Plüss 1999, p. 3) serves to illustrate not only the willingness of Hong Kong people to be religiously tolerant, still evident in the contemporary life of the city, but also represents the long history of Hong Kong's intercultural mix and exchange. It shows, in commonplace terms, the accommodation of others and their ways of life.

It would, however, be disingenuous to claim that this group of Muslims were accorded respect on these grounds alone. It is more likely that these sailors and traders were both respected and feared. Certainly the close connection of Indians to the British gave them an elevated status in the territory above that of the local Chinese. In one sense their excellent language skills made them the preferred subjects of the British. From a colonial point of view the Indians were a useful and significant way of policing the boundaries of society. The Manichean divide of colonialism, as Fanon (2004, p. 3) labels it, enabled Indians to become important in occupying roles in the bureaucracy, the police, and security forces. Quite simply, there were intermediary jobs that the colonials did not want to do. Indians therefore often acted as a go-between using their language skills and status to mediate the authority of the British to the Hong Kong Chinese. Lethbridge (2003, p. 534) states that, despite the great wealth that many Indians achieved, they remained socially ambiguous and were typified by their liminal position between the Europeans and Chinese.

During the early years of the colony, it was not uncommon for successful Muslim merchants and administrators who settled in Hong Kong to take local wives. This community is referred to by Weiss as 'local boys' and many of these families still live on in Hong Kong today. In Weiss's work, she details the protocols of marriage for these local Indians. Some who were already married brought their wives from India to Hong Kong, while others married local Chinese, or other Hong Kong residing Indians. In general, Chinese families would consent to these marriages because of the status and wealth of the Indian suitors. Indian women rarely married local Chinese men, preferring instead to marry into other Indian and occasionally European families (Weiss 1991).

The seamen and traders had by the 1850s formed a Muslim community that was recognised by the British government. They established the first Islamic organisation in Hong Kong known as the Incorporated Trustees of the Islamic Community Fund. This group appointed four representative members from different Islamic communities in the territory as trustees to overlook any land given to them for religious purposes. On 23 September 1850 the trustees were given land for their religious needs in Shelley Street (Weiss 1991, p. 425). A small mosque was completed there by 1890 and enlarged again in 1905 (Incorporated Trustees of the Islamic Community Fund). This mosque, now named the Jamia Masjid, is popularly called the Shelley Street Mosque and is considered Hong Kong's first mosque. In July 1870 some land in Happy Valley was given to the trustees for a Muslim cemetery. When this was developed, it also had a small mosque. In Kowloon, land was given in 1884 to meet the needs of the Punjab regiment stationed at Whitfield Barracks off Nathan Road. This, through years of transformation, eventually became the Kowloon Mosque that greets commuters at the B1 exit of the Tsim Sha Tsui MTR. The contributions of the Islamic community in Hong Kong, over a hundred years ago, converge on the rhythms of life in the present city. A city personified by rapid change and impermanence. These origins show that by the start of the twentieth century Muslims in Hong Kong were considered a permanent and valued community. They were free to practise their religion and entitled to have land on which to do so.

Protecting, policing and guarding

A cursory stroll around Hong Kong's Museum of Coastal Defence provides some insight in to the longstanding relationship that South Asians had with the military. Dioramas depict battles in southern China with turbaned soldiers. Paintings and photographs, well over a hundred years old, portray Hong Kong's Indian servicemen. These images of the early British colony serve to provide a foundation to understand how South Asian Muslims became an integral part of Hong Kong's security forces for many decades. Towards the end of the nineteenth century Indians in Hong Kong were increasingly sought after as Hong Kong protectors in the army, police force and prison service.

The prominence of Indians in these roles meant that they became associated with a certain type of authority. It was common for the local

Chinese to strongly dislike and fear Indian police constables. Lethbridge claims this was partly due to the Chinese dislike of dark skin and also the rumour that Indians were a sexual threat to local women (2003, p. 534). These beliefs were generated in the early years of the colony with events such as the San-yuan-li incident. This occurred during May 1841, as part of the battle of Canton. British soldiers camped around Guangzhou for several days and patrolled the nearby villages. During this time, Indian soldiers were accused of defiling graves and sexual assault on local women. Such was the outrage felt by the Chinese at these occurrences and, more generally, the British presence that a civilian uprising erupted as over 8,000 local residents retaliated (Wakeman 1966). One of the results was an association in the collective memory of the local Chinese population between Indian soldiers and sexual violence. More broadly speaking, there has been a longstanding connection between South Asians and intimidating authority that has been fostered through the visible roles they have played in Hong Kong society. The dynamic has a legacy still evident today as many South Asians are employed as security personnel, night watchmen, and hotel doormen. Indeed, as I mentioned in the introduction, a number of participants have fathers who work as night watchmen. The evolution of these roles is well captured by White (1994) who gives an overview of Sikhs, Muslims, and Ghurkhas in their various security roles in the territory.

By 1844 a number of Indians released from the army had become private watchmen, patrolling in the evenings to prevent robberies along Queens Road (White 1994, p. 107). At the same time the British administration felt unhappy with tensions in the police force between Europeans, Indians, and Chinese. There were particular challenges because of the language barrier between the Chinese and non-Chinese in combination with the mounting corruption caused by triad affiliations (White 1994, p. 107). For many years the British increased the number of Indians serving in the police force. Sikhs were prominent in the force and their numbers became so large that the British actively sought to recruit Muslims in order to balance the affiliations of these public servants. This decision has come to be rather significant with regard to the development of a South Asian Muslim community in the territory, and also to the type of occupation that Muslims have been associated with. One aspect of this legacy is the ubiquitous 'shroff' office found throughout the territory, often in car parks.

This word is very much a part of everyday life for Hong Kong people, yet its origins are not generally well known. The term 'shroff' is an Anglo-Indian term derived from Gujarati, Urdu, and Arabic, meaning cashier. White (1994, p. 112) notes that in 1872 the actual Shroff was a police court official to whom monies were paid. Even in post-colonial Hong Kong the ceremonial post of the Grand Shroff is represented in the New Year's parade. The popular use of the term 'shroff' is thus a longstanding aspect of Hong Kong's colonial legacy and mixed cultural heritage.

Many Indian police officers settled permanently in Hong Kong, although the terms of their employment forbade them to marry local Chinese women. The constraints on marriage were dropped briefly during the Japanese occupation of the territory in World War II. Over the years, and during more normal conditions, a number of officers brought their wives and children to live with them. Some police stations even had special family quarters. This transformation solidified ties with the territory and a new generation, of what White (1994, p. 66) terms 'local Indians', emerged who were born, raised, and educated in Hong Kong. Importantly, White distinguishes 'local Indians' differently from Weiss's term, 'local boys'. For White, a local Indian is anyone of Indian ancestry born in Hong Kong. Weiss defines 'local boys' as a group that has emerged from generations of Indian Muslims who have intermarried with non-Indian women.

By the 1880s the prominence of Muslim men in the army and police force began to alter the character of Islam in Hong Kong. Muslims working in one form or another as security personnel now outnumbered the original Muslim community of sailors and merchants. Interestingly this new era, although distinctively different from the former, served to strengthen the presence of Islam in the territory. These men tended to preserve close ties with India and as such continued to observe their religious rites. As a community, they were able to sustain their everyday Islamic practices with the support of the colonial administration. Reviewing this new era of a Muslim presence in Hong Kong also now serves as an allegory for the story of Hong Kong, a place of permanent flux, of cyclical change and transformation. Weiss argues that unlike the Muslim sailors, merchants, and police officers, Indian soldiers were distinctly expatriate, never learning Cantonese or marrying locally, and generally returning home after their service (1991, p. 427). Their presence and the businesses that were established to meet their needs were mainly concentrated near the Kowloon Mosque and have left a lasting mark on the area. In particular, Tsim Sha Tsui's infamous Chungking Mansions has become a microcosm of cosmopolitan trade and travel where South Asian shops and halal restaurants are numerous. When this building first opened in the 1960s a number of South Asian businesses in the Tsim Sha Tsui area began to move there. This iconic locale is explored more fully in Chapter 4 where we come to learn of its connection with the everyday lives of Muslims in the territory.

Another important security function that Muslims have been associated with is the prison guard service. Initially, Punjabis were employed in the 1880s for Victoria Prison (Weiss 1991, p. 432). However, Muslim officers grew to be more strongly associated with Stanley Prison, constructed in 1935. Such was the prominence of Muslim guards at Stanley prison that land on the site was given for the construction of a mosque for the guards. This mosque still stands today, despite the fact that there are now few, if any, Muslim prison guards left. The mosque is seldom used and as a result it is a contested space which the prison service would like to use for other purposes. Weiss reports the unusual circumstances experienced by the prison guards during the Japanese occupation of Hong Kong in World War II. At this time, the Indian workers were called on to service the boundaries of the social divide. The Japanese kept the Indian prison guards in their jobs, but now they were overseeing the British as inmates. It is understood that the Indian guards treated their previous masters with such compassion and respect that the majority retained their employment at the end of the war when the British regained control of the colony (1991, p. 433).

Many new recruits to the prison service came through kin networks. Often officers returning home would enlist young men from their home regions. This practice, also used in the police force, generated Hong Kong Muslim and Sikh communities with strong transnational ties to particular parts of the Indian sub-continent. In the prison service the majority of the guards, being either Muslim or Sikh, shared two surnames: Singh and Khan; they were commonly referred to in their job by their service numbers (White 1994, p. 115). One Muslim rose through the ranks to become chief officer in the 1970s. However, the post-war period signalled a dramatic change in the employment of expatriate Indian staff. India achieved independence in 1947 and with that came partition and the creation of Pakistan, leaving many South Asians in Hong Kong in a precarious position. Did they want to return to a home that was now in a new nation? The end of colonial rule in India also altered the terms by which the British recruited their police and prison guards. A deal was struck between the Hong Kong government and Pakistan which allowed police to be recruited from the country on condition that salaries were raised and that either Sikhs or Muslims be employed, not both (Weiss 1991, p. 434). All Sikh policemen were returned to India in 1951 and over 150 Pakistani Muslims were recruited in the following decade; this expatriate recruitment finally ceased in 1961. At this time the restrictions on local marriages were again dropped although few Pakistani officers took local Chinese wives. By 1991 Weiss estimates that there were around 30 Muslim prison guards in service, the majority regarded by her as 'local boys' with Chinese wives (1991, p. 435).

Transformations following the end of World War II dramatically altered the trajectory of Hong Kong, not just from the perspective of the Muslim community, but also in terms of the commerce and development of the colony. Of huge consequence was the decolonisation of the British Empire. In the twenty years following the end of World War II the number of people under British colonial rule fell from 700 million to 5 million, of whom 3 million were in Hong Kong (Louis 1999, p. 330). Muslim workers in Hong Kong transformed their roles in society, adapting their heritage to the new social and economic climate of the territory. Jobs as security guards, doormen, road workers and salesmen became the visible roles of South Asian men in the territory. As a result of these transformations, a number of South Asian families have seen two de-colonisations by Britain: first of India and then fifty years later that of Hong Kong itself.

Institutions and organisations

Hong Kong's Islamic institutions and organisations afford an interesting comparison to the history of Muslims in the territory. The mosques, cemeteries, and cultural organisations provide insight into the different groupings of Muslims in Hong Kong, their geographic concentration, wealth and status. This can be understood in reference to the three mosques we have already discussed. The first two mosques established in the territory, the Shelley Street Mosque and the Kowloon Mosque, are distinctly central in their locations. These two buildings highlight the importance of the Islamic community in historic colonial Hong Kong. The Stanley Mosque by contrast shows the specialisation of Muslims in the running of the Stanley prison and is arguably also an important historic location in that it highlights the value of Muslims to the colonial regime.

Another important Mosque for the Islamic community is the Masjid Ammar located in the Osman Ramju Saddick Islamic Centre. This complex in the Wanchai district impressively houses prayer halls for males and females, a restaurant, library, kindergarten, the Islamic Union and the Islamic Youth Association offices. Its origins date back to the time when land was given to the Islamic community as a burial site in Happy Valley in 1870. As previously mentioned, a small mosque was built on this site and it was later redeveloped following World War II. However, by 1978 the land on which it stood had been taken back by the Hong Kong government and used to build the Aberdeen Tunnel designed to connect traffic from the north to the south side of the island. As compensation for the removal of the mosque, the Muslim community was given a plot of land on Oi Kwan Road to build a new mosque along with HK$2.5 million compensation for the construction. The mosque was completed in 1981 and is quite unlike the Shelley Street, Stanley, and Kowloon Mosques (Ho 2001, p. 66). In appearance, the Islamic Centre and Mosque does not at all look out of place in its surroundings. Like its neighbours, it is a tall uniform building but with subtle nods to Islamic architecture. It is, without a doubt, the mosque most strongly associated with Hong Kong's Chinese Muslims. However, it is also the most diversely multicultural and unisex of all of Hong Kong's Islamic institutions.

The Wanchai Osman Ramju Sadick Islamic Centre is an important location with regard to Hong Kong's various Islamic organisations. It is here that much of the public relations, community organisation, and education of Muslims and converts take place. The Islamic Union is housed on the seventh floor of the complex. This organisation was initially founded for commercial interests to facilitate Indian Muslims and trade with China. It has developed over the years to provide a host of services for Muslims within the territory. The Islamic Union oversees the running of the Masjid Ammar (the mosque housed within the Wanchai Islamic Centre), and also the kindergarten, library, free tuition for Muslim students, Islamic courses, and medical clinic. It manages publications, and provides annual support to the Islamic community in Macau.

The most important Islamic organisation in Hong Kong is, however, the Incorporated Trustees of the Islamic Community Fund that oversees the running of Hong Kong's mosques and Islamic cemeteries. This group co-operates with the government to further the interests of the Islamic community. As previously mentioned, the Trustees became the first Islamic organisation entrusted in the late nineteenth century with land given by the government for a Muslim cemetery and subsequently the Shelley Street and Kowloon Mosques. The Board of Trustees has gone through a number of changes, but for much of the last 60 years it has comprised six members and one observer. These members are nominated by the Pakistani Association of Hong Kong, the Islamic Union of Hong Kong, and the Dawoodi Bohra Association of Hong Kong. The observer is nominated from the Indian Association of Hong Kong. The Trustees, and as a result Islamic affairs in Hong Kong, are largely represented by South Asians. The inclusion of a representative from the Chinese Muslim Cultural and Fraternal Association has been historically considered but blocked by the desire of various members not to lose any of their own ethnic representation and influence (Plüss 2000, p. 22). However, the interests of Chinese Muslims are well represented by the Islamic Union of Hong Kong, which is comprised of local Indians and 'local boys', Chinese Muslims and a variety of other ethnicities. The strong representation of South Asian Muslims on the board of trustees has largely continued as other Muslim organisations have decided that by being separate to the trustees, they are able to organise their own mosques (often small-scale converted apartments or offices) and madrasas (Plüss 2000, p. 23).

Hong Kong's Islamic organisations shed light on the different Muslim ethnic groups in the territory and their alignment with one another. The Dawoodi Bohra Association, for example, is a relatively insular group that has been working and trading in the territory since its early days as a British colony. Plüss states that their inclusion on the board of trustees is largely related to the fact that the Bohras were very wealthy and prominent in business, an asset to any organisation in Hong Kong (2000). Aside from this, the Bohras manage their own Islamic affairs; they perform their prayers and celebrations at their own association and do not attend the local mosques. They do, however, bury their dead at the Muslim cemetery where a small allotment is reserved for the Bohra community.

There is an array of other smaller groups with a variety of ethnic affiliations. The growth of the African community in Hong Kong, for example, has also led to the establishment of their own Islamic association. This has proved to be a useful ally when mediating the affairs of African Muslims in the territory. These smaller organisations have a variety of personalities that work to espouse Islam in their communities and often have small fraternity-based mosques. Some of these are merely rooms in an apartment block, but they assist in providing support for Muslims in some areas, like the New Territories, that are not serviced by any mosques under the governance of the Trustees. This is a more recent occurrence and moves us towards the discussion in the following chapter.

A diverse history

Looking through some photographs of historic Hong Kong I came across a very interesting picture. It showed the Peninsula Hotel in Tsim Sha Tsui, an icon of luxury in the territory that opened in 1928. The photo in question dates from this era and pictures the building as it could be viewed from the platform of the Kowloon Canton Railway station. A sign boldly reads Kowloon in English. The right hand section of this sign has the Chinese characters for nine dragons, which is what Kowloon essentially means in Cantonese. The left-hand section of this sign has Arabic script that phonetically reads Kowloon. The use of the Arabic script in street signs signifies the importance of Muslims in this era. This simple, almost banal sign, in front of the grandeur of the hotel resonates with the spirit of this chapter. Muslims were part of Hong Kong's history, a commonplace and everyday part of the colonial past.

The history that has been covered in these pages speaks not only of the long involvement of Muslims in Hong Kong. It also addresses the fact that everyday life in this small territory often encompasses a complex nexus of cultures, politics, and histories. As one strolls through the streets of Hong Kong, there is no end to the contrasts of old and new, East and West, and wealth and poverty that are encountered. The prominent dome of the Tsim Sha Tsui Mosque is, therefore, not simply a reminder of Islam's long-standing presence and importance to the territory; it is also an affirmation of the inherent multiculturalism that continues to play a role in propelling and sustaining Hong Kong.

The role of Muslims as soldiers, police, merchants, and sailors has left a mark on Hong Kong. Islam has become part of daily life, an element in the rhythm of the territory. As a very small part of Hong Kong's history, it has often been overlooked. While I believe that this history is useful to Hong Kong studies, it is also unquestionably important to orient this same past in any contemporary study and analysis of Muslims in the territory. This chapter's aim has been to explore the past, examining the origins and legacy of Muslims in Hong Kong. The following chapter looks at the key events that have come to bear on the Islamic community since the 1997 handover.

3
Transformations

Much of the history discussed in the previous chapter is tied to the British colonial regime. It is therefore important to bring this story up to date and to chart the significant transformations that have occurred within Hong Kong's Islamic community in the post-colonial era, not least because these new developments are representative of the *zeitgeist* in which this book has been written. What follows is a discussion of some events significant to Muslims since the handover of Hong Kong to the People's Republic of China. The date of 1997 is used solely for practical purposes providing a very contemporary overview. It is not intended to suggest that the date was a catalyst for a different era for Muslims in Hong Kong, although Ho (2001, 2002) has argued that the affairs of Muslims and the importance of the Islamic community has seen a notable decline since 1997. This is because the fortunes of this community were in part tied to the colonial government. Many Muslims held positions at various levels in the civil service, roles that have since altered and in some cases vanished. But it is also fair to argue that these were a minority of individuals who were already due to retire from many of these posts.

It is not fair to suggest that Muslims have not done well since 1997. At present, more Muslims than ever before profit from earning a living in the territory. Government statistics for 2009 report the Muslim population of Hong Kong at its highest ever figure, with over 220,000 Muslims residing in the territory (*Hong Kong Yearbook* 2009b). However, the profiles of the community have altered considerably. In contrast to their previous occupations as prison guards and police officers, many Pakistani men now work as security guards at offices and residential complexes, as delivery goods truck drivers, or road construction workers. Similarly, the largest proportion of Muslims now living and working in Hong Kong are Indonesian foreign domestic workers, employed as maids, childminders, and cleaners. There are also a number of South Asian Muslims who work illegally in Chungking Mansions, and increasing numbers of Muslims are asylum seekers. However, these are a minority of the broader Muslim population.

There are five different developments which have had a significant effect on the Islamic community since 1997, and which highlight their transformations. These are (in chronological order) the immediate political and governmental changes post-1997, 9/11, the SARS pandemic, the Danish cartoon row, and anti-racism legislation. These various events and issues are not representative of the most urgent and important concerns of the Islamic community, but they do provide a measure by which change can be observed and understood. The final parts of this chapter look at Hong Kong's new anti-racism law, and also the rise in numbers of Indonesian foreign domestic workers, and their connection to the SARS crisis. The stories of these Indonesians are new to Hong Kong and also quite different from many other accounts in this book.

End of the colony

As Hong Kong was returned to China on 1 July 1997 the world watched in anticipation of what might occur. The evening of the handover was quite unremarkable besides the drizzly weather. The event is perhaps best understood as a formal recognition of change rather than the political and social changes that pre-empted and followed that very date. For the various Muslim groups that lived in Hong Kong at that time, 1997 posed the question of belonging. Where was their home going to be? Were they, for instance, Indian, British, or Hong Kong belongers? Many South Asians were awarded British National Overseas (BNO) status but this is not transferable to their children. Those that became BNO before turning 18 years of age found that the status expired when they became adult. Many young South Asians continue to have issues with passports and residency in Britain. Some Muslims in the territory found that with the transfer of Hong Kong's sovereignty they effectively became stateless. One way in which this has been remedied is through Chinese national naturalisation enabling locally-born ethnic minorities to have a recognised state and preserve their right of abode in Hong Kong. The first successful case of Chinese naturalisation by a Hong Kong South Asian occurred in 2002. Since this time applications from South Asians for Chinese naturalisation exceed 500 annually.

A very local account of one of the few times the Islamic community made headlines in Hong Kong prior to 9/11, involves an argument with the government regarding a date palm tree. In April of 2001 an elderly *Hui* woman was angered by government plans to build a road that would require the removal of her 47-year-old date palm. The tree in question had been brought back from Mecca by her mother-in-law after she had made the pilgrimage, or *hajj*. It was feared that the palm, at over 15 metres in height, would not survive the relocation that the government offered. The news of this affair spread locally and throughout the Islamic community and diaspora. Eventually the story was picked up in the Middle East and the Saudi administration offered to pay for the palm's relocation and send three further date palms to the lady as a gift (Wan 2001). This rather quaint story is representative of the mundane profile that Muslims had in the years following the handover.

9/11

The events of 11 September 2001 shocked Hong Kong and its Islamic community, but had little negative impact on their daily lives. In contrast, the increased interest in Islam that came in the aftermath of the terrorist attacks resulted in a record number of conversions to Islam within the local Chinese population (Lee 2003). Islam became particularly appealing to a number of individuals looking for organised and structured religious activity and an alternative to the pervasive materialism of Hong Kong society. Throughout this period, Hong Kong's Islamic community were spared the scrutiny and vilification that was visited upon Muslims and South Asians in Europe, Australia, and the United States. Hong Kong media tended to focus on the international threat of Islamic terrorism rather than domestic concerns (Law 2002). However, efforts to build a mosque in the Sheung Shui area of the New Territories revealed a variety of concerns and prejudices towards Muslims locally. Hong Kong Chinese residents in Sheung Shui argued that the new mosque would be unsightly, and that Muslims as Middle Eastern people, had 'bad habits'. There was also increased animosity because of the events of 9/11, and the destruction of Buddhist statues by the Taliban (Lee 2001). Much of the opposition to the construction of the mosque appeared to be based on racism and not really concerned with Islamic extremism, terrorism, or what is more generally referred to as Islamophobia. Leung (2004) has noted that following the events of 9/11 Muslims in Hong Kong have become more socially marginalised, but again, religion is seldom articulated as a reason for animosity towards Muslims in Hong Kong. This is certainly the dynamic that is found throughout this book; while Muslims experience discrimination in Hong Kong, it tends to be racially and ethnically based, rather than focussed on religion.

In conversation with one of the *Hui* volunteers at the Islamic Youth Association I was told how shortly after the events of 11 September 2001 the organisation was contacted by an American official. The man never revealed his title or for which department he worked, but he asked a series of questions about the radicalisation of Muslim youth in Hong Kong, and attitudes towards the United States. The volunteer insisted to the American official that in Hong Kong Muslims are not political, that they tend to be safe and free and that the discontent associated with Muslim youth in the West is not something that is replicated in Hong Kong. There were no further visits from the United States consulate, and similarly no local stories of Islamic extremism, terrorism, or subversion.

While much of the world set about the business of tightening controls on their borders following the events of 9/11, in Hong Kong business remained much the same as usual. Up until recently only the citizens of very few countries required visas in order to enter Hong Kong. Notably, visitors from African countries were able to enter freely. As a result, Hong Kong became an important intermediary place for many Muslims from African nations involved in trade with the then expanding Chinese market. So while 9/11 signalled a moment when immigration rules were tightened and minorities scrutinised in many Western nations, in Hong Kong it coincided with the increased presence of African traders visiting and trading in the territory.

The SARS pandemic

One central component in the rising number of Muslims in the territory was SARS. The Severe Acute Respiratory Syndrome (SARS) pandemic in 2003 was a watershed in recent Hong Kong history. The SARS outbreak between November 2002 and July 2003 claimed 299 lives in Hong Kong and more than 1,700 people became infected. The disease had a huge impact upon the local economy as tourism declined, property prices plummeted, businesses closed and unemployment soared to 8.3% (Benitez 2003). This landmark incident in Hong Kong's first post-colonial decade was to distinctly alter the demographic profile of Muslims in the territory. Foreign domestic workers have long been part of Hong Kong's economic and family structure. The majority since the 1970s have come from the Philippines. However, concerns over their health and the economy in Hong Kong resulted in large numbers of Filipina workers returning home during the SARS crisis. In March 2003 Philippine president Gloria Macapagal-Arroyo imposed a ban on new foreign domestic worker contracts between the Philippines and Hong Kong. Between February and May 2003 the number of foreign domestic workers decreased by 17,000 to a total of 216,810 (Benitez 2003). Increasingly, Indonesian workers became more popular as they had no ban imposed upon them by their government and they were often willing to work for wages lower than the legally prescribed limit. Since 2003 the number of Indonesian foreign domestic workers has steadily grown and now female Indonesian domestic workers account for the largest single population of Muslims in Hong Kong (*Hong Kong Yearbook* 2009a).

The new community of female Indonesian migrant workers represent an interesting contrast to the longstanding Chinese and South Asian Islamic culture in Hong Kong. These workers are presenting a new image of Islam in the territory, one that is youthful, and female. As a group, Indonesian domestic helpers have become popular in Hong Kong because of their willingness to work for low wages, their perceived obedience to authority, and their spoken Cantonese. These women go through intensive training in Indonesia where they are taught how to speak Cantonese and how to manage domestic matters. In the final part of this chapter, I discuss the social experiences of these Indonesians in Hong Kong.

The SARS crisis, at a time when Muslims were experiencing rising social and political marginalisation as minorities around the globe, was actually a catalyst for an increased presence and appreciation of Muslims in the territory. These changes are also representative of the transition in migrant labour in the globalised era, where young women have increasingly become popular as surplus workers in a variety of employment sectors. While young men originally arrived as sailors and soldiers in Hong Kong, now the majority of Muslims arriving to live and work in the territory are young women trained in domestic labour. As yet, they are a temporary community with few remaining long term in the territory, marrying, or raising their own children here.

Danish cartoons

While domestically SARS provoked distinct social changes, social issues in other countries also had repercussions for Muslims in Hong Kong. In February 2006 Muslims in the territory rallied against caricatures of the prophet Muhammad that had originally been published in a Danish newspaper in September 2005. These were then subsequently reprinted across the world. This event is noteworthy for two reasons: firstly, the Danish cartoon row was one of the few incidents to bring Hong Kong's Muslims onto the city streets to demonstrate.

Secondly, the question of how to protest polarised the community as Chinese Muslims refused to either demonstrate or to speak out about the

Figure 3 Muslims demonstrate in Kowloon over the Danish cartoon depictions of the Prophet Muhammad in 2006 (photo by Alex Hofford)

incident. It is without question that the caricature incident caused upset across the different Muslim communities within the territory; however, the *Hui* were very concerned not to be seen as militant, and to avoid losing face in a public display that did not matter to the larger Hong Kong population (Crawford 2006). Thus, the Danish cartoon row highlighted the tension between the dual, and sometimes contradictory, identities of being Chinese and Muslim.

The demonstrations came at a time when social tensions among and surrounding Muslim minorities in the West were high following not only 9/11 but also the wars in Afghanistan and Iraq, and suicide bombings in Bali, Madrid, and London. During the demonstrations protestors held up a variety of placards, some exhibiting the torture photos taken by American soldiers of the Iraqi inmates at the Abu Ghraib prison. Thus, the demonstrations were presented as an act of solidarity with the plight of Muslims internationally rather than locally and responded to far more than simply the Danish cartoon row.

Figure 4 A protestor takes the opportunity to complain about discrimination and the treatment of Iraqi prisoners at Abu Ghraib prison in Iraq (photo by Alex Hofford)

Following the May 2011 assassination of Osama Bin Laden by American forces in Pakistan, a series of animated videos were released by *Next Media*, the newsgroup that publishes Hong Kong's *Apple Daily* newspaper. These videos presented lurid animations of Bin Laden's death. In one of the short videos, Bin Laden is killed and then urinated on by American troops. We then see him sent to hell where he meets Sadaam Hussein and Adolf Hitler. He is then escorted into a bedroom where a legion of pigs attack him. The video was quickly condemned and removed from the internet. Hong Kong's chief Imam Muhammad Arshad was concerned about reactions to the video and comparisons were drawn with the cartoon protests (Tsang 2011). As soon as the video was removed, the controversy died away.

These quite different events allow us to gain a broad contemporary overview of some of the transformations in Hong Kong society that have affected the everyday lives of Muslims. Two other areas of discussion remain. They represent, arguably, the most significant transformations for Muslims since 1997. The introduction of anti-racism legislation by the Hong Kong government is a key issue, which is explored below. The most significant parts of this debate relate to education. Therefore, elements of this discussion recur in Chapter 8.

Hong Kong's anti-racism law

In reviewing texts on Muslims in Hong Kong one resounding impression is evident; in over 169 years of history, Muslims have repeatedly encountered racial rather than religious prejudice. In the early years of the colony, religious, and cultural differences were often acknowledged and respected. In contrast, negative attitudes towards dark-skinned people have been a longstanding feature of life for South Asians in Hong Kong. As the colonial era came to an end, it became increasingly clear that the prejudice and discrimination visited upon some ethnic minorities represented outright racism.

This story begins prior to 1997 with the first formal recognition of discrimination coming with the establishment of the Equal Opportunities Commission in 1996 as an independent statutory body. Despite the Hong Kong government having signed the United Nations International Convention on the Elimination of all Forms of Racial Discrimination

(ICERD) in 1969, there had never been any formal acknowledgement of racial discrimination in the territory. There was therefore no law prohibiting acts of racial discrimination in work, public housing, or government policy. Following the handover, this omission was repeatedly challenged by the United Nations High Commissioner for Human Rights and local NGOs concerned with equality in Hong Kong. This criticism about the absence of anti-racism legislation in a twenty-first century cosmopolitan 'world city' eventually led the government to concede to demands. In 2003, it instigated an investigation into the feasibility of introducing anti-racial discrimination legislation to cover both public and private sectors. The long process of public consultation meant that the Hong Kong government did not propose a race discrimination bill until 2006 (Constitutional and Mainland Affairs Bureau 2006). This bill, based on the UK 1976 Race Discrimination Act, has encountered numerous challenges. It deliberately protects civil servants and exempts government policies and has been repeatedly contested by the United Nations (Hui and Shamdasani 2006; Wong 2008). In July 2008 the bill was passed by the Legislative Council, but then lawmakers argued that its exemption of language discrimination was unacceptable. It finally became law in July 2009 and remains controversial, particularly with regard to the education of ethnic minority youth (Wong 2009).

Ostensibly, the long battle for anti-racism legislation has been won. However, there is a general feeling that the battle continues because of shortfalls in the legislation. One of the key groups and channels for the representation of ethnic minorities has been Hong Kong Unison, which has fought for all levels of inclusion for ethnic minorities in the territory. The NGO was originally established in 2001 and became a limited company and charitable organisation in 2005. The growth in interest surrounding ethnic minorities has been championed by the long campaigns of NGOs and ethnic minorities in Hong Kong.

One important aspect of these campaigns has been for the inclusion of Mainland Chinese migrants within the provisions of the ordinance. Such migrants often experience discrimination in Hong Kong society. Following the handover there have been differing levels of animosity to Mainland Chinese. Some of the tensions between Mainland Chinese and Hong Kong Chinese come from cultural issues with the latter, at times, regarding the former as backward and coarse. Immigration issues and the trend for pregnant Mainland women to give birth in Hong Kong, thus over-stretching Hong Kong's public hospital maternity wards, have caused deep resentment. In recent years, the large amounts of conspicuous wealth that many Mainland Chinese have accrued has resulted in local Hong Kong Chinese being elbowed out of the property market. Demand for luxury flats by wealthy Mainland Chinese has inflated housing prices throughout the territory from 2009 onwards. The scope of this interesting topic is beyond our debate here. Suffice to say that Mainland migrants to Hong Kong have experienced discrimination. It is not based on colour, like much of the racism aimed at South Asians and Africans, but is based on differences in culture and the fear of being overwhelmed.

The issue of racial discrimination is repeatedly articulated as a concern that affects the education, employment, and prospects of Hong Kong's locally-born and raised ethnic minorities, many of whom are Muslim. A variety of studies and media reports (Ku et al. 2003; Yang Memorial 2000; Yau 2009; Yeung 2002) have described the problems that ethnic minorities face in learning Chinese and being streamed into English language education which limits their prospects to access even vocational courses. As a result, many school leavers find they are unable to find and secure skilled work or access higher education. Many are thus employed in menial labour. Of further concern is how marginalised minorities are also at risk of involvement with criminal gangs, substance abuse, or quite simply social and economic deprivation. Even with language skills jobs are scarce for South Asians and Africans.

Such issues came into sharp relief when an unarmed homeless Nepali man, Dil Bahadur Limbu, was shot and killed by police officers in March 2009 (Tsang and So 2009). Further insult and controversy was generated when the inquest into the shooting was held in Cantonese, meaning that the family of the deceased was unable to adequately follow the proceedings (Tsang 2009). The shooting is an extreme example of how ethnic minorities can become dismissed outcasts in Hong Kong society.

Shortly after the shooting incident, the Racial Discrimination Ordinance became law. The new legislation was first put to the test by a Pakistani man who, despite speaking fluent Cantonese, could not gain employment (Yau 2009). The 25-year-old Mr Husain reported that any job interviews he managed to secure were always very brief in comparison with other candidates despite the fact that he reported being well received in telephone communications. He argued that as face-to-face meetings were by contrast abrupt, it was clearly racial discrimination that was obstructing him gaining employment. Another complaint raised following the implementation of the law concerned some of the street names on Hong Kong Island. Mosque Street where one can find the Shelley Street Mosque is referred to in Cantonese as *Mo Lo Miu Gai*. The phrase *Mo Lo* is, for some, a derogatory term for South Asians which seems to be an anachronism from early colonial days in which Indians were thought to be Moroccan by the local Chinese. *Miu Gai* translates simply as Temple Street (Kadison 2009a, 2009b). Despite the fact that this identification occurred, and reached the local press, there seems to be little support to rename the street. Part of the issue is that there is little knowledge or consensus regarding how offensive the term *Mo Lo* is.

So, despite the introduction of the Racial Discrimination Ordinance, the issue of racism will continue to be a topical concern in the territory. While there are many individuals who believe that Hong Kong is largely an harmonious society, one cannot disagree with the need for appropriate legislation to protect the interests and contributions of ethnic minorities. Due to the importance of the issue of racism for ethnic minorities, this debate is touched upon again in Chapters 4 and 10. It is within these debates that I explore how Muslims in the territory react to racism and how they believe that Islam is regarded in Hong Kong. Their stories deviate considerably from this overview of the fight for legislation and instead talk of the everyday experience, and, at times, acceptance of racism.

Indonesian foreign domestic workers

Every week the largest gathering of Muslims in Hong Kong occurs not in the capacious Kowloon Mosque but in Victoria Park. Indonesian domestic helpers who have left their home country to work for Chinese and expatriate families descend on Hong Kong Island's most well-known park to meet with friends on their day off from household chores and childminding. During this day Indonesians alter the demographics of this public space making it almost wholly a female occupied locale. In addition, the park also becomes a nominally Muslim space although this may not be palpable as it is clear that many of the women present do not dress conservatively or wear headscarves. The park is situated in Causeway

Bay and it is close to the Indonesian consulate. Since 2003 a number of Indonesian businesses have become concentrated on the outskirts of the park. Approaching from Sugar Street there are Indonesian supermarkets, money changers, and mobile phone stores that cater to this predominantly female community. At the entrance to Victoria Park on Gloucester Road young women fill the streets wearing colourful headscarves and masculine punk fashions, all in their very best clothes for conservative socialising or debauched partying. The average age of the migrant workers is 27, though the majority are in their early twenties and a number arrive as teenagers (Sim 2009, p. 10).

Inside the park, groups of Indonesian women can be seen sitting on plastic sheets on the floor, sharing food, listening to music, cutting each other's hair, reading letters, and catching up on emails back home using the free WiFi available in hotspots around the park. Some groups of women sit in a circle and read the Qur'an together throughout the day; some congregate in activities such as practising competitive dance routines, singing songs, or selling products shipped from Indonesia in an effort to supplement their meagre wages. On Sundays during Ramadan, very little changes. During daylight hours, many women take the opportunity to eat and celebrate with their friends, while many others appear quite sober in dress and attitude. Such is the connection with Indonesians and Victoria Park that when the festival of *Eid* arrives at the end of the month of Ramadan, the consulate organises prayers in the park en masse. Videos uploaded on YouTube serve to document for the Indonesian community in Hong Kong and friends back home the large crowds the event draws each year. The importance of this public space for Indonesians has also been recognised back in Indonesia. A 2010 Indonesian film all about the trials of being a migrant worker in Hong Kong is titled 'Minggu Pagi Di Victoria Park' or 'Sunday Morning in Victoria Park'. One of my respondents, Amisha, spoke of how she disliked this representation of the Indonesian experience of Hong Kong. Amisha felt that the movie just shows Indonesians as lesbians, or engaging in romances with Pakistani men. It does not present a good Islamic portrayal of life for Indonesians in Hong Kong.

The experience of Indonesians in Hong Kong represents a different account of Islam in the territory. They are the first large group of migrants who are mainly Muslim women. The ways in which these Indonesian domestic workers have engaged with Hong Kong society varies. Some have discarded their Islamic traditions, and others have converted to Christianity. Their behaviour has been scrutinised by Muslims of other ethnicities in Hong Kong, and also the Indonesian community and government. In 2006, visiting members of the Indonesian parliament were shocked to see how female Indonesian migrant workers were living in Hong Kong. These visiting officials were most concerned about the blatant displays of homosexuality that these women exhibited and their sexual promiscuity in general. Similarly, they reported a concern over the excessive materialism which has locked many Indonesian women into debt (Ma 2006).

The lifestyle of the Indonesian migrant worker is thus fractured between their culture, their job, and Hong Kong's freedoms and excesses. One Indonesian domestic helper, Tarini Sorrita, has become notable for her writings that capture this existence. She has a number of short works published and is popular among the Hong Kong community of Indonesians. Her work speaks of the everyday scenarios of working for her wealthy employers and her nights spent chasing romance while dancing among friends and suitors in the bars of Wanchai (Lai 2010). While her writings capture the experiences of many of her peers, for numerous other Indonesian women, life in Hong Kong has only made them more attentive and observant of their religion.

In essence, one of the key ways in which we can understand Indonesian foreign domestic workers is through the prism of transformation. This is because the whole process of migration for many of the women has been quite traumatic. Due to a confluence of differing circumstances, Indonesian foreign domestic workers are actually quite vulnerable to physical and sexual abuse, exploitation, debt, imprisonment, and deportation. For many of the young women, the transformations begin as they travel from their homes to the training centres in which they are taught the skills necessary for employment in their host country. There are a variety of stories which detail women being molested as they make this journey, many of them leaving their families for the first time. The Yonasindo Intra Pratama is one business that has training centres where these women may spend weeks or months being taught before they are placed in a job. They have an extensive web site and also videos on YouTube showing training sessions.

The living conditions in the numerous training centres throughout Indonesia vary enormously. Generally, the women spend daily life in very close proximity to their fellow trainees. They sleep and often bathe communally and as such many women develop intimate emotional and physical relationships. These close bonds form in part because of the absence of males in their daily lives but are also a rejection of men due to the abuse and molestation that some of these women experience in the process of being recruited and leaving home (Sim 2009).

Women travelling to Hong Kong are taught Cantonese so they can communicate with their employers adequately on arrival. Over 91% of Indonesian foreign domestic workers end up working for local Hong Kong Chinese families (Sim 2009, p. 9). Even though Hong Kong is a desirable destination as it has a minimum wage, employment contracts, and laws covering domestic helpers, the Hong Kong Chinese are sometimes regarded as the least desirable employers. There are many justifications for this. One complication is that although most Indonesians have a basic competence in spoken Cantonese, they do not tend to read Chinese or English. They are therefore in a precarious situation legally in that they are not always able to access information on all their rights. Quite simply, they are signing contracts that they cannot read. Some employers therefore pay them below the legal minimum wage for foreign domestic workers (HK$3,740 per month at the time of writing). It was certainly the willingness (or at least the lack of objection) to accept the payment of lower wages that increased the popularity of Indonesian domestic workers during the economic instability of the SARS crisis. A complication of the low pay that some of them receive concerns the employment bond they sign with their training house. This requires them to repay the cost of their recruitment process and tutelage. Generally, this cost amounts to around seven months' pay in Hong Kong (Sim 2009). Many find this a burden particularly since they accrue further debt in Hong Kong.

Amisha, a 31-year-old from the Banyumas region of Java, spent three months training in Indonesia. She spent the first seven months after her arrival in Hong Kong repaying HK$3,000 a month to the training centre. This left her with about HK$500 a month for her own needs. She explains that this is a very difficult situation for Indonesians arriving in Hong Kong. Those being paid under the legal limit are subject to a great many financial complications, especially if their employer is unreasonable and abusive.

Aside from wage exploitation these Indonesian women are also frequently denied their statutory holidays of one day per week (generally Sundays) and also public holidays. I have spoken to many Indonesian domestic helpers who only get one day off every fortnight; some have even fewer regular rest days. Generally, Indonesian foreign domestic workers are considered to be pliant to the demands of their employers. Verbal, physical, and sexual abuses are all real issues that many of these women encounter in varying degrees.

The sometimes strict demands of employers also impact upon the way these women follow Islam in Hong Kong. In conversations with Indonesian women in Victoria Park, the same themes recur. Generally speaking, Islamic dress, in particular the headscarf, is not permitted by their employers. Even when they do wear this dress, such as on Sundays, local Hong Kong Chinese will often question them, asking, 'Isn't it too hot to wear that headscarf?' Many women report that they are unable to pray during the week. They have neither the time nor the permission of their employers. Perhaps the most surprising element is that a number of these women report that they have been made to eat pork by their employers. Undoubtedly, this is an issue that highlights the employers' ignorance about the position of pork in Islamic culture and also the very obedient behaviour of Indonesian women. Jawa, a 28-year-old Indonesian domestic helper, says that she 'only eats a little pork'. Another woman, Suri, reports that her previous employer asked her to eat pork with the family. She did for the two-year duration of her contract and at the end of the contract searched for a new employer.

For these women sustaining their employment is a much higher priority than maintaining the same types of religious observation that they would in Indonesia. On the whole, the general consensus from the Indonesian foreign domestic workers in this research is that halal food is easy enough to acquire in Hong Kong, but they simply cannot access it because of the demands of their employers. In terms of Islam in Hong Kong, it appears that many Indonesian foreign domestic workers experience processes that make their religion less important for them during their stay in the territory. In many cases, the fact that they cannot eat halal food or pray throughout their working week becomes a catalyst for a more cursory observation of Islamic rules in general.

Amisha explained to me that her second employer in Hong Kong would not allow her to pray at home, or allow her to wear her headscarf.

She found it hard to follow her religion in these circumstances and started to go to Victoria Park and consciously decided to 'dress sexy'. Amisha noted that when Indonesians are not behaving well in Hong Kong, it is not always their fault. It is the circumstances that they find themselves in. Although Amisha is strict with her religious observation now, this does not stop her having friends who are lesbians, or who have boyfriends. In the case of one of her lesbian friends, she has had to perform the role of mediator with the girl's parents. They are aware that she is a lesbian but want her to return home and get married. In conversation with her friend, Amisha has argued with her, asking her friend what she imagines her future will be like without a husband or children. Amisha feels that lesbian Indonesian girls are simply playing. They are toying with sex and promiscuity in ways which express a political, social, and for some, even a religious stance. Amisha believes the lesbian relationships occur because of the dense compression of public space in Hong Kong. Unlike Indonesian foreign domestic workers in Malaysia or Saudi Arabia, the small territory of Hong Kong equals enhanced freedom. Due to Hong Kong's compressed space, it is easy for Indonesians to congregate together en masse, an option not available in the same way in other countries. For many Indonesian women, arrival back in Indonesia brings an end to behaviours like not praying, eating pork, or having lesbian relationships. The issues of transformation in Hong Kong are for many women temporary and many revert to more traditional behaviour once they return home.

Sunday morning in Victoria Park is a prime time to witness how these women spend their free time. The prominence of lesbian relationships among Indonesian domestic workers is undeniably visible in and around the park. It is estimated that up to 20% of these women are lesbian (Fenn 2010). Through these relationships Indonesians redefine gender roles. Some girls take on 'tomboy' roles, dressing in funky baggy clothes with short, cropped spikey hair. These fashions are quite distinct and unlike Islamic dress, and do not seem to bother local Hong Kong Chinese employers who tend to be quite approving of the suppression of femininity in their domestic helpers. This is a theme picked up by Constable (1997) in reference to Filipina domestic helpers in Hong Kong. Many female employers do not want to be in competition with a young and attractive woman living in their household and thus approve of short hair, and baggy clothes. Indeed, a Malaysian Chinese work colleague I once had compiled a long list of rules for her new Indonesian domestic helper that she allowed me to read through. It included the following types of demands: no make-up, hair must always be tied back, no tight clothes, no skirts, no praying at home. The list went on to make some very peculiar demands about acceptable times to eat, rest, and return home on days off.

Lesbian relationships tend to be viewed among the Indonesian women in a variety of ways. In some senses, they make up for an absence of Indonesian men; in other ways, they respond to the intimacies of co-dependence that have arisen since they began training communally in Indonesia. Some women regard them as a way of regaining power, playing out gender roles that they have little capacity to do in their normal everyday lives in Hong Kong because of their new status as migrant domestic workers. The sexual component of these relationships is something that varies considerably. Some consider that sex can only take place with a penis and equate lesbian sex as 'not really sex'. In another fashion, some of these relationships have very little to do with sex. There are also different values and behaviours with the different gender roles assumed in these homosexual relationships. Some of the 'tomboys' take their male role as a licence for promiscuity and maintain a variety of relationships and trysts with different girls.

In contrast, heterosexual relationships are also common among Indonesian women and other ethnic minority men. While some, especially those with English language abilities who are not opposed to being with non-Muslims, may form relationships with Western men, it is often the case that Indonesians take Pakistani and African men as boyfriends. On a Sunday lunchtime stroll around Chungking Mansions, you are likely to encounter numerous Indonesian girls in short skirts gleefully soaking up the attention of countless men. These women are often enjoying the liberty and freedom that they have on their days off and in turn they are experimenting with Hong Kong's intoxicating permissiveness.

A trip a few hundred metres up the road from Chungking Mansions delivers a very different image; hundreds upon hundreds of Indonesians women thronging around the Kowloon Mosque and occupying the floors, steps, and benches of Kowloon Park replete in Islamic dress and brightly coloured headscarves. Across the harbour at the Wanchai Mosque, it is a similar story. On Sundays, the whole of the Osman Ramju Saddick

Figure 5 Sunday replaces Friday: Indonesian foreign domestic workers spend their day off at the Kowloon Mosque (photo by author)

Islamic Centre becomes a female and Indonesian space. Ascending to the women's prayer hall via the stairwell involves navigating dozens of women sitting together discussing, praying, and reading the Qu'ran. It is as if Sunday has become the holy day for these Muslim women. They seem to have thrown themselves into religion as a way of protecting themselves from the excesses of life in Hong Kong and the exploitation they may risk.

Sadly, there are many stories of rape, unwanted pregnancies, imprisonment, and illness. Mathews reports a young Indonesian woman who became blind and paralysed on one side of her body (2011, p. 99). Her Ghanaian boyfriend had only recently died of AIDS. It took some time for her and her friends to comprehend what had happened eventually understanding that she too had developed AIDS. She was sent home to Indonesia to die. In general, Indonesian women tend to be fairly naïve about contraception and protection from sexually transmitted diseases.

The norms of their Indonesian culture dictate that they should not take a decisive role in these matters. As a result, there are often tragic stories of unwanted pregnancies, abortions, adoptions, and broken families.

A very new development within the Indonesian foreign domestic worker community is the increasing numbers of them claiming asylum in Hong Kong. From what has been explained to me, there are several reasons why this is happening. Firstly, some Indonesian women who have become pregnant and have boyfriends are encouraged by their boyfriends to claim asylum. In some cases, these men may also be asylum seekers from South Asia working illegally. Some encourage their girlfriends to leave their employers, then persuade them to work with them, sometimes in the restaurants where they work. In a second set of circumstances, some Indonesian women decide to cancel their employment contracts and claim asylum in order to remain in Hong Kong and work as prostitutes. The prime motivation here is thought to be money and considering that some of these women are in debt, this provides them with at least some autonomy in clearing their debt and becoming independent. Another situation is that some lesbian couples will decide that there is simply too much hardship in the work they do. They decide to claim asylum and with the small amount of money they receive they can move in with their girlfriends and no longer have the burden of work.

The whole process of claiming asylum as foreign domestic workers is fraught with contradiction and questionable ethics. Many of these women claim that they cannot return home because of violence, maybe because they have had a child out of wedlock, or that they are in debt. Nevertheless, it is clear that these women arrived in Hong Kong in order to work, not to flee dangers in Indonesia. At the same time, the social circumstances I have described above do suggest that there are particular hardships and risks that make Indonesian foreign domestic workers vulnerable.

On the topic of Islam in Hong Kong, Indonesian foreign domestic workers provide a unique focus. Much of what is urgent and immediate for these women is set apart from their religion. The Indonesian women who come to Hong Kong to work are currently redrafting the story of Islam in Hong Kong. Over a few short years, they have altered the perception of Victoria Park. They too have disrupted the gender balance of Muslims in the territory, making Islam in Hong Kong noticeably female in character. How long this community will remain in Hong Kong is uncertain.

The territory changes and adapts so quickly that what is observed today may be obsolete within a few years. Thus, this discussion has explored the circumstances of transformation to which they are currently subject. It is these issues that are important to understand and address if we are to recognise this new, largely young, female group of Muslims, the largest group in Hong Kong.

More fully, this chapter has covered an intersecting variety of transformations that have come to affect the everyday lives of Muslims in Hong Kong. These changes bring us up to date in our Hong Kong history, showing the important and wide-ranging effects of the SARS crisis and the drawn-out and continuing controversy of racial discrimination in Hong Kong. The discussion delivers us informed into present-day Hong Kong, able to engage with who Hong Kong's Muslims are and how they have become imagined.

4
Islam, Chungking Mansions, and otherness

Chungking Mansions may be one of the places most readily associated with Muslims in Hong Kong. Only 270 metres separate the Kowloon Mosque and Chungking Mansions. Indeed proximity to the Kowloon Mosque, its legion of Pakistani shop owners, halal restaurants, and African Muslim traders prove that the Islamic association is rightly deserved. It is also the case that while Chungking Mansions is important to discuss, and while it is a fascinating and compelling topic, it represents only a small aspect of the lived experience of Islam in Hong Kong. If we are to grasp Islam in Hong Kong as it currently exists, we shall have to look beyond the walls of this building and engage in the daily events of Muslims throughout the territory. Nevertheless, Chungking Mansions provides a vibrant first step towards understanding how Muslims are considered in Hong Kong. Indeed, for a great many Muslims, Chungking Mansions represents a huge part of their Hong Kong experience.

A recent and excellent book on the building by Gordon Mathews explores the notion that Chungking Mansions is an 'island of otherness' in Hong Kong (2011, p. 3). The place is a physical part of Hong Kong, but it is not 'of' Hong Kong. Indeed, the dizzying mix of people passing through this location will ultimately tell us little of how Islam and Muslims engage with everyday Hong Kong life. Many of the daily exchanges in this building operate with an impetus and focus on places beyond Hong Kong. African trade with China, illegal Indian workers sending remittances to Calcutta, Somalian asylum seekers endlessly waiting to be granted refugee status in North America are all common occurrences within the building. Its Muslim occupants treat Hong Kong as a checkpoint, waiting room, or temporary encampment in the greater projects of their lives. These Muslims rub shoulders with a vast array of people of other religious affiliations, of unalike cultural backgrounds, and dissimilar tongues. In talking with Muslims in Chungking Mansions, we can begin to explore how Islam is imagined in Hong Kong and also a little of how it is lived.

The building holds a special place in the lives and imaginations of an eclectic range of people. It is perceived by the local community, more often than not, as a den of iniquity filled with a darkness that they see as a metaphor for both the skin shade of most of the inhabitants and their ethics and pastimes. This association is changing among a younger generation and I often encounter local Hong Kong Chinese diners in the restaurants I frequent. For travellers and backpackers across the globe it is a notoriously exciting location of intrigue and adventure. For African and South Asian traders it is both a key site where business can be located and a springboard into the Mainland. In recent years, they have all come to rely on Chungking Mansions as an in-between space. It is here they gather information, procure cheap accommodation, change money, renew visas, and instigate their trade. The building is also widely associated with vice. Certainly, inside and outside of Chungking Mansions, South Asian drug dealers will furtively offer you cannabis or other drugs. Similarly, the sex trade exists directly outside and within the establishment and many women on tourist visas use Chungking Mansions as a base to accrue money that will amount to a small fortune in their home country. I was told of one Kenyan woman who after three months was able to buy three used cars which she shipped back to her home country to set up a taxi business. Her brief stint in Chungking Mansions has enabled her to access status as a middle-class businesswoman. For some, the dream matches reality and they return home able to set up a lucrative business. Other women visiting Hong Kong are tricked and coerced into this sex trade, often by acquaintances in the villages and towns they come from (Choi 2011).

These dynamics speak not only of Chungking Mansions but also relate to the imagining of ethnic minorities, particularly male ethnic minorities in Hong Kong. While white or European minorities in Hong Kong are typically considered wealthy, non-white minorities are associated with poverty and developing countries. This is the prism through which Chungking Mansions is understood, despite the fact that in reality the building represents a crossroads for the developing world bourgeoisie (Mathews 2011, p. 213). Even many of the illegal workers trading in the shadows of the law are actually well-educated professionals in their home

Islam, Chungking Mansions, and otherness

Figure 6 A cultural crossroads: Chungking Mansions on Nathan Road in Tsim Sha Tsui (photo by author)

countries. In Hong Kong, the pittance that they are paid dwarfs the salary that they would have as a legitimate professional in India.

Many of Hong Kong's Muslims are South Asian and in the local imagination it is with the dynamics of ethnic otherness personified by Chungking Mansions that Islam is often associated. Chungking Mansions and its locale are saturated with non-Chinese, many of whom are recognisably Muslim. Therefore, Chungking Mansions is by default part of our discussion on Islam in Hong Kong.

This chapter provides readers with an insight into the daily lives of Muslims in Chungking Mansions. It begins by discussing Chungking Mansions as a metaphor for larger Hong Kong. This articulates at a different level its importance as a local site of difference. Interesting and compelling accounts of Muslims connected to Chungking Mansions are then presented and highlight the very different links to and understandings they have of Hong Kong. In the light of these accounts, it would seem that Chungking Mansions has become largely a transient space of Islam in Hong Kong and one that tells only a fraction of the story of locally-born and raised Muslims.

A metaphor for Hong Kong

There is no doubt that Chungking Mansions is well-known beyond Hong Kong. Its notoriety extends to numerous people who have never visited it, in addition to those who never will. Newspaper reports and travel guides feast on its legendary status as an exotic and dubious stopover in the largely clean and safe metropolis of Hong Kong. What is particularly interesting is how commonly Chungking Mansions is used as a metaphor for Hong Kong at large. This dynamic persists despite the common identification of Chungking Mansions with 'otherness' and despite the fact that few Hong Kong Chinese can be found working in or visiting the premises. One cult representation of Chungking Mansions is Wong Kar Wai's 1994 film *Chungking Express*. The director confesses that his interest in Chungking Mansions relates to its frenetic activity and mix of cultures. He specifically notes that the overpopulated building and hyperactivity of the space is a 'great metaphor' for Hong Kong itself (Ciment in Huang 2004). Indeed, Chungking Mansions is architecturally a compressed and puzzling maze, like urban Hong Kong. In both places, people come and go at alarming speeds and trends in commerce change daily. Chungking Mansions and Hong Kong are both liminal, in-between spaces providing an important service as hubs to get to other worlds. They are exotic but also safe havens from which further commerce and travel can continue. This is also noted by Mathews who states that 'Chungking Mansions thus plays the same role that Hong Kong has itself long played—it is an entrepot between China and the world' (2011, p. 118). What we see in these understandings of Hong Kong and Chungking Mansions is a recognition of their versatility, both deftly able to adapt to the often harsh caprices of global trade, social change, and political transition. I am fascinated by Hong Kong's hybridity which is at its most obvious in the day-to-day interactions of the diverse people that live in this city. Additionally, it is a hallmark of the urban landscape. Abbas describes Hong Kong's fusion as a result of the hyper-density of the city managed by 'aggressively mixing up ... not rigidly separating public and private, commercial and residential space. The result ... is heterogeneity, vitality, complexity. For example Hong Kong may be one of the few cities in the world where one finds people in pyjamas strolling in shopping malls' (1997, p. 88). The mix that he describes could be cut and pasted into a description of Chungking

Mansions. Such is the persistence of the metaphor that it guarantees that a cursory exploration of this building and its people is valuable not only in our broader understanding of Muslims in Hong Kong, but also of Hong Kong itself.

Muslim denizens of Chungking Mansions

Only a small portion of my research focussed on Chungking Mansions. As this book is really about Islam in Hong Kong, there is much that happens in Chungking Mansions that is at a tangent to the crux of our story. However, a number of informants in Chungking Mansions spoke to me about their experiences as Muslims in the territory and the relationships they have with co-workers and peers connected to the building itself.

Leaning on the glass counter of a small phone shop I discuss the multicultural character of Hong Kong with the shop owner, Arif, a 42-year-old Pakistani Muslim man who has been living in Hong Kong for a little over 20 years. He has a Chinese wife and together they have a 4-year-old daughter. He declares loudly and proudly that Hong Kong is multicultural. I challenge him by saying that 95% of Hong Kong people are of Chinese descent (*Hong Kong Yearbook* 2009a). He argues back that despite the territory being perceived as mostly Chinese, there are deeper issues of cultural mix. He reconfirms, 'Hong Kong is incredibly multicultural.' It is hard not to agree with him amidst the traders and tourists mingling around us on the first floor of Chungking Mansions.

Arif's shop is positioned between two others, a Chinese trader to his right, and an Indian trader to his left. It is with pride that Arif discusses the good terms that all of them share. He points further down the corridor and identifies a large Indian man sitting on a stool. The man sees us talking and gives us a friendly nod. 'That man,' Arif tells me trying eagerly to make his point, 'he is Indian, he is the boss over there and all his workers are Pakistani.' People from various backgrounds work with one another in situations that would simply not occur in their home countries. It is actually a characteristic of cosmopolitanism that is increasingly being shared by groups of ambitious workers from developing countries focussed on improving their lot. Mathews describes the process as 'low-end globalization' and Mayaram suggests the social outcome is 'subaltern cosmopolitanism' (2009, p. 24). It is Hong Kong's commitment to the primacy of commerce that proffers the circumstances through which religious, caste, kinship, and ethnic difference can be managed with equanimity. Therefore, the accommodation of different ways of life so evident in Chungking Mansions is in varying ways replicated throughout the city. For Muslims, and particularly Pakistani Muslims, this means they can quite comfortably get along with Indian workers in their daily affairs. Of course, conflicts exist. They often surface due to petulant business disagreements, or personal conflicts. What Arif and many others underline is that when there are disagreements they do not tend to fester and cause feuds; instead, they get resolved. Arif states that conflict in Hong Kong is 'humdrum'; common ground is found and grudges are not held.

Arif explains that he has lived in Britain, Pakistan, and spent time in New York. In all his time abroad Hong Kong remains his favourite place, the only place he wants to live. He notes that as a Pakistani in England, life was not easy; it was hard for him to feel comfortable there. Racism is part of this challenge, but so too is the lack of diversity and the bitterly cold weather. In Pakistan, there are so many complications with politics and religion. Again, Pakistan is a place in which Arif feels anxious and unsettled. It is simply too dangerous in Pakistan for him. Hong Kong, in contrast, is a place that has 'security', a place where he feels safe physically, mentally, and politically.

He acknowledges all these factors while also accepting that racism is very common in Hong Kong. In justifying how Hong Kong can be understood as a good place for him to live, he explains that racism here is not threatening. Importantly, the racism he experiences never relates to Islam. As a basic rule in Hong Kong, he confirms to me that religions are respected. These beliefs are reflected in Arif's family. His local Hong Kong Chinese wife has accepted him and his religion. Their daughter is thus being raised in a culturally hybrid environment speaking Cantonese, Urdu, and English while attending a local Chinese kindergarten. When she is older, she will also learn to read the Qur'an. She will be heir to the diversity and cosmopolitanism that Arif promotes as a crucial part of Hong Kong life.

Arif celebrates Ramadan with his extended family in Hong Kong as his brother and cousins also live and work in the city. The feast of *Eid ul-Fitr*, which marks the end of the month of fasting, is for him a private family affair. Along with celebrating Islamic festivals, he also celebrates the local Chinese festivals, Chinese New Year, and the Mid-Autumn Festival.

Arif's only real complaint during our conversation was that halal food was a complicated matter in Hong Kong. Where he works in Chungking Mansions, and the surrounding area of Tsim Sha Tsui, it is easy to get reliable food that one can trust as halal. It is a different story in Tuen Mun where he lives. Some businesses say that they are halal when in fact their food is not trustworthy. Listening to Arif, it is easy to believe that the most challenging aspect of life in Hong Kong for a Muslim is in obtaining decent halal food. This is quite remarkable as he spends the majority of his days in one of the few places where nearly every food stall sells halal food. Muslims who work and attend school in less multicultural areas experience the challenge of halal food more acutely.

There are many features in Arif's testimony that we will revisit again in the accounts of Muslim youth later in this book. These opinions of racism, freedom, conflict, and halal food can be regarded as generally indicative of the Muslim experience of Hong Kong. While Arif has spent most of his life in Hong Kong and Chungking Mansions, Hong Kong is to many other Muslims a temporary home, a place which they are just passing through.

Let me now provide a contrast to Arif's words with accounts from African Muslim asylum seekers who are often, one way or another, in the orbit of Chungking Mansions. The issue of asylum seekers in Hong Kong has increasingly become more heated. From around the year 2000 onwards, more and more Africans have become visible in the Tsim Sha Tsui area. In many senses, they found Hong Kong a good point to do business because it has a very open immigration policy. The citizens of many African countries do not need a visa to visit Hong Kong and could enter and renew their stay quite simply. Following the world-changing events of 9/11, Hong Kong became one of the most accessible and attractive destinations to those in need of asylum simply because they could easily enter. At the time of writing, there are currently 6,740 asylum seekers in Hong Kong and the numbers are climbing. A great many are entirely bogus and use the special status as a means to prolong their stay in Hong Kong and to work illegally. We saw part of this dynamic previously when discussing Indonesian asylum seekers in Chapter 3. Currently, restrictions on visas continue to change as the Hong Kong government gets increasingly concerned about the numbers arriving to claim asylum. During the course of my research I met a number of Muslim asylum seekers from African countries. Many arrived as young men in their early to mid-twenties, typically articulate, educated, and eager to have their lives back on track.

As Muslims, as Africans, and as new arrivals to Hong Kong their stories are of interest here.

When Franky first arrived from Ghana asylum seekers were still an unusual oddity. Only a few police officers knew anything about claiming asylum, and Franky had great problems in officially getting asylum status. During his first two months in Hong Kong, he slept rough sometimes in a charity office in Chungking Mansions, at other times just a stone's throw away at the Cultural Centre overlooking Hong Kong harbour and the awe-inspiring skyline of the city. Here, he would sleep under the large architectural plinths that are a characteristic of this imposing landmark. Franky, who is now 32, would wake in the mornings, pack his bags, and walk to Kowloon Park where he could get a shower. Life was very hard for him, but he persisted with his daily prayers.

> **Franky:** I make my prayers five times a day—every day. I cannot stop. It is like the prayers have married me. Even if I am sick or late for something I still pray.

Much of the adversity that Franky encountered when he first arrived in Hong Kong was due to racial prejudice. He still feels strongly that the Hong Kong Chinese are callow racists and is forever promoting Mainland Chinese as paragons of tolerance from his brief visit over the border.

> **Franky:** Hong Kong has not got a problem with religion. I have been here for six years, I have been to lots of different societies and institutions and I can say Hong Kong has no problem with religious matters. The problem is racism. When I came here, people didn't want to talk to me. When you ask people for directions, they don't want to speak to you. If they have a slight problem they call the police. When you are in the lift with them, they hold their nose, as if we smell. It is very bad for us brothers. Any slight mistake a black dude makes is very bad for us. A friend said to me, 'Any black man in Hong Kong is guilty until you prove yourself innocent.' That's the way it is.

Franky also told me that he has approached police for information on the street and had them simply ignore him and walk away. On another occasion, he was at his flat when the police knocked on his door, only to check if he lived there. It turns out a resident in the building was alarmed to find a black man entering and immediately called the police. Iftikhar, a 23-year-old Somalian from Mogadishu, is not as caustic as Franky about the racism of Hong Kong people. He presents a more balanced appraisal of what he has experienced.

Iftikhar: There are lots things going on, language is one of them. People want to speak to you, but Hong Kong people don't speak very much English. They don't know much about Africans and they don't know who these new people are in their city. They are ignorant of us. Hong Kong is a cosmopolitan city and that is what I want it to be, an international city. But in the Chinese context it is not like that. People need to learn who we are.

In debating further the ignorance of Hong Kong people towards Africans, Franky and Iftikhar spoke of a university student they had met who was enrolled in a master's programme. To their annoyance, this young student believed that Africa was simply one country and believed all Africans shared the same nationality, language, religion, and culture.

Much of our discussion centred on these themes. A recurring element was the challenge of language as Iftikhar notes. He also mentioned that Cantonese was blocked off to African asylum seekers. Iftikhar knows many Somalis who arrived in Hong Kong knowing no English. Within a year they were fluent English speakers simply because they were in an English-speaking environment around Chungking Mansions and among the African and Islamic community. This is largely true; English is a common and shared language in Chungking Mansions, while Cantonese is a distinctly local language in Hong Kong. Iftikhar bemoans the irrationality of it all, 'we are in Hong Kong, we should be speaking Cantonese', but it simply does not work that way.

These Muslim asylum seekers experience the most extreme forms of social marginalisation, though it has little to do with the fact that they follow Islam. It has much more to do with their legal status, their ethnicity, and their home country. For Mahmood, another Somalian from Mogadishu, religion has proved to be a true resource in his claim for refugee status.

Mahmood: Most of the time I pray five times. Being an asylum-seeker and losing your family is more than you can tolerate. If I was non-Muslim I would have committed suicide before long. Because of Islam I have many good things in my life.

Each of these men have spent a few years in Hong Kong; due to the incredibly slow process of verifying asylum seekers, they may stay much longer. 'In 2008, of 1,547 refugee claims evaluated by the UNHCR only 46 were recognized as valid' (Mathews 2011, p. 118). They sometimes visit Chungking Mansions for provisions and meals from some of the charities based there. It is in this location that they can also meet up with friends and others in the African community. Many other Muslims passing through Chungking Mansions may spend just a few days, or months trading and working based in the building.

In this matter, the metaphor of Hong Kong arises again. Not only is Chungking Mansions a global place, it is also very much a transient place. What is a well-known and common practice in the building in one year may be quite unrecognisable the next. My argument is that while there are a great many Muslims connected to the building at any given time, Chungking Mansions is not very representative of the Muslims who go about their daily lives in the wider Hong Kong context. Thus, the iconic understanding of the building as a place of 'otherness' fails us in grasping the everyday realities of Hong Kong for Muslims who live, work, and are educated beyond this zone.

In the subsequent chapters of this book, I take a closer look at thematic issues of everyday life for young Muslims in Hong Kong. The idea of the everyday is important to explore here and contextualise for these subsequent discussions in order to elaborate on the diversity experienced by Muslims in Hong Kong and provide a tangible account of their hybrid world.

Hong Kong's hybridity

Chungking Mansions is an important site for the discussion of Muslims in Hong Kong, but the building and its occupants tell us little of the world outside its dilapidated edifice. Chungking Mansions is best understood as a metaphor for Hong Kong. It is a compressed space, a maze, with ambiguous ownership and governance; it is exotic but very safe for visitors and intoxicating for the *flâneur*. We might also consider Hong Kong in a similar light, an intensely hybrid and dynamic middleman between East and West commerce and culture. While hybridity is popularly contested in the social sciences, Hong Kong may be one place where it is undeniable and consistently self-evident.

Hybridity is a term that is used in reference to a variety of Hong Kong issues like education (Luk-Fong 2006), language use (Wright and Kelly-Holmes 1997; Pannu 1998; Lin 2005), and cinema (Marchetti 2004). Hong Kong films in particular are notable for their hybridity because they not only represent Hong Kong's hybrid culture (Cheung 2004, p. 268), but also export and market this hybridity locally, regionally, and internationally (Erni 2001). The image of Hong Kong beyond the territory is often influenced by this hybridity. Gladney (2004, p. 40) reports a conversation with a tour guide in China who argues that Hong Kong people are not Chinese, as 'they have been entirely influenced by Western culture and their customs are very close to Western customs'. Arguably, this image of Hong Kong is reversed when gazing from the West with the territory appearing entirely influenced by Chinese culture. Even politically, as a special administrative region of China, Hong Kong is in a liminal position, neither directly separate from, nor part of Mainland China.

The idea of Hong Kong's hybridity is not one that is universally or uncritically accepted. Ip (1998, p. 45), for example, discusses his dislike of the term hybridity; he believes that it has connotations of marginality, weakness, and irrelevance. At the same time, he notes that hybridity and marginality are the 'most salient characteristics of Hong Kong's cultural identity'. The unique social and political circumstances of Hong Kong that have created such fusion and mix are ones that a number of cultural theorists argue are not easily represented by post-colonialism and its accompanying connotations of hybridity (Abbas 1997, pp. 1–2; Law 2000, p. 227; Erni 2001, p. 391). Part of the problem is that Hong Kong has become post-colonial only very recently and also the territory has not achieved independence. For some, the territory remains colonised as 1997 simply marked the transference of the territory between colonial masters (Chow 1998, pp. 148–167). Others, like Law (2000, 209), even consider that Hong Kong culturally colonises and exploits China and other countries in South East Asia through media exports and business models. Post-colonial, colonised, coloniser; it appears that Hong Kong is unable to be appropriately discussed within these frameworks.

But what we see in Chungking Mansions and in our exploration of Muslims in Hong Kong is a particular trope of hybridity, a commonplace, everyday hybridity. The salience of hybridity in daily life is simply too usual to attract much scrutiny as whatever new mixture is encountered is only a nuance of what has already been observed. This banality of hybridity in Hong Kong is one that is often articulated by theorists, novelists, and filmmakers. For example, Forman (2004) discusses the little-known Hong Kong writings of James Dalziel, who, he argues, represents an authentic view of the particular type of cultural hybridity that exists in Hong Kong. Dalziel's works date from 1907 and show that the cultural mix that personifies hybridity in the territory has, for a long time, been part of the Hong Kong story. Forman argues that Dalziel's writings undermine the notion that the empire was a 'bourgeois enterprise' as his European characters have hybrid identities and 'inhabit multiple and far from uniform positions of class, religion, and geographical origin' (2004, p. 547). Forman not only provides an argument that hybridity is historically relevant to Hong Kong culture, but also that hybridity in Hong Kong is unglamorous and commonplace.

With regard to Chungking Mansions, hybridity in Hong Kong is very much an unglamorous affair. It reminds us that the daily business of cultural exchange and inter-mixture happens in mundane spaces and is entwined with the most practical and at times unseemly of affairs. Hybridity resounds in the daily activities of Muslims in Hong Kong, be that speaking multiple languages, pursuing halal food, or learning about Islam in a Chinese cultural space. So, as we move on in this book, it is these dynamics, and this form of hybridity on which a representation of Islam in Hong Kong is built.

Section 2

Religious Practice

5
Learning to be Muslim

A dear Bangladeshi friend tells me that all individuals enter the world as Muslim. Elaborating on this declaration, he explains that all humans are born knowing only purity and goodness, delivered from god. He argues that life, with all its distractions, the very many things to do and experience, ends up taking us away from this initial state of innocence. In reading the Qur'an and following Islam he asserts that one becomes Muslim again. This is not an unusual belief, Sardar (2004, p. 54) discusses an English convert to Islam who loathes the label of convert and tells people that he has returned to his 'natural state', Islam. It is a common practice for converts to Islam to refer to their conversion as a 'reversion', that it is their return to Islam. While this understanding might be seen as a promotion of a type of Islamic essentialism, in other words that everyone is born Muslim, it is for me a reminder that Islam needs to be learnt. It identifies an important issue, that religion is something that needs attention, learning, and study. The popular tendency to see Muslims as one-dimensional characters united in their sense of religious commitment and understanding is profoundly damaging (Hopkins 2009, p. 36). Arguably, no other religion is understood in such limited terms. An enquiry into everyday life offers a means to address the ways in which Muslims learn about Islam and to consider the factors that contribute to their understanding of the religion.

All the individuals in this research were born Muslim. But what is being addressed here is the social and cultural sense of being Muslim. They were born into Muslim families and raised amid Islamic culture in their homes. Some even lived for a time in Islamic countries and were thus immersed in the Islamic world. Despite these circumstances, all of these individuals have had to learn about Islam. It is important to recognise that Islam is learnt and taught, and that everyday activities mould the understanding that young people acquire. In this chapter, we observe how Muslim youth in Hong Kong learn about their religion. It provides a much needed insight in to the religious biographies of Muslims in Hong Kong.

Learning about Islam takes place in three main domains: the home, the mosque, and school. In each of these environments, the participants are exposed to different experiences of their religion and develop their understanding of both Islam and Hong Kong. The processes of learning about Islam in secular Hong Kong are similar to those recounted by youth living as minorities throughout the Western world. What distinguishes the accounts provided in this chapter is their setting in Hong Kong's cultural mosaic, a factor which continually influences what can be learned.

Home and family

The research findings suggest that the home environment plays a crucial role in establishing Islamic education for Muslim youth. Initially, Muslim children learn about religion by watching their parents praying, fasting, and preparing food. As they become older, a more formal approach to religion is adopted as religious study of the Qur'an is introduced. There are some distinct differences between ethnicities regarding what sort of role parents take in organising religious education, and how ideas of home, nation, and gender influence what and how young people learn about Islam.

The first memories of Islam for many of the participants relate to watching parents praying and beginning to learn from them through observation. Sharif, a 14-year-old Pakistani boy, remembers watching his parents pray at home when he was four years old and spoke of his enjoyment and intrigue about the practice. At the age of six he was being taught how to pray by his parents and was slowly learning to participate in religion at home. Elisha reports a similar pattern; her mother taught her the 'basic stuff' when she was young as preparation before she began education at the local mosque. Similarly, some participants discussed their interest in fasting during Ramadan and their excitement about being allowed to gradually join in, as they have grown older. All but one participant begun learning to read the Qur'an in Arabic by the time they were seven. For Pakistani youth, there is a clear transition between a familiarisation with Islam at home and then the commencement of formal education at the mosque.

Those participants who did not attend the local mosque as young children tended to continue their religious education at home. Both Ashja, a 15-year-old Indian boy, and Qaaria, a 13-year-old Sri Lankan girl, learnt to read the Qur'an at home. Ashja initially attended the mosque but felt uncomfortable as Pakistani peers continually questioned his authenticity as a Muslim because of his Indian ethnicity. It was because of this that he refused to attend the mosque and his father subsequently taught him to read the Qur'an at home.

Dil, a locally-born 14-year-old Pakistani girl, illustrates another dimension of home education. During the time that she attended the mosque, she also received supplementary religious instruction in an extended visit to Pakistan to stay with her grandmother. This was a special visit made just by Dil, her sister, and mother. It was also an opportunity for her grandmother to teach her younger female family the nature of being a Pakistani Muslim woman. In addition, Dil was taught domestic responsibilities such as elements of childcare and food preparation. Although these are not strictly religious in content, they are considered crucial skills for Pakistani Muslim women. This visit represents an extension of 'home' education, consolidating the role of the family in the transmission of both religious and culturally specific knowledge. It also underlines the importance of Pakistan as a place of belonging and a place of religious significance. The home can be understood as a space of cultural authenticity that in a variety of ways establishes the foundations of Islamic knowledge and values for young Muslims.

The Mosque

Most participants went to either the Kowloon or Wanchai Mosque for their Qur'anic lessons. It is within these places of worship that Hong Kong's Muslim youth learn to read the Qur'an in Arabic. Their initial experiences of attending lessons underline the importance of the mosque. For the youth in this study the space of the mosque not only represents religious authority, but also relates to an aspect of their Islamic identity that is seldom visible in Hong Kong. That is to say while Islam permeates their daily life, it is actually quite absent from the broader arena of everyday life experienced in the city. Entering a new space, a specifically Islamic space is therefore a significant moment. This is vibrantly captured by Waqi in his recollection of the day when his father took him to the Kowloon mosque to begin his religious education.

> **Waqi:** Well when I entered, I felt very, very good. I was happy and very interested. When I entered I saw so many things all new to me. I entered and met my teacher who gave me a small book. Then he taught me how to read this book. This very small book has the main points that teach us how to read the Qur'an. We learn that first and then we go on to the Qu'ran.

The presence of Waqi's father is notable as it highlights the transition taking place. Domestic tutelage takes a secondary role and the formal learning of Islam begins. For Aseelah a locally-born 15-year-old Pakistani girl, the trip to the mosque on that first day was filled with anxiety and excitement.

> **Aseelah:** I went with my brother the first time. There were so many children there and it was so noisy. All of them were reading the Qur'an and some of them were sitting at a low level. I was kind of scared. I thought where should I sit? In the middle of the room there was the teacher, he would teach us and listen to us recite. I was really scared because I saw him hitting students who made mistakes.

The vast majority of participants attended classes like this at their local mosque once or twice a week and learnt to read the Qur'an over a few years. Aseelah's nervous first encounter at the mosque contrasts with Waqi's awe and excitement. Elisha, who is also a 15-year-old locally-born Pakistani girl, reports a similar experience to that of Aseelah. She recounts lessons at the mosque as a busy noisy affair in which the teacher would sometimes hit students who did not recall the Qura'anic text properly. For most of the participants, however, this was a thing of the past as adolescence represents the end of formal education and the commencement of religious obligations. Seven participants in this study were continuing to attend the mosque for Qur'anic instruction. Two, Hadaf and Sharif, visit the mosque every afternoon for up to three hours as part of their extended study to become a *hafiz*, one who has committed the entire Qur'an to memory.

When I first met Hadaf he was 20 and had been studying for the title of *hafiz* for five years. At the time of our first interview, he could recite the first sixteen sections of the Qur'an from memory. Speaking to him again some five years later, he recounts how it took him eight years in total to memorise and learn to recite the entire Qur'an. He now uses the skill mostly during Ramadan and visits Muslim homes on request to recite the holy book to families. *Hafiz* training typically breaks the Qur'an down into thirty segments, the purpose being that the Qur'an can be completely recited throughout the month of Ramadan, each segment representing a portion of the Qur'an to be read or repeated in a single evening. It is a rote process of learning and should not be confused with theological study.

There is little information available to indicate how common the attainment of the title of *hafiz* is for Muslims who are political minorities. It is, however, interesting to note that four of the Pakistani boys involved in the research are studying to become an *hafiz* and each told me of friends or siblings who have already completed their study. The honour of *hafiz* is one that is enjoyed particularly by parents. This is in part due to the perception that the commitment of the Qur'an to memory is a benefit or service to Islam. Lewis (1994, p. 82) discusses the seventy men that made up the *ulema* (Muslim scholars) of a Bradford mosque. He describes the thirty *hafiz* as having a fairly low status in comparison with the other religious experts; they have a perfunctory Islamic knowledge supplemented by a skill in recitation. A *hafiz* is utilised by the community to give recitations during religious festivals, rites of passage and during prayer meetings and religious gatherings.

The study and attainment of the *hafiz* title is notable. It provides an insight into the level of religious education available in the territory. This specialised focus on recitation is something that is offered, available, in demand, and utilised in Hong Kong. It also demonstrates a cultural difference between young Pakistani men and more generally the rest of youth in Hong Kong who are encouraged and funded by parents to pursue academic achievements. For example, many young Hong Kong people attend extra-curricular classes for additional help with academic study, or to participate in sports in their free time after school and at weekends (Lui 2004). The religious focus, commitment, and education that young Pakistani men pursue show that they have quite different priorities to other youth in Hong Kong. Pakistani men maintain the importance of their religion in an environment where, for many youth, religion is a low priority. Similarly, this investment in the rote learning of a religious text is a notable commitment amidst the numerous social and technological distractions of contemporary Hong Kong.

For many Pakistani boys who have finished their formal religious instruction the mosque continues to be important in their day-to-day religious lives. It is a place where they sometimes meet with friends and relations to pray together, or part of the area in which they eat, work, and socialise. The contact Pakistani girls have with the mosque decreases sharply as their religious education comes to a close. The space surrounding the mosques in both Tsim Sha Tsui and Wanchai, are areas in which young Pakistani men might be found eating food from Pakistani takeaway businesses, playing cricket in the surrounding parks, or simply meeting and chatting with friends. In these spaces, a common element is often the proximity of the mosque.

The mosque is also a significant place of learning for some Indonesian foreign domestic workers, as we have already seen. Sunday at the Wanchai Mosque provides an opportunity for Indonesian women to meet with friends; it is also a place where they spend a day in prayer, listen to lectures, and take lessons in Qur'anic Arabic. Amisha, a 31-year-old Indonesian foreign domestic worker whom I discussed in Chapter 3, spends her Sundays in this way. She tells me that when she was young in Indonesia, she was 'naughty' and avoided her religious study. She now greatly values the fact that in Hong Kong she can learn more about Islam. Specifically, Amisha is learning to read the Qu'ran in Arabic, something she never achieved as a child in Indonesia. When she previously worked for a Chinese family in Malaysia, she was not allowed to pray or wear Islamic dress. So, despite the fact that Malaysia is a Muslim country, she has a more Islamic everyday life in secular Hong Kong, a territory driven by the ideology of rapacious capitalism. There is thus an interesting juxtaposition in this development. Amisha's knowledge of Islam is expanded by her move away from other Islamic countries, one of which is her birthplace and home.

The mosque is significant as it is a place wholly Muslim amidst bustling Hong Kong, a city of unique Chinese and Western fusion. Much of what Muslim youth experience and learn at home and in the mosque relates to interaction with other Muslims, often of their own ethnicity. Importantly, this focus delivers us an account of the mosque that is a departure from representations of it as a place of extremism and subversion. In this analysis, we see the mosque as another aspect of everyday life for young Muslims. We see Muslim youth as real social actors, not simply caricatures contextualised by broader concerns about Muslims as minorities. Simply addressing the fact that Islam is learnt undermines many of the associations of Muslim youth with an inflexible Islamic culture that is opposed to multicultural living.

What is learnt about Islam beyond the home, mosque, school, work, and in street-level negotiations, moves us beyond the sphere of Islamic culture and places Muslims amidst the Hong Kong multiculture. Learning about Islam in these other spaces relates to the management of cultural and religious difference. In these spaces among Muslims of different cultures and non-Muslims alike, multiple opportunities arise by which Muslim youth can reflect on their status as minorities and their religion. Harris's (2009, pp. 191–192) comment that multicultural youth tend to be in positions where they are unable to avoid intercultural transactions is relevant here. We observe that youth learn about Islam through their compulsory immersion in Hong Kong's cultural hybridity.

School and beyond

The majority of the participants attend three different schools, all of which are government-subsidised and cater for Hong Kong's working-class ethnic minorities with an English-language curriculum. There are a few exceptions; Qaaria attends an English-language private international school that provides education for the wealthy sector of Hong Kong's ethnic minorities, largely the expatriate community and middle-class local Chinese families. Fazeelah, who has completed her schooling, previously attended a Chinese Christian school where she was taught in Cantonese and English. The Indonesian domestic workers are all over 20 years of age and the African respondents are all long past their schooling, though many aspire to further study at university.

The type of religious instruction available to participants at their different schools varies considerably. Two schools have little to no religious education, and as a result offer little scope for furthering the students' knowledge of Islam. One school, however, a Chinese Islamic secondary school which six of the participants attend, has Islam on the curriculum. The Pakistani girls that go to this school have a unique opportunity to prolong their formal Islamic education and learn about Islam in a different cultural context. Many of the students to whom I spoke stayed after school for additional lessons on the Qur'an and Arabic pronunciation. Kiran, a 14-year-old Pakistani girl, enjoys going to the Chinese Islamic school because she feels it is less strict than her primary school. She states that her religious education has given her more confidence to wear the headscarf. At primary school where her friends were mostly non-Muslim, she sometimes felt discouraged about wearing the headscarf and was conflicted about what to do. Since learning more about Islam at the Chinese Islamic school, this uncertainty has gone and she now feels confident, as she understands the significance of wearing the headscarf.

With this increased knowledge, a number of students have also developed an insight into the cultural differences that exist in the practice of Islam. Kiran notes how the Chinese teachers practise Islam differently from Pakistani people. One example she gives is that she has been taught to pray to the ground while Chinese Muslims pray with their faces looking upwards. Jumana claims that these differences pose a challenge to daily religious practice as there is no way to make a clear decision about who is right and who is wrong.

> **Jumana:** I learn something here at school in my Islamic education class and then I go home and talk to my mother about it. Sometimes what our teacher has told us is different to what my mother tells me. Then it just gets mixed up and I don't know what to do.

This account shows how two different sources of Islamic authority in Jumana's life contradict each other. Yet, despite this confusion, the female students at the Chinese Islamic school have a depth of understanding about Islam that makes them particularly well-informed in contrast to the other respondents whose education on Islam was mainly focussed on learning to read the Qur'an. In some respects, their knowledge is deeper because they have a prolonged Islamic education. Their exposure to Islam from other, non-Pakistani sources broadens their understanding of the religion. This mixing of Chinese and Pakistani Islamic traditions is an excellent example of Hong Kong's very commonplace, everyday hybridity. The school is actually an example of lived hybridity; it is a place where cultures converge and mix and learn together.

This account shows young Muslims learning about Islam at a Chinese Islamic school and developing an awareness of religion that goes beyond the experiences of the Pakistani community in Hong Kong. The girls wear headscarves in the style of *Hui* women, not the traditional South Asian *dupatta*. Daily life thus requires youth to be versatile and adapt to ambiguity and contradiction. The experience of this cultural mix does appear to present some difficulties and confusions for young Muslims. At the same time, the mix of cultures that they navigate also provides them with opportunities to make their own decisions about religion, to be autonomous and creative in their choices, and to educate others.

Some authors have argued that learning about Islam in a non-Islamic country sometimes encourages youth to engage with pan-Islam and not the culturally-specific Islamic traditions of their family; Modood (1997, pp. 157–158), Dwyer (1998, p. 58), and Bouma, Daw and Munawar (2001, p. 69) provide examples of this in the British and Australian contexts. The focus on Islam beyond cultural ties is, however, less evident in the responses of the other participants and is mostly a characteristic of the students who attend the Chinese Islamic school.

Not all the Muslim students at the Chinese Islamic school feel that their Islamic education is as good as it could be. The fact that the majority of the enrolled students are non-Muslim makes a difference to many of the girls. Sahira, in particular, plans to attend an Islamic college in Pakistan when she is older so that she can learn about Islam in a 'proper' Islamic school where the curriculum is all about Islam and there are 'no other Chinese non-Muslims'. It is interesting to note that Muslim students at this school are a minority; most students are non-Muslim Chinese. In Britain, the United States, and Australia, there are many faith schools that offer the type of segregated education that Sahira desires, where all students are Muslim and boys and girls are taught separately. The Chinese Islamic school is unique as, despite the fact that integration is limited, it provides a space for dialogue and familiarisation between youth of different cultures.

Despite such circumstances providing opportunities for youth to learn more about their religion, the reality of living in a culturally-mixed environment dictates that there are both positive and negative sides to each situation. Sahira's comments highlight that cultural mix should not be uncritically esteemed and this contributes to the project of making hybridity tangible (Noble, Poynting, and Tabar 1999, p. 31; Ang 2001, p. 194). Why should everyone celebrate cultural difference? Why should individuals not want to be surrounded just by their own culture? Her reaction to the environment of the Chinese Islamic school is precisely this. It has created a hunger for more Pakistani Islamic authenticity in her education. This is clearly a legitimate and arguably a common aspect of everyday life within multicultural communities. In such cases a cultural mix sometimes results in a move towards cultural specification as it has in this case with Sahira wishing to become more authentically Pakistani in religious understanding and practice. This is an aspect of multiculturalism, plurality, and cultural hybridity that needs to be acknowledged, as it challenges the idea of an harmonious cultural mix and celebration. Therefore, the mobility of the multiculture and its constant flux can both renew and sustain culture. This can also be regarded as a challenge to arguments that multicultural communities erode or homogenise cultures. It shows how no culture, society, nation, or religion can ever realistically be considered static.

Many of the young Muslims interviewed understand that religious life in Hong Kong is free in comparison to life back in Pakistan, Indonesia, Sri Lanka, Somalia, Ghana, and India. Participants from these countries acknowledge that they can do things in Hong Kong that would not be possible in these other countries. Particularly in Pakistan, girls note that their freedom is strictly circumscribed. They acknowledge that life for friends and relatives in Britain encompasses a lack of freedom. This is due to the fact that many Muslims feel unsafe, threatened, and victimised there. Waqi claims that all people in Hong Kong are free and safe and can go out as late as they please without fear. Sometimes when Waqi is working at a Pakistani grocery store in To Kwa Wan, Chinese workers in the neighbouring businesses ask him about Islam and describe their own religious practices. Waqi says that these workers give respect to Muslims because of their commitment to pray five times a day. These workers appear to be impressed at the conscientious nature of the Pakistani grocers, demonstrated by their commitment to pray so frequently. In many ways, it is an oddity to them, but it is not one they disparage. They receive a practical education on and from Muslims in Hong Kong, and the Pakistani workers appear to be treated affably as a result.

In all of these everyday scenarios, the experience of living in Hong Kong teaches the participants about their religion and their identity as a Muslim. These everyday exchanges also teach them about what it is like being a Muslim in Hong Kong, and that they have a different experience of being Muslim than their peers in other countries. At the Chinese Islamic secondary school, Pakistani Muslims learn about Islam through English in a Chinese cultural space and they develop an awareness of religion that goes beyond the experiences of the Pakistani community in Hong Kong. The students to whom I spoke at the school tacitly appear to be distinguishing Islam as a religion, in contrast to Islam as part of the culture into which they were born. Kiran's new understanding of why she wears the headscarf, and the contradictions that Jumana encounters between school and home, highlight how differing interpretations of Islam encourage the girls to make their own choices about Islam and religious observance.

Qaaria stands out among the participants as one of the few from a middle class background. Unlike the other respondents she is socialised and educated in a wealthy, internationally-aligned community, largely what may be termed 'expatriate'. She attends an international school with a curriculum based on the British secondary system which provides for her extended cross-cultural religious instruction. She is also the only Muslim in the study who does not have Muslim friends; her social circle is entirely non-Muslim. She is in a unique position in the study as she is the only participant who has two parents in full-time employment; all of the other mothers in the research are housewives. At school, her religious education covers a variety of world religions and coincidently at the time of interview she was learning about Islam in her religious studies class at school.

Qaaria states that it is only since she has been at secondary school that she has become more aware of herself as a Muslim. She says that learning about different religions was something that was not done in any depth at her primary school and that this provision at secondary school enables her to reflect upon her own religion. Rather than seeing Islam as a separate and distinct part of her life relevant mostly to the family and the home, learning about it with peers in a non-Islamic context has been an important way for Qaaria to broaden the way she understands herself and her identity as a Muslim.

Learning about Islam at school is important to Qaaria as it blends boundaries; she has been able to learn about Islam in another context, one in which the majority of her time is spent, that is in the English-language and with her Westernised non-Muslim peers. Valuing the authority of the school she also appears to find verification in the content of the lessons. She exhibits pride in the fact that she knows 'almost everything' and that she *is* a Muslim. The process itself is similar to that which

Abbas (1997, p. 25) refers to as reverse hallucination in that what has always been present and evident is not always necessarily recognised or understood. Highmore (2002, p. 142) argues that this same process, the familiar being unrecognisable, is an important element of the scrutiny of everyday life. His argument is that procedures that have always been part of our daily routines are often accepted uncritically, not revisited from different perspectives or analysed. By learning about Islam in another context, Qaaria begins to see herself as a Muslim with greater clarity. These multiple sources of information allow young people to construct their own reflexive understanding of Islam, enabling them to ask different questions about their religious background and to develop a deeper understanding of it.

Qaaria also discusses the Islamic education she receives from her mother and from her prayer teacher. The fact that her secular secondary school adds context to these teachings suggests that the classroom provides a space for her home culture and peer culture to be observed together for the first time. One of the key points that Qaaria makes with regard to learning about Islam at school is that she is being taught nothing new; instead, she is being provided with a different perspective.

> **Qaaria:** My mum and my prayer teacher are the ones that teach me about Islam. We also learn in school and right now we are learning about Islam and fasting during Ramadan. I already know half the things we learn.
>
> **Paul:** Is it strange learning it when you have this taught to you at home?
>
> **Qaaria:** Yes, it is strange because they teach us differently. I know almost everything they teach us at school because my mum has taught it to me or my prayer teacher has taught me. At school they show us videos and they explain it differently.

Qaaria's account above shows how learning about other religions enables a broader understanding of one's own religion. But for many young Muslims in Hong Kong, religious education at school is either unavailable, or focussed on one particular religion. Fazeelah, for example, a 30-year-old female *Hui*, attended a Christian school and sought Islamic education independently at the Wanchai Mosque. Her case highlights how there is a conflict between academic education and Islamic education. At her school, she kept her Islamic identity secret. She followed the

Christian prayers during school assemblies and Islam was very much absent in her education. Her parents, like many *Hui*, prioritise academic work and success above religion. Thus we see that the choices, resources, ethnicity and social class of parents strongly influence how their children learn about Islam and in turn how their children understand their religion, engage with, and practise it.

Many of the participants have finished all forms of institutional or formal religious education. Pari, a 14-year-old Pakistani girl, is the most influenced by local Chinese culture of all the non-Chinese respondents. For her, the end of Islamic education has had repercussions upon her behaviour. She feels she has forgotten all her Islamic education to the extreme that when she is with her Chinese friends, she forgets that she is a Muslim. Pari's parents are worried about her Islamic education because she does not pray. In particular, this is a concern that she raises because she feels she is getting older and growing up. She feels she must become more responsible as she matures. Her parents remind her that she is a Muslim, that she is not Chinese, that she must read the Qur'an. When Pari is scolded in this manner she begins to remember what being a Muslim is about and what she should do. Pari reveals that two of her three brothers are just like her and that it is only her eldest brother who is really committed to Islam. Pari's parents persist in telling her and her two brothers to pray, continually trying to encourage them. This, however, seems to have little effect, as they are, at least for the time being, far more influenced by their Chinese friends and less so by Islamic practice.

School provides a spectrum of different types and methods by which youth continue to learn about Islam. It holds the potential to extend religious education and in addition broaden young people's engagement with and understanding of the cultural melange of which they are part. Waqi discusses religion with his friends at school, especially when they are messing around and wasting time. He reports that he often uses this as an opportunity to talk about how they make prayers and to learn from each other. Jumana also shares an interest in talking about religion with friends and pursues further education independently by reading various books on Islam in her free time. School for the majority of the participants provides a place where they can be with and talk to Muslim peers. Despite not always having access to religious education, or prayer rooms (see Chapter 6) at certain schools, young people can continue to have a religious dialogue and informal education among friends of the same faith while at school.

However, for those participants who have not received religious education at school and who no longer attend the mosque, there is a notable break in their learning about Islam. This was most tangible in the accounts offered by girls. Pari, Elisha, and Inas have all finished their religious education and spend much of their time with non-Muslim peers. What they now learn about Islam and being Muslim corresponds more and more frequently with their everyday experiences of life in Hong Kong.

Muslims made in Hong Kong

These youth have been learning to be Muslim their entire lives. Primarily, parents have provided the initial introduction to Islamic practices at home; they also organise the structure of institutional education at the mosque, or arrangements for Islamic teachers to visit the home, or in some cases they provide the education themselves. For some individuals, formal education extends to their secondary school or prolonged Qur'anic study in pursuit of the title of *hafiz*. In sum, these accounts show how youth learn to be Muslim in Hong Kong, and how their cultural backgrounds and gender influence how and what they learn about Islam.

For the majority, formal education seems to be closely related to the cultural traditions of their ethnic community and family. Pakistanis go to study the Qur'an at the mosque, while some non-Pakistanis, like Ashja and Qaaria, learn at home. In contrast, Fazeelah, like many *Hui*, did not learn about Islam until she was older. A number of the respondents reported that there occasionally was a Chinese Muslim in their Qur'anic classes. None of the respondents, including the Indonesian domestic workers, actually had any real contact with *Hui*. The opportunity to learn about religion from more than one source is a factor that appears to facilitate autonomous learning about Islam by young people.

These youth have learned about Islam in Hong Kong, and as a result they have acquired a specific understanding about what it means to be a Muslim in the territory. For example, Ashja learnt in his brief time at the mosque that as an Indian Muslim in Hong Kong he is in a double minority, marginalised by Pakistani peers who appear to have hegemony over particular religious spaces.

These accounts make us question how the discourse of 'Islam in the West' may influence Muslim youth in Western nations. The many negative portrayals of Islam in the media (Hopkins 2009, pp. 35–36) contribute to how Muslim youth in the West understand and conceptualise Muslims and their religion. In the Hong Kong context, with little negative portrayal of Islam locally, Muslims construct a religious identity that is less influenced by post-9/11 politics, and the monotheistic religious frictions it so often exploits.

Alternatively, Fazeelah has learnt how to compartmentalise her life, how she, as a Chinese Muslim, can be a secret Muslim in Hong Kong (this is a dynamic explained more fully in Chapter 9). Jumana and Kiran have experienced different cultural interpretations of Islam in their education and everyday experiences. For many this type of learning is subtle; it takes place through discussions with friends abroad, or contact with Muslims from other cultures. In essence, the processes that young Muslims go through in Hong Kong as they learn about Islam are much the same as those experienced by Muslim youth in the West (Baumann 1996; Lewis 2007; Jacobson 1998). Muslim youth encounter many of the obstacles and issues that colour the experiences of other multicultural youth (Phillips 2009, p. 2). What is crucial to underline is that while the processes remain much the same, the context delivers explicit and tangible differences. Muslim youth in Hong Kong are free to be Muslim and experience this freedom in the processes of walking through the city, attending the mosque, and going to school. Arguably, religious education performs an important role in a multicultural society. It enables youth to reflect on their own religious and cultural identity and to understand that of others. Furthermore, the everyday component of living as a minority has educated the young Muslims in this research about their religion and influenced the type of Muslims that they have become.

6
Daily practice

Everyday life is characterised by de Certeau (1984, p. 43) as a 'vast ensemble' of *'procedures'*. Islam, perhaps more so than any other religion with the exception of orthodox Judaism, places a great focus on orthopraxis, the following of correct procedures. The daily lives of Muslims involve an array of religious obligations, and as such, these procedures have come to be more indicative of Islam in the non-Muslim sphere than the actual tenets of Islamic belief to which they relate. The five pillars of Islam dictate the obligations Muslims must attend to continually, daily, monthly, annually, and in reference to *Hajj*, once in a lifetime. This chapter looks at two of these obligations, that of daily prayers and the annual fast during the month of Ramadan, both of which set Muslims apart from their non-Muslim peers during everyday activities. The following discussion shows how individuals manage their religious obligations in everyday situations and circumstances. We see in these accounts how our sample of young Muslims encounter a variety of external expectations and demands regarding their time and religious behaviour. These testimonies highlight how religious practice is tied not only to family traditions and ethnicity, but also to how daily life in Hong Kong influences religious observance. Islamic practice is identified as part of the rhythm of everyday life in Hong Kong. These accounts of religious practice add context to an emerging theme in this book; that is, Islam is not a contentious or volatile issue in Hong Kong and Muslims are free to observe their religion both legally and socially.

Of all daily commitments a Muslim makes, prayer is the one that sets them apart from the regular processes of the day in non-Muslim communities. Unlike consuming halal food, which can be performed alongside non-Muslims however problematic this may be, prayer fixes a moment where Muslims must leave their non-Muslim peers and perform as a Muslim alone. It is a daily obligation that must be made five times. There are specific rites about how each prayer should be performed and at what time. Prayer times vary seasonally and relate to ambiguous Qur'anic guidelines which are supplemented by the example of the prophet Muhammad as outlined in the Sunnah. In a Muslim country the call to prayer by the *Muezzin* from the mosque minaret releases Muslims of the need to be mindful of these times themselves; they are informed. In a non-Muslim society the time must be obtained from the local mosque, through Muslim friends, or sought out independently online. From the beginnings of the religion of Islam, it was understood that prayers could not always be made at their exact times and so if Muslims are unable to perform one of the daily prayers, they are given the concession that they can make them up another time by adding them to a later prayer.

The circumstances of the participants in the research vary in terms of their willingness and ability to perform the daily prayers. The vast majority of the youth pray every day and on average manage three of their daily prayers. At least nine have a daily routine in which they complete all their prayers each day. Out of the 37 respondents, seven are infrequent prayers who prefer to leave the precise details of their prayer life ambiguous. In some cases this is due to other commitments in their daily lives, while in others prayers are simply a low priority. School obviously presents an obstacle in attending to prayers. For Indonesian foreign domestic workers, prayers are simply not possible during the busy demands of their daily work.

The extent of the difference in the performance of daily prayers is immediately apparent when we address how the first prayer of the day is approached. This prayer is called the *fajr* prayer, the dawn prayer, and can be performed between first light and sunrise (Qur'an S 24:58). At the time of writing the Islamic Union of Hong Kong's website (http://www.iuhk.org), which lists the time for the daily prayers, says that *fajr* starts at 04:24 and that sunrise is at 05:47. Ashja wakes early each morning and performs his prayers with his father and brother. Along with praying, Ashja uses this early start to the day to do extra studies and homework before he has breakfast and travels to school. For Qaaria, the morning prayer is also an important part of her daily routine. However, she feels that her busy schedule prevents her from participating in the other prayers over the course of the day.

> **Qaaria:** ... I've got so many other things to do. After school stuff, so I don't really pay much attention to my religion *(said as starting laugh)*.
>
> **Paul:** That's fine.
>
> **Qaaria:** I mean I do. But I don't pray five times a day or anything like that.

It is sometimes difficult for non-Muslims to grasp that Muslims do not always attend to their prayers because Islam is generally essentialised in terms of orthopraxy. Not all Muslims worship regularly; many Muslims pray simply when they feel like it (Basit 1997, p. 41). These responses highlight again how young Muslims have considerable autonomy regarding how they choose to follow Islam.

Prayers are an important part of Jumana's daily routine; the morning prayer is a central focus in her morning schedule of waking and preparing for school. Elisha also prays every day when she wakes. However, a number of other girls do not always manage this prayer and omit this observation entirely. Many feel that the *fajr* prayer is simply too early. Sahira generally does not perform her morning prayers. Her mother often wakes her at 05.30 to pray, but despite this, she just stays in bed and falls back to sleep. For Pari the situation is much the same, in relation to the first prayer of the day she says that 'in the morning I can't get up from my bed'. Many respondents are a little guarded about how frequently they pray, but for Dil this is not an issue, she is happy to declare that she prays when she can and that this is sufficient for her.

> **Dil:** Actually I can manage only three of the daily prayers because the two prayers I miss, one is very early in the morning. I can't wake that early, and the second one is about one o'clock to two thirty and I am in school at that time.

These accounts not only challenge an essential or monolithic idea of Islamic culture, they also show young Muslims being innovative about their religious practice. Here, we see Muslim youth exercising a choice. Prayers are simply a part of everyday life; they do not define Muslim youth any more than any other everyday factor.

In contrast to the morning prayer, which for all the participants is something to attend to at home, many of the other prayers performed throughout the day occur during school time. The different schools that the participants attend all have differing levels of support for Muslim students. The Chinese Islamic school makes provision for students to perform all their prayers during school time and to also have a special communal *Jumu'ah* prayer for Muslim students to attend together. *Jumu'ah* prayer is the most important prayer for Muslims each week and takes place on Friday lunchtimes. The importance of this prayer is also acknowledged and facilitated by the principal of the government school that Waqi, Elisha, and Inas attend. Their school in contrast to the Chinese Islamic school is a secular government institution. It is, however, a school closely associated with South Asians in the territory. Each Friday the school makes a room available for the *Jumu'ah* prayers but has no space or time allowed in the school day for the other Muslim prayers. The lack of Islamic provision or guidance at this school and the other secular government school included in the research contributes to a variety of negative feelings that have been reported by some parents. These concerns have been voiced alongside other complaints regarding the school system which focus on a lack of discipline, poor monitoring of school uniforms, and students' informal interaction with staff (Ku et al. 2003, pp. 50–51). The school that Dil, Hadaf, and Ashja attend had little support for students' daily prayers when I first visited in 2006. Hadaf told me at that time that students who wanted to pray on Friday for the *Jumu'ah* prayers had to travel to a local mosque either in Sham Shui Po or Tsim Sha Tsui. This was allowed by the principal although there were some concerns that some Pakistani boys might just take Friday afternoon off as a break. Now the situation has changed and Muslim pupils are allowed to perform their prayers in the school gym in between classes and are given full use of this space for *Jumu'ah* prayers on Friday lunchtimes. The international school that Qaaria attends has the least provision for prayers with neither time nor space available for the few Muslim students they have.

At Waqi's school, students are given the use of a classroom for their weekly *Jumu'ah* prayers. This provision is one that seems to be used exclusively by Pakistani boys, as Waqi explains.

> **Waqi:** Most of the Pakistani boys go, we have some boys from Malaysia and Indonesia they are Muslim but they don't come. They are Muslim, they know they are Muslim and they should come to pray, but they don't. Most of the Pakistani boys come.

While religion in Hong Kong is generally accepted without conflict, it is interesting to note that among Muslims, Islamic practice is sometimes used as a way of criticising other ethnic groups. Waqi's comments are thus reflected back on to his own ethnicity by Inas. She provides an interesting insight when talking about prejudice and anti-racism at school. Despite her school having over 40 different nationalities on the register, she states that there are no real activities raising awareness of different cultures or combating racism. She reveals that there are certain issues of difference and prejudice at her school.

> **Inas:** The Pakistanis are so straight, they have to wear the headscarf and long clothes. Sometimes they don't talk to the Christians at school, some hate them.

In numerous discussions with Muslims at the mosques, schools, and with asylum seekers at Chungking Mansions, I encountered similar remarks regarding how Indonesians, Pakistanis, Africans, or Filipinos practised Islam. This again shows the diversity of Islamic practice, that it is versatile and adaptable to different cultural spaces and traditions. These comparisons never debated the tenets of belief, but instead were critical of practices and observance. Muslims in Hong Kong therefore appear to be perfectly aware that there are different ways to follow Islam, though they may not always be tolerant, or positive about them. It is very clear that Pakistanis, Indonesians, and *Hui* have different attitudes and beliefs regarding Islam. In light of these comments, it is also worth noting that some ethnic groups exercise hegemony over religious spaces. The *Jumu'ah* prayer room at Waqi's school and Ashja's reticence about attending the mosque underline these factors. Those who do attend the mosque are male and they refer to the mosque as a part of their social territory. They meet friends, eat, play games, and shop in the areas surrounding their local mosque.

The mosque that Insaf occasionally attends is a converted office space in the Indonesian consulate and as such is exclusively patronised by Indonesians. In this respect, practising Islam in Hong Kong for Insaf is ultimately a monocultural experience; he does not worship, or discuss Islam with other Muslims and only visits Muslim institutions that are connected to his homeland. Through various questions I came to understand that Insaf infrequently visits the 'office' mosque. He clearly does not go during the week and states that he is unable to perform *Jumu'ah* prayers because of his school timetable. He usually only goes to the mosque during festivals or celebrations. Despite this, Insaf appears very humble, earnest and softly spoken on the subject of Islam. Whatever can be taken from these responses needs also to be placed in the context that Insaf has only lived in Hong Kong for one year and is due to return to Jakarta in three more years. I speculate that Insaf considers Islam a mostly stable and secure part of his life and it therefore does not require the attention that school and social activities do in his new home. For Insaf it appears that learning English, being among peers from a variety of different cultures, and becoming familiar with Hong Kong are the most pressing of daily concerns. In light of this, I gathered that while his religious practice has altered since arriving in Hong Kong, his beliefs, and Islamic principles have not really changed since leaving Indonesia.

Ramadan

Each year during Ramadan, Muslims take on an additional daily religious obligation to fast throughout the month. During this month, Muslims are required to abstain from food and drink during daylight hours; they must read the Qur'an and be more mindful of religion in their daily life. Amisha, an Indonesia domestic helper, finds that Ramadan is very special in Hong Kong. She takes the time to think about others less fortunate than herself and to read the Qur'an. Her employers have no objection to her fasting and she feels supported in her religious commitments. Ramadan for Amisha is just as special in Hong Kong as it is in Indonesia. While many Indonesian foreign domestic helpers do not observe fasting while in Hong Kong, this does not bother Amisha. She simply asks that her friends not eat around her during the hours of fasting. The celebration at the end of Ramadan is termed *Hari Lebaran* by Indonesians and Malays. The communal prayers that take place at this time in Victoria Park are popular among all types of Indonesian foreign domestic workers, whether they are observant or not. Amisha noted that many Chinese employers support the religious festivals and commitment of their Indonesian helpers. She had even heard of some cases where women have been working in Hong Kong for several years and their employers have paid for them to make *hajj*, the pilgrimage to Mecca.

Waqi provides a contrast to these accounts. He has lived in Hong Kong for many years and provides an illuminating insight into the challenges of Ramadan as a male Muslim in the territory.

> **Waqi:** In Hong Kong it is really very hard to have this month. Each day we eat in the morning but we don't have anything else to eat until six or seven o'clock in the evening. Everything, even our eyes, ears and lips they can't do bad. Our lips can't say wrong things, ears can't hear bad things, and eyes can't see bad things. But here in Hong Kong it's very hard to protect our eyes and our ears, because girls wear short skirts and easily you can see a girl who is wearing a short skirt. In Pakistan they wear the full dress and it's different from here than in Pakistan.

Waqi's account provides context to understanding the practice of Islam in a non-Islamic country. Hong Kong has been described as a 'louche and lascivious city' (Morris 1997, p. 55) and in many ways Waqi has tacitly acknowledged this in his comment. It could also be argued as an insight into the heightened visibility of contemporary Westernised femininity and sexuality, on display and to be gazed upon. In reviewing research on Muslim minorities, I have never encountered such an articulation of the challenges during Ramadan. It is an informative insight into a different type of test during Ramadan, which, instead of relating to pangs of hunger, details the difficulty of avoiding lustful thoughts. His response is presented with the awareness of having lived in an Islamic country. It highlights a concern about being a good Muslim during Ramadan that is particular to his experience of growing up as a young man in both Hong Kong and Pakistan. It is a street-level insight about an everyday issue.

Waqi, however, was not alone in highlighting such conflicts. Iftikhar from Somalia joked with Franky from Ghana that there were plenty of temptations and distractions in Hong Kong during Ramadan. Franky explained that he has spent Ramadan in various different countries. He once spent the month of Ramadan in Saudi Arabia and cherishes this special time. He also recalls fondly how Ramadan is celebrated in his home country Ghana. Even though the country has a religious mix, Christian businesses respect Ramadan and adapt to the daily fast and open in the evenings instead of the daytime. For Franky, Hong Kong during Ramadan is only reflected in the services at the mosque. For him, everyday life pretty much remains the same. With this normalcy comes distractions and obstacles.

> **Franky:** Something you don't want to see, you see. Something you don't want to hear, you hear.

This is clearly challenging for Iftikhar too. He explains that 'where I am from everyone is Muslim' and as a result no food, or restaurant, is available during daylight hours in Mogadishu. Everyone experiences Ramadan together. In Hong Kong, by contrast, Ramadan is a non-event. Unlike many of the other respondents, Franky and Iftikhar, as asylum seekers, experience religious festivities in a lonelier manner with no family to celebrate with. As a result, their experience of Ramadan speaks of the street-level absence of festivity, change, and the typical religious solemnity experienced at home.

Family is central to the accounts of Ramadan given by many of the young women. Elisha visits the mosque with her family during the two *Eid* celebrations and brings beef as a gift to give to family, friends, and relatives. Elisha's visits to the mosque are now no longer ones in which to learn, they have become occasional visits of religious significance during festival times. She attends with her family, not independently, and the focus is not upon prayer but upon celebrating, eating, and meeting with friends and relatives. A similar account is given by Qaaria in which she details what the women's prayer hall in the Wanchai Mosque is like.

> **Qaaria:** We only go once every year during Ramadan. I think it's the same in all mosques, but there is this separate section for women and men. We are on the top floor, then men are just below us and the guy that conducts the prayers is downstairs. There is a hole in the floor in the women's prayer room. We can hear what he says in the men's prayer room below and you can see the men. We all stand together and we start praying.

Qaaria does not note any particular obstacles to fasting during Ramadan, but many others describe fasting when friends are eating as the greatest challenge throughout this month. Pari, who considers herself Chinese in many respects, explains Ramadan to her Chinese friends and tells them when she is fasting. They appear to respect this and let Pari do as she pleases. Aseelah also fasts among many non-Muslim friends, in particular outside of school with her best friend who is Chinese. She comments that friends are sometimes curious about fasting and her best friend tries to fast also. This is a very good example of youth engaging with the diversity that surrounds them and learning about the different cultures with which they come into contact. Aseelah's friend learns from her about fasting during Ramadan and even participates in the religious practice in a basic manner. Aseelah provides a contrast to suggestions that Muslim youth are radicalised by Islam and encouraged to strictly follow the faith by their parents. Like many others, Aseelah spoke about her enthusiasm to fast as a young child, though her parents encouraged her to put off fasting until she was older.

> **Aseelah:** When I was young I used to be interested in fasting. I would say I am going to start fasting. This is easy to say but it's hard when you feel hungry … When I was young my parents wouldn't allow me to fast because my dad felt we were too thin. He thinks that we are too thin and it's not healthy to fast.

When she was younger, around the age of 12 when children are expected to join in fasting, her parents would let her only fast for one day during the month of Ramadan. Aseelah's account highlights again the presence of parents in overseeing the religious affairs of their children. Such behaviour relates to the findings of both Basit (1997, p. 40) and Bauman (1996, p. 85) that children are eager to be involved in religious practice and parents often want to protect them from religious responsibility too young. While it is often the case that enthusiastic young children want to participate in Islamic practice, these same parents often encounter another issue when their children become adolescents. Parental interference with how frequently their children pray or read the Qur'an is very common. Many participants report that their mothers chase them up about prayers and fasting.

> **Dil:** My mum is always after me that I should pray but sometimes I just skip it because I am tired … My dad doesn't pray but my mum makes her prayers everyday.
> **Paul:** So does she tell your dad off as well?
> **Dil:** She does but my dad just says, 'I am a working man.'

Elisha gives a similar example.

> **Elisha:** Sometimes I skip the prayers because I am tired. Really, really tired. My mum gives me this lecture, telling me that she used to pray five times a day and that she learnt to cook at the age of eight and she did all the housework.

Such responses again underline the argument that women are the transmitters of culture (Yuval-Davis 1997, p. 196): a pattern that is also discernible in the role that mothers play in the early education of children regarding prayers and the fundamentals of Islam. For many of the Pakistani girls, Ramadan is another topic that illustrates the importance of their home life. Elisha, Dil, Aseelah, and Kiran all speak with warmth about their family and the pastimes that they share collectively.

Kiran provides a rich description of her close relationship with relatives while referring to the practice of eating prior to sunrise. Each morning of Ramadan, families wake up very early to have large meals to see them through the day. Kiran's mother knows that the family often does not want to eat a hearty meal at such an early hour and therefore plans the meals carefully. Each morning the family is presented with their favourite foods to ensure that they will eat lots in order to give them stamina for the day ahead. Kiran also describes *Chaand Raat* night (meaning 'the night of the moon') which is a particularly popular Pakistani celebration on the last night of Ramadan.

> **Kiran:** My cousins come to my house. Before the night of *Eid* we have the Pakistani culture called *Chaand Raat* Moon night. All the girls get together and dance and do henna painting. We check out our clothes and everything like that. In the morning we have to pray and then all our cousins come to visit and we get a lot of money and eat a lot of food. All the girls go shopping and have dinner together.

During this shopping spree Kiran buys stationery or 'girls' stuff' and visits some of the big shopping malls or department stores with her female relatives. Kiran's account blends a number of different themes together. It highlights a transnational theme in the persistence of a culturally specific Islamic celebration *Chand Raat* in Hong Kong. It also reveals the enjoyment she has celebrating with her aunties and cousins, and shows that there are strong bonds between them. Kiran also gets the opportunity at this time to fully indulge in girl consumption patterns, the hallmark and confirmation of contemporary female youth (Harris 2004, pp. 121–123).

Living Islam in Hong Kong

At the start of Ramadan in 2010, a group of beggars gathered outside the Tsim Sha Tsui Mosque on Nathan Road. The group, an annual presence, had grown in size since the previous year as a number of Mainland beggars had now joined the local Hong Kong beggars. The new additions caused friction among the veteran Ramadan panhandlers and a scuffle took place. This bizarre anecdote provides a very basic truth about Islam in Hong Kong; it is part of the rhythm of everyday life. It is recognised and incorporated into the workings of the territory. These beggars understand that during Ramadan many Muslims contribute to charity; performing *Zakat* is one of their religious rites. This knowledge of Islam in Hong Kong, and this annual performance outside the Kowloon Mosque, demonstrates Islam as a living part of Hong Kong's hybrid culture.

The varied accounts of the participants in this chapter provide a rich insight into the different ways in which young Muslims follow and live Islam in Hong Kong. Anecdotes regarding prayers and fasting show how the youth navigate a variety of obstacles and circumstances in religious observance. These descriptive accounts of religious practice illustrate the fact that Islam in Hong Kong is for many Muslims a sphere of life which is tied to their ethnicity. It also shows that many different types of Islam are practised in Hong Kong, not just in terms of national and ethnic cultures, but also individual practices that are constantly in flux. These accounts support the argument that Islam is a facet of culture and identity that is cultivated in innumerable ways over an entire lifetime (Zine 2001, p. 404). We see that the participants practise their religion amidst an array of differences and ambiguities regarding religious obligations. The fact that the Muslims in this study choose to attend to all their prayers, few, or none at all, appears to be something that fits with their day-to-day lifestyle and the actions of their peers. While parents and particularly mothers encourage Islamic observation among their children, it is not strictly enforced, and as such youth have a good deal of autonomy and freedom to follow Islam within certain boundaries. In the case of Insaf, Hong Kong's diversity appears to have little impact on his religious observation. Insaf's cultural mix permeates his life, but it currently makes a shallow impact on the way he practises Islam. Individuals are not uniformly culturally mixed; hybridity is uneven, and not every aspect of their daily life and culture is a fusion and representation of the mixing of cultures.

In acknowledging the discourse of Muslims as minorities we can again consider how everyday hybridity facilitates a broad understanding of the lived experiences of young Muslims. Here, we engage with the daily practice of religion and we are reminded that Muslims are not defined by Islam, that it is simply a part of the ensemble of their lives.

Media reportage and fears concerning Islamic ideology have obscured these truths. Muslims are too frequently only understood through a distorted lens regarding the challenge and threat of Islam. Many Muslims never manage to pray five times a day, or seldom read the Qur'an. These representations of Muslims, mundane and banal as they may sometimes be, are necessary to counter the overwhelming amount of information that addresses Muslims as individuals and communities only in terms of conflict. The next chapter closely examines the issue of halal food for Muslims in Hong Kong, revealing once more a variety of different attitudes to everyday religious observance.

7
The ambiguity of halal food in Hong Kong

Preserving a halal diet is one of the obligations that Muslims have that highlights their presence as minorities among non-Muslims in a distinct way. Keeping a halal diet in a non-Islamic country reminds Muslims of their religious identity. Unlike the wearing of the veil that reveals a woman publicly as a Muslim, halal food requires a Muslim to be conscientious of their own difference from the non-Muslim majorities they live among. While it is an aspect of religious observance, it is also a very practical reminder to Muslims of their minority status. It is therefore odd for those who have no special dietary requirements to imagine what sort of impact an abstinence from pork might have on everyday life. In Muslim countries the injunction against pork is of little consequence, as the meat is not available because it is neither a part of the region's diet nor culture (Pillsbury 1978, p. 659). Muslims in the West are, however, living amid a culture in which pork is popularly accepted and they are therefore constantly on guard about what they eat.

This chapter highlights how problematic a halal diet can be for Muslims living amid a Chinese food culture, where pork is a cherished ingredient in Chinese cooking. Against the culinary cultural background of Hong Kong, young Muslims make conflicting decisions about what foods are suitably halal and what is not acceptable for them to consume. In some ways this is compounded by language ability; most non-Chinese Muslims have better English-language skills than Chinese skills (Tang 2006, pp. 25–26; Detaramani and Lock 2003), which presents another barrier in obtaining information about the spectrum of food available to them. While racism is an issue for many Muslims in Hong Kong, halal food poses a distinct obstacle that is perhaps more tangible and problematic than incidents of prejudice. The everyday challenges of living as a Muslim in Hong Kong are arguably most distinct with regard to keeping a halal diet. That is not to say that it is impossible or even very difficult, it is however awkward to live, as many of the participants do, away from Islamic businesses and attend school or work with non-Muslims, and to socialise in the city eating only halal foods. Pillsbury's anthropology of *Hui* in Taiwan highlights the realignment that Islam takes in fusion with Chinese culture. She notes that in conversation with one elderly *Hui* it is claimed that the need to avoid pork is more important than the requirement to pray five times a day (1975, p. 142). Vigilance for the Chinese Muslim is thus reoriented not on attention to prayer, but upon avoidance of pork. In highlighting the central nature of pork in Chinese cooking and culture, Pillsbury explains that the Chinese ideogram for 'home' (家) contains symbols for both 'pig' (豕) and 'roof' (宀) (Pillsbury 1975, p. 142). This example shows precisely how important and fondly the pig is viewed in Chinese culture. The pork proscription is arguably the key cultural signifier of *Hui* in Chinese society.

Writing on the large *Hui* community in the Chinese city of Xian, Gillette gives some in-depth detail about the lengths that Muslims will go to in order to avoid the perceived polluting effects of pork. Crucially, this leads to an abrupt boundary construction between *Hui* and Han in that they are unable to eat together and therefore socialise. The polluting effects of pork are felt to even prevent *Hui* from drinking tea from a cup in a Han house or restaurant as it will have most likely been washed in water that cleaned utensils that cooked, held, or cut pork (Gillette 2000, p. 121). Stereotypes and prejudicial proverbs from China again show that pork is a fundamental boundary between *Hui* and Han identity. One Chinese proverb suggests that a Muslim travelling alone will become fat, while two travelling together would waste away (Israeli 2002, p. 302). This proverb, like others which speak of Muslims, shows how the Han perceive them to be duplicitous secret pork-eaters. Offence and avoidance of pork is even entwined in the way *Hui* choose to speak, avoiding the word 'pig' even when discussing its representation in the Chinese zodiac, but articulating it as a profane and derogatory expression when using foul language (Gillette 2000, p.122). Highlighting once more the association between Han Chinese and *Hui*, Gillette states that *Hui* who move out of the Muslim quarter of Xian are often believed to have compromised on their halal diet and have begun to eat pork (2000, p. 52).

Most of the information regarding being Muslim in a Chinese cultural climate refers to those who are nominally Chinese Muslims, the *Hui* and the Uyghur. The Hong Kong context provides an opportunity to also consider how Muslims from Southeast Asia, Africa, and the Indian subcontinent engage with Chinese cuisine and try to keep a halal diet. Therefore, it is helpful to clarify just what halal food, or allowed food, encompasses. Halal food is not simply that which does not contain pork. All meat to be consumed by Muslims must be slaughtered ritually, cut across the neck while a spoken acknowledgement of god as creator is given. Meat not slaughtered this way is considered *haraam*, forbidden, and food that contains traces of non-halal meat is also *haraam*. Other foods that may appear halal can also be suspect as they contain ingredients such as gelatine or monosodium glutamate which can contain non-halal meat products. Cross-contamination of foods in preparation can also make food *haraam* so some Muslims are cautious and avoid utensils that have been used in kitchens where halal food laws are not followed. For some Muslims, factory food may also be considered *haraam* because of the threat of cross-contamination from machinery or workers. In a broader sense, *haraam* can also relate to other forbidden items and actions such as alcohol, drugs, and adultery. Regarding food there is great variance between Muslims both culturally and individually as to the extent with which they follow halal laws. For instance, Pakistanis in this project voiced the greatest concerns about halal food. The Africans I spoke to were on the whole more relaxed than Pakistanis regarding halal food. It was only among Indonesian foreign domestic workers that I found respondents who admitted to knowingly eating pork.

In this chapter we see what issues are involved in following or keeping a halal diet. The testimonies reveal how ambiguous the title of halal is in the daily processes of eating foods within the city. The ambiguity requires young Muslims to make a variety of decisions about how fastidious they should be in their halal demands when navigating Hong Kong, and socialising with friends. This ambiguity is accompanied by concerns about family and cultural norms and religious belief and commitment. These accounts resonate with the point made by Ang (2001, p. 143) that 'ambivalence pervades the micro-politics of everyday life in a multicultural society'. However, '*ambiguity* is a category of everyday life and perhaps an essential category' (Lefebvre 1991, p. 18). So it is worth remembering that while the multiculture is a prime site for recognising such challenges, such difficulties are diffused throughout everyday life. While it has been popular to consider food a key way to celebrate and engage with other cultures (Hage 1997) in everyday hybridity, food can also be a site where the differences between minority and majority cultures are at their most distinct and most banal. Indeed, 'nothing is more variable from one human group to another than the notion of what is edible' (de Certeau, Giard, and Mayol 1998, p. 168).

Halal in practice

The primary patterns of keeping halal for young Muslims in Hong Kong are largely related to the norms associated with food at home and also the time the youth spend at home. Accordingly, there are slight gender differences to be noted as the use of home space varies considerably between male and female participants. The ambiguity of eating food outside of the home illustrates that many youth are quite flexible with their definition of halal food and that these definitions are often negotiated among peers. Many young Muslims in Hong Kong avoid Chinese food altogether, while some frequently eat particular types of Chinese foods. By contrast, all the participants eat fast food, commonly McDonald's, but also including *dim sum* and halal food from Pakistani takeaways. As a result, the discussions about halal food focus on food prepared at home and the consumption of fast foods.

Through the issue of halal food we see young Muslims approaching their religious and cultural values in quite different ways, dealing with real issues of difference in pragmatic terms. In many cases the accounts highlight differences already noted with regard to class and gender, and similarly they illustrate the everyday social patterns and spaces youth encounter. In addition, much of what follows in this chapter provides some of the keenest insights into the everyday lives of young Muslims in Hong Kong. Halal food is one aspect of being a Muslim, but the topic of food itself encompasses a whole range of everyday scenarios. We learn much more about where these young people spend their time, who they are with when they eat, and what kind of a budget they have for food and social activities.

Where to eat?

Throughout Hong Kong there are a variety of different establishments that provide halal food products for cooking, and restaurants that cook and sell halal meals. In many cases these businesses are at their most concentrated in areas which Muslims frequent, often close to some of the established mosques. On Hong Kong Island there is a halal butcher in the Bowrington Road wet market in Causeway Bay. Currently, this is the only one on the island, although there have been others in the past such as one in Happy Valley. The Bowrington Road wet market is opposite Chan Tong Lane which houses the Chinese Muslim Cultural and Fraternal Society, which is itself approximately 150 metres away from the Wanchai Islamic Centre on Oi Kwan Road. At the Islamic centre there is a halal restaurant that is open daily, and in the vicinity there are a number of South Asian halal restaurants and Pakistani grocery stores. At one stage there was a popular halal dim sum restaurant close by on Morrison Hill Road, but it

Figure 7 The halal butcher at Bowrington Road Wet Market (photo by author)

is rumoured that the gambling debts of the *Hui* owner forced its closure. Around the Kowloon Mosque it is much the same story. Grocery stores and restaurants are numerous, particularly in the nearby Chungking Mansions where South Asian food stalls are scattered among DVD shops selling Bollywood and Nollywood movies and South Asian run mobile phone stores where one can purchase digital versions of the Qur'an to read 'on the go'. In smaller groupings throughout the territory, a variety of restaurants and grocery stores provide halal food in areas such as To Kwa Wan, Sham Shui Po, and Yuen Long. Some halal restaurants are located in the central business district and attract mainly non-Muslim customers. Examples are the popular Habibi restaurant that also sells foods to supermarkets, and Al Pasha which markets itself as serving 'Silk Road cuisine'. The latter establishment is actually owned by a Uyghur woman, who is a renowned 'oriental' dancer and occasional actress. The majority of the Muslims in the research tend to eat at the less expensive businesses in Wanchai and Tsim Sha Tsui. It is significant to note that the concentration of these businesses in specific areas means that for many Muslim youth, who may live and attend school away from these districts, obtaining halal food can at times be challenging.

'But yes, if it has pork in it, we won't buy it'

The most widely understood aspect of a halal diet is that pork is forbidden. For many Muslims old and young alike, abstinence from the consumption of pork is the only way in which they really observe halal food laws. Even among individuals who believe they are quite relaxed about halal food there is an ambiguity about what they feel is acceptable. In the Hong Kong context an uncertainty exists among Muslims, sometimes tacit, that the foods they consume do not have pork in them.

Qaaria follows halal food laws in a way that does not conflict with her engagement in the consumption and social patterns of contemporary girlhood (Harris 2004). Her explanation shows how the norms within her family have largely dictated how she chooses to follow halal guidelines.

> **Qaaria:** We don't buy anything with pork in it. If it is chicken and doesn't have the pork in the ingredients list, we don't stress about eating it. But yes, if it has pork in it, we won't buy it.

Not 'stressing' about halal food is also a characteristic of Pari's approach to eating. When she is with her Chinese friends, she feels it is easy to eat halal food. Wherever she goes, there are both halal and *haraam* choices. For Pari, halal options are chicken or vegetarian dishes. This provides some indication of the degree to which she follows halal laws. Pari is not very concerned with how food is prepared or how meat is slaughtered. Some of her Pakistani friends at school are less flexible, however. She gives the example of dining at McDonald's where her friends argue that none of the meat in the burgers is halal. Pari finds that such attitudes are troublesome and she resents the need to be so concerned with what she sees as overbearing rules. It is circumstances such as eating with Pakistani peers that has made Pari develop a preference for Chinese friends over Pakistani ones. She is quite adamant that she is a Hong Kong person and appears to find the following of Pakistani Islamic cultural norms in Hong Kong peculiarly out of place.

Qaaria and Pari's approach to halal food is fundamentally a no-pork approach; it is a basic interpretation and allows them greater freedom in eating with their non-Muslim friends than the stricter interpretations of halal food laws to which many other young Muslims in the territory adhere. Both of these girls represent different social and cultural alignments, Qaaria being middle class and very Westernised has no Muslim peers and Pari, who is working class and schooled among many Pakistani peers, considers herself Chinese. Their cultural and social alignment is reflected in the way they choose to follow halal food laws and is strongly influenced by their family, but also, and importantly, peer and friendship groups.

Qaaria and Pari exhibit a *laissez-faire* attitude to halal food. Elisha, however, provides a more typical and average South Asian account of maintaining a halal diet in Hong Kong. The norms within her family extend beyond simply avoiding pork; if meat is not prepared correctly then they pursue other options. For Elisha the question of how the food is cooked is clearly important.

> **Elisha:** We don't worry actually. Normally we just get what is halal and sometimes we get vegetarian food. We ask the restaurant to cook it all in vegetable oil.

Like the others, Elisha states that she does not worry too much, but clearly goes to greater efforts than Qaaria and Pari to ensure what she consumes is halal. Collectively, their accounts highlight how ambiguous the issue of halal food is as they all consider themselves fairly laid-back and carefree about how they follow their halal dietary obligations. Each girl has very different ways of finding and selecting halal food.

There is a very clear association between Chinese food and pork among the majority of Muslims I have spoken to during my research. Qaaria states that it is sometimes difficult to find halal food in Hong Kong because Chinese people 'love pork'. For Dil the distinction regarding Chinese food is clear: it is simply not halal and therefore Muslims must avoid it.

> **Dil:** I don't eat Chinese food. Muslim people can only eat halal, and Chinese food often uses oil that doesn't contain halal ingredients.
>
> **Paul:** So tell me about keeping halal in Hong Kong, is that quite hard?
>
> **Dil:** I think so. Usually restaurants don't use vegetable oil. Even McDonald's didn't until recently. McDonald's are now using vegetable oil after some non-Chinese people requested for using vegetable oil.

Dil explains how even though Muslims are not vegetarian they sometimes have to eat as vegetarians do because they can only eat meat that has been slaughtered in a halal manner. Hong Kong is a pervasively meat-eating territory. I have on a number of occasions found that some vegetarian meals come with non-vegetarian dressings or condiments. Dil states that as the majority of food in Hong Kong is prepared by non-Muslims; it often makes her family dine as vegetarians when eating outside of their home. When Dil's family eats out they tend to only visit Pakistani or Indian restaurants as it is those places that serve reliably halal food.

Franky also sees Chinese food as questionable. His outlook, which is shared by Iftikhar and Mahmood, is that all Western food is acceptable. This he justifies because Western people are *al Kitab* or 'of the book'. This phrase is used to show that Jews, Christians, and Muslims share the same monotheistic origins in the covenants that are revealed in the Torah, Bible and Qur'an. Food that is prepared by people from these backgrounds, Western food, is halal for Franky. So fast food chains in Hong Kong like McDonald's, KFC, and Pizza Hut, are all acceptable places to eat. He will eat Chinese food, but carefully chooses only to eat noodles and rice with vegetables or fish.

Gender difference

Generally, access to halal food between Pakistani participants differs across genders. The Pakistani young men often eat out at South Asian restaurants near either the Wanchai or Kowloon Mosques. They also often get halal takeaways from these establishments with their friends. In contrast, the majority of Pakistani girls eat out only with their family. Though in some cases they eat at McDonald's, a choice that seems to be as much about easy access as it is about avoiding being seen hanging out with Pakistani boys. Access to halal food for them is more typically represented in discussions of purchasing groceries to cook at home. Jumana does not eat Chinese food and believes that halal food is easy to get because the Islamic community has shops and businesses to provide such services (Islamic Union of Hong Kong 2007, Hong Kong Tourism Board 2008). Despite feeling that there is easy access to halal food, Jumana lives some considerable distance away from their local halal butcher at Bowrington Road market. Although it is practical for her housewife mother to travel this distance to do the grocery shopping daily, it is a stark contrast to the lifestyle of many other Hong Kong families who shop locally and access convenience goods and stores regularly. Access provides greater context to understand how young Muslims and their families encounter and engage with space. It is not uncommon for Muslim families to live far away from Pakistani stores, mosques, and halal butchers. Unlike Britain, for example, where Muslims often live in particular suburban areas (Amin 2002, p. 962), Muslims in Hong Kong are not concentrated in any one locale; they are dispersed throughout the territory. Access to halal food highlights spatial gender differences that we shall encounter again in Chapter 11. Young Pakistani men have a different experience of halal food in Hong Kong to Pakistani young women. These gender differences are most distinctly a South Asian experience and quite unalike the experiences of *Hui* in the territory.

McHaraam

The popularity of McDonald's in Hong Kong is widely recognised with over 200 of the restaurants dotted across the territory. The subject of halal food with many of the participants led to some reference of eating or avoiding eating particular items at McDonald's. There is much debate among Muslims in Hong Kong as to what, if anything, is halal in these widely accessible and inexpensive fast food restaurants. Both Dil and Elisha say that they eat the fries that are sold at McDonald's as they are now cooked in vegetable oil.

> **Elisha:** We normally get the fries and we tell them to fry them in vegetable oil.

In 2000 the *South China Morning Post* reported on comments made from the Muslim community about the oil in which McDonald's fries were cooked. Mohamed Alli Din, then chairman of the United Muslim Association of Hong Kong argued that McDonald's in Singapore and Malaysia ensured food was halal and so should McDonald's in Hong Kong (Lo 2000). A letter to the same newspaper in May of 2000 requested that some halal food should be put on offer at Hong Kong's international airport, which is regularly voted the best in the world. The letter made the particular request that McDonald's provide some vegetarian options.

McDonald's state that within Hong Kong none of their food is certified halal, however, they point out that some of the food they offer is vegetarian. It must be added that while all this information is obtainable through contacting the corporation, it is not readily available to customers in the same way in which their food is. This confusion over what Muslims can eat is still apparent in the way respondents like Elisha request fries to be cooked in vegetable oil. McDonald's in Singapore received halal certification in 1992 and signs on the doors of the restaurants explicitly inform the customers of what to expect (McDonald's Singapore 2011). McDonald's in Hong Kong remains *haraam* and unlike Singapore Hong Kong's halal certification, provided by the Trustees of Islamic Community Fund, is not widely used. To date, they have only awarded certification and inspected restaurants who have requested validation. There is no government body to oversee the use of halal labelling in food shops, butchers, and mainstream food chains such as McDonald's. The concern that arises from such a situation is that any business or product can claim to be halal in Hong Kong. A number of issues regarding false labelling of halal produce, and of varying interpretations of halal guidelines at Hong Kong restaurants, have highlighted the enduring ambiguity that Muslims have with regard to their food choices in the territory. Arif who works in Chungking Mansions states that there are a number of businesses that claim to be

The ambiguity of halal food in Hong Kong

halal when they are not. He declares that you have to be careful, particularly near where he lives in Tuen Mun.

One example of the contested nature of halal food in Hong Kong is presented in a picture taken at Ebeneezer's in Wanchai. This popular takeaway which offers kebabs, curries, and pizzas is certified as an halal establishment. All the meats they use are halal, even their Hawaiian pizza has turkey instead of ham. But at the front counter next to the halal certificate a collection of different canned and bottled beers are displayed. A sign requests that customers do not consume the alcohol on the premises. But this does not seem to deter people from doing so. It is also not difficult to find drunken customers in the takeaway at any time of day. For some Muslims this is unacceptable. This would simply not be an issue in an Islamic country as there would be no alcohol on sale, but also there would be no halal certification required. Thus the ambiguity that accompanies the issue of halal food in Hong Kong can be understood as simply an element of the social complexity that Muslims as minorities are living in. Alcohol is an element of everyday life for a number of Muslims. Franky observes that among the Muslims he knows at Chungking Mansions there are always some that can be spotted drinking beer or smoking cannabis. The presence of bottled alcohol is thus not as contentious as the question of pork meat, food sourcing, and cross-contamination.

Figure 8 Halal and *haraam* on display in a Wanchai takeaway (photo by author)

One of the key issues for Muslims in Hong Kong is the lack of government or big business recognition with regard to their special dietary requirement. McDonald's move to make vegetarian products such as fries vegetarian in production signals an acknowledgement of vegetarian consumers as a valuable sector in which minor concessions can increase or at least retain profits. Statistics from the Hong Kong Vegetarian Society estimate that there are around 80,000 committed adult vegetarians in Hong Kong (2008). It is noteworthy that numbers of Muslims in Hong Kong exceed the estimated numbers of vegetarians in the territory by three times. McDonald's however, is careful about how it adapts locally and halal food does not seem to be a priority on their agenda. Similarly overseeing halal food certification is not a priority of the Hong Kong government who, despite growing numbers of Muslims in the territory, are not concerned with legislation that supports ethnic minority interests. Perhaps the candid truth of the issue rests in the economic profile of the Muslim majority of Hong Kong. The largest group is Indonesian foreign domestic workers who are characteristically not wealthy. Many Pakistanis are also working class and like Indonesians, they have their own businesses to provide them with their own cultural foods. They are not regarded as an important business target for the necessary adaptations to be considered worthwhile.

Regardless of the ambiguities of McDonald's, it is still a popular choice with Muslims in the territory. Franky told me that 'Pakistani guys always come to McDonald's and choose number five', the *Filet-O-Fish* sandwich. They say that choice is safe as fish is halal. This is confirmed by 13-year-old Murtaza who says that the fish burger is the only safe thing to eat at McDonald's. On this point Qatadah elaborated that Muslims were allowed to order this set but must remove the cheese before they eat the burger. When I asked him why the cheese is unsuitable, Qatadah replied only that his religious teacher had told him not to eat it.

On the subject of McDonald's Iftikhar swooned when describing the food there. 'I love McDonald's,' he declared, 'I would happily eat there for every meal.' Reviewing the responses of the Muslims in this research it is clear that Iftikhar is not alone. There is no shortage of Muslims at McDonald's in Causeway Bay each Sunday. The restaurant on Yee Woo Street, a stone's throw from Victoria Park, bustles with Indonesian foreign domestic workers during their weekly day off. So it seems that even without halal certification, and even with accompanying ambiguity regarding meat, cheese, and cooking oil, McDonald's is still a popular choice for Muslims in Hong Kong.

Eating local, concessions and complexities

Generally, the Pakistani participants (with the distinct exception of Pari) are quite vigilant about keeping halal laws. Although they often eat at McDonald's, they rarely eat Chinese food. There are, however, a number of circumstances in which they feel comfortable eating certain Chinese foods. Sahira, for example, eats only the Chinese food that her father cooks. He, having lived in Hong Kong for over 20 years, has learnt from friends and colleagues how to prepare a number of Chinese recipes and uses only halal ingredients. Sahira's experience of Chinese food is solely that of the fish her father cooks in the Cantonese style he was taught by co-workers, and it has become a meal that she has also learnt to prepare.

Hadaf, in contrast, avoids Chinese food altogether, emphatically stating on two occasions that he does not eat any type of Chinese food, 'Chinese food I don't like any. Nothing, nothing at all.' He also underlined this when offering advice at the close of our interview about what he would tell other Muslims about life in Hong Kong. Despite his avoidance of Chinese food, Hadaf feels that non-Chinese should take the time to talk and get to know Chinese people and enjoy their culture. This is an interesting contrast as the celebration of Chinese food in Hong Kong is a key way to enjoy, show respect for, and become involved with Chinese culture. One of the standard greetings in Cantonese poses the question, 'Have you eaten yet?' It is a pleasantry that gives the acquaintance the opportunity to discuss a shared love: food. In this light, Hadaf provides a reification of everyday hybridity. It is remarkable because he rejects one aspect of Hong Kong Chinese culture that is very important. He utterly rejects Chinese food considering it entirely *haraam*, yet he proudly encourages other people to enjoy getting to know Chinese people and understand their culture. The celebration of Chinese culture through food is entirely absent in Hadaf's lived multicultural experience. His hybridity indicates that people of different cultures can interact and mix without conflict even if they reject major aspects of each other's cultures. Therefore, the challenges that Muslims face in Hong Kong with regard to food are also important to read in the context of food and multiculturalism.

The use of food as a signifier of 'cultural capital', is something that Hage (1997, p. 145) argues is a common way in which people feel they are engaging with other cultures and being multicultural themselves. Hadaf's commentary reveals how superficial such claims of multiculturalism can be. He represents an engagement with Hong Kong culture that appears to be deeper than that of dabbling with Chinese culture by doing things like taking *yum cha* on a Sunday or giving *lai see* at Chinese New Year. This is not the level at which Hadaf is involved. He respects Chinese people and culture; he speaks Cantonese and watches local television. Yet, he refuses to eat any Chinese food. In day-to-day exchanges he is surrounded by Chinese people and Chinese culture and he remains a committed Muslim.

In Hong Kong, a number of Chinese festivals are celebrated as public holidays throughout the year. These sit alongside public holidays for national days and Christian religious celebrations such as Easter and Christmas and also the Buddhist celebration of Buddha's birthday. Many of the young Muslims eat mooncakes during the Chinese Mid-Autumn Festival which is a key part of the celebration. Waqi, Elisha, and Pari all enjoy doing this either with friends or family. Aseelah, in contrast, says that when she celebrates the festival, she avoids mooncakes as she believes they have pork in them. This example shows that while young Muslims may have different ways of following halal rules there is also often a lack of consensus on what foods are clearly *haraam*. While a number of participants will eat meat that has not been slaughtered following halal guidelines, all (apart from some Indonesians) report that they avoid pork. Although Aseelah rejects mooncakes, she does enjoy eating Chinese *dim sum* fast foods like fishballs, but worries about eating them as some of her friends say they are not halal. I questioned her further about how there are many different opinions on what is halal.

> **Aseelah:** If it's got pork it's not allowed that is the main thing. If food is cooked in dishes that previously were used to cook pork, that is not halal. But how are we able to know how some foods are made? The machines that pack food, are they used to cook other things? If you know it, if you can see pork next to fish then you can tell this is not halal at all. But if you don't know, if you can't see, then you can't be blamed for not knowing.

Cross-contamination for *Hui* in China is quite serious and Muslims perceive that even the cleaning of utensils used in the preparation or serving of pork cannot rid them of their pork contamination (Gillette 2000, pp. 125–130). This is a concern for Indonesian Amisha as she often has to prepare food that she eats alongside that of the food for her Chinese employer. She tries to keep surfaces clean and to use different knives for her food and the pork she prepares for her boss. Ultimately, Amisha does not mind handling pork, but she is vigilant not to eat it. Aseelah summed up her criteria for halal food by saying that 'as long as I can't see any pork I am not bothered by it'. But this is contradicted by her rejection of mooncakes which do not clearly have pork in them. Many of the youth enjoy eating mooncakes during the lantern festival, and they make sure that they buy cakes that have no meat ingredients. Aseelah's choice of halal food remains ambiguous with reference to *dim sum* fishballs stating that she used to eat them until a friend told her that they are not halal. As our discussion on the topic closed, she concluded that '[i]t's made of fish so I think its halal.' She justifies this in reference to the Qur'an which states that if you eat *haraam* food accidentally it can not be held against you (Qur'an S 16:115).

Dealing with this ambiguity, Fazeelah decided to take matters into her own hands with regard to a popular *dim sum* snack, fish *siu maai* (魚肉燒賣) which is widely available in convenience stores such as 7-Eleven and Circle K and also street foodstalls. On suspicion of the ingredients which listed no pork content she took the food to a laboratory and organised a test to find if any pork traces were present. She found pork fat in the *siu maai* used in her samples and she now abstains from eating them. Fazeelah is arguably the most informed and pragmatic regarding the consumption of halal food. She does not really have any conflicts about the ambiguity of different types of foods and in the case of her suspicion regarding the *siu maai* she was able to investigate in order to satisfy her curiosity. Fazeelah tends to eat vegetarian options the majority of the time so she can avoid *haraam* food and the accompanying complications she encounters when explaining her peculiar diet to her non-Muslim Chinese work colleagues. Her mother also prepares home-cooked mooncakes during the Mid-Autumn Festival using vegetable oil. Fazeelah and Benny are the only participants in the research who speak Cantonese as their first language and can read Chinese. Fazeelah is in a privileged position to make precise enquiries regarding food choices. Some of the ambiguity of halal food in Hong Kong is made more difficult by the fact that many Muslims have a limited proficiency in speaking Cantonese and generally very little ability in reading Chinese characters.

Eating local food is thus connected to a variety of issues. For Sahira Chinese halal food is something that her father is able to provide, while Aseelah chooses to eat Cantonese fish street snacks because she perceives fish to be a safe choice. As we saw in Chapter 3, Jawa eats a little bit of pork during meals with her Chinese employer. Among all of the respondents it was the Indonesian foreign domestic workers that ate the most local Hong Kong Chinese food. It was also this group that had the least ability to choose what they ate in day to day scenarios. For Hadaf though, all Chinese food is unacceptable, and he encourages his friends to be cautious about what they eat. Fazeelah, in contrast, is able to use her Chinese language skills to make informed choices about what is halal. As a collection, these accounts provide an insight into some of the accompanying issues surrounding Chinese food for young Muslims in Hong Kong.

Halal Hong Kong

Through the everyday experiences of food, of following a halal diet, we gather an even deeper understanding of the lives of young Muslims in Hong Kong. The challenges that they face on a daily basis, navigating Chinese food, choosing which items and which establishments are safe for them to eat in provide an interesting and little known image of Muslims in Hong Kong. As religious minorities, and specifically Muslims, their experiences of life in the territory are not determined by their Islamic culture. While it undoubtedly provides certain obstacles and challenges, we see through the topic of food that Muslim youth are animated by such quotidian issues of where to eat, how to share food with friends, and even how to participate in local Chinese festivities. This is a refreshing change from accounts that persist with the notion that Muslims are marginal social subjects as religious and political minorities and that this marginal status combined with Islam is a catalyst for radicalisation.

The issue of halal food is an interesting one to discuss because it provides an understanding of a unique aspect of the everyday experience of Hong Kong's hybrid culture. The participants reveal that they are able to make their own choices regarding how they follow halal food laws, but it also shows how there is no consensus over certain types of food and the extent to which they should be concerned about what they are eating. Halal food in Hong Kong is therefore an issue that represents the ambiguity and ambivalence of the lived intercultural encounter of being a Muslim in Hong Kong. Consistently, the issue of halal food has been cited by the respondents as an obstacle and challenge in living in Hong Kong where meat is a pervasive ingredient in many foods. The lifestyle and culture of the participants is also typical of other contemporary urban youth. Many like to access convenience and fast foods when with friends. Peers are therefore an important influence on what and where they choose to eat, but so too are religious teachers and employers. The participants show that they learn and consult with friends about what is and is not halal, highlighting how they are forging their own Islamic cultural norms, apropos of life in Hong Kong.

In the next section of this book, the focus moves away from explicit themes of religious practice and takes a closer look at some of the social themes important to young Muslims and their everyday lives. The following chapters explore language, identity, racism, and the use of urban space by young Muslims.

Section 3

Language, Space, and Racism

8
Muslim youth, language, and education

Everyday life in Hong Kong involves the navigation of a variety of languages. Many people can go about their daily lives without having to speak anything other than their mother tongue. However, more often than not, daily exchanges, work, and schooling necessitate communications and transactions in other languages. During the colonial period, English was the key language in the territory in terms of administration and law. Cantonese has always been an integral part of daily life in the city and has displaced English since the handover. Cantonese now functions as the official language while English occupies a secondary role as an alternative administrative and somewhat elite language. This change has been accompanied by the rising importance of Putonghua (or Mandarin) as a focus for integration and commerce with Mainland China.

Within Hong Kong young people are educated and socialised in an environment that is trilingual. There are accordingly many demands and confusions for young people and their parents about which language should be their priority. This is complicated, as we shall see, by the academic demands of Hong Kong schooling that require students to push very hard for the very best results. On top of these dynamics we have the reality that there are many other languages important to the 5% of ethnic minorities that live in the territory. For young Muslims, who are largely ethnic minorities, language is one of the key concerns and challenges that they face.

In Chapter 3, I discussed the transformations that have recently had an impact on Hong Kong's Muslim communities. One aspect of this was the introduction of the Race Discrimination Ordinance in 2008. This legislation has been widely criticised for failing to address one of the key challenges for ethnic minority youth in the territory, access to education. Put simply, many young Muslims are placed in English-language schools and learn little Chinese. Their access to Chinese-language schools is obstructed at a variety of levels and at the end of their schooling they have limited opportunities to access higher education and vocational training. This is a significant concern as eight of the Pakistani respondents were born in Hong Kong and many of the others have lived here for the majority of their lives. It is clear in this respect that Hong Kong is their permanent home.

In this chapter these issues, which are of central concern to many young Muslims and their parents, will be discussed. At the same time, we shall explore the culturally hybrid world of language that young Muslims navigate in their everyday lives. Despite education policies obstructing the integration of some ethnic minority youth into Hong Kong life, many young Muslims are proficient in spoken Cantonese, have local Hong Kong Chinese friends, and consume local Cantonese-language media.

The chapter begins by exploring the relationship between language and culture particularly in relation to cultural mix, a key issue for ethnic minority youth. This is followed by a discussion about education for ethnic minorities in Hong Kong. This, of course, is pertinent to the general debate about Muslim youth. It shows how many young working-class Muslims have limited academic success and highlights the concerns of some ethnic minority families with regard to education policies towards minority youth or non-Chinese-speaking youth. The chapter then progresses to look at the daily 'language lives' of the respondents. It answers a variety of questions regarding what languages the participants speak, their social status, and their experiences of speaking Cantonese. The final section of the chapter examines Cantonese-language media consumption and suggests that many young Muslims are invested in local Hong Kong Chinese popular culture and share some of the recreational pastimes of the larger population. The chapter concludes with an overview of the issue of language among Hong Kong's young Muslims as ethnic minorities.

Language and culture

In terms of cultural knowledge, a language has great significance. As a collection of words used to communicate, and a repository of values and etiquette, the cultural meanings and nuances woven deeply into the idioms and intonation of spoken words makes language an unrivalled cultural signifier. The tie between language and culture is one that Eoyang clearly articulates. He states that 'language and culture are indissoluble: there can be no language without culture' (1998, p. 11). Thus, the languages that Muslims speak can be taken as an indicator of their cultural heritage and daily experience. Language use tells us which cultures young Muslims have been immersed in and similarly the cultural spaces in which they socialise and interact with others. Eoyang goes on to say that 'to learn a language is not just to acquire a skill, like typing or computer programming, it is to negotiate and to comprehend a certain kind of human experience' (1998, p. 14). Language can therefore be seen as a way to understand and comprehend others.

Language is too readily considered essential, static, or fixed. Languages can in fact be fluid and versatile. There are countless examples of how language is responsive to the culture and environment in which it is used. Evidence of young people being multilingual, swapping between languages or even mixing them depending on context, can be viewed as a tangible representation of the hybridity in which they live. Language is clearly an aspect of daily life that can aid our recognition and understanding of cultural diversity, and ethnic minorities. Language and intercultural exchange highlight the meeting and understanding that can be fostered between people of different cultures. There is even a political stance to this significance of language as Eoyang states that 'we cannot afford to envision a future that is mono-cultural and mono-lingual … there is a fallacy rampant throughout the world … which sees accord as achievable only with uniformity, and suggests that diversity is always divisive' (1998, p. 19). Through the focus on language we can come to understand how cultures meet, combine, renew, and sustain themselves and each other.

The language use of ethnic minorities in multicultural communities presents a way to engage with the type of cultural mix they encounter. In the work of Noble, Poynting, and Tabar (1999), the Arabic language is focussed on as a way to engage with a dominant cultural trait among a variety of culturally hybrid young Australians. Their study shows how Lebanese and Syrian youth are brought together through their shared culture of the Arabic language. This work provides a key contribution to challenging the ways in which we discuss and understand Muslim youth. Ang's (2001) account of herself as an English, Dutch, and Bahasa-speaking

Chinese Australian is an excellent example of how language reveals a cultural complexity about someone that race and nationality, or more fundamentally appearance, cannot. The link between language and culture has been one that some Australian sociologists have promoted. In the British context the link has not been so clearly demonstrated, despite the fact that research often highlights issues of language mix. Jacobson (1998, p. 96) states that there is an almost exclusive division between spoken languages among Pakistani youth in Britain. Within the home Urdu is spoken to relatives, but at school and among peers and siblings English is the dominant language. She also acknowledges that while there is a division between the context in which youth speak their different languages, there are times when recreational language mix, making jokes, and linguistic juxtapositions are employed with other Urdu-speaking peers (1998, p. 97). Pakistani parents in the UK tend to emphasise the importance of four languages for their children: Punjabi, Urdu, Qur'anic Arabic, and English. The ways in which these languages are taught can often mean that some young Pakistanis fail to become literate or conversant in one, let alone all four languages (Lewis 2007, p. 43). The space of the mosque, where Arabic is taught, seldom engages with English language in which the youth are taught formally at school. Similarly, the ghettoisation of Pakistani communities in some northern English cities has meant that their exposure to English is marginalised; some youth therefore only learn to speak slang and have no formal competence in the language.

Language is always a topical debate in Hong Kong and there is a great deal of research on English, Cantonese, and Putonghua use in the territory. For ethnic minority families the trilingual environment of Hong Kong holds an added complexity as their youth navigate a family language in combination with the variety of languages that are used in Hong Kong in everyday scenarios. The acculturation to English by Indian youth in Hong Kong is discussed by Patri (1998) who notes that at some of Hong Kong's international schools there is a stronger preference for English language use by Indian teenagers than their Hong Kong Chinese peers. In stark contrast, through research undertaken at some of the territory's English-language government schools, Pannu (1998) studied the language use of Indian teenagers in Hong Kong. Her research shows a considerable preference for conversing with South Asian peers in Cantonese despite the fact that their family languages are often South Asian and that they are educated in English. Her findings also show that nearly 40% of all conversations that these young people have involve the mixing of at least two languages (1998, p. 229). Language mix appears to be widespread in the lives of South Asian youth in Hong Kong.

Language and ethnic minority education in Hong Kong

Returning to the early years of Islam in Hong Kong, it was the children born from the initial Muslim migrants in the nineteenth century who became the first Muslims to require schooling in the territory. The most prominent institution for educating Indians has historically been the Sir Ellis Kadoorie School, founded in 1890 by the Kadoorie family. The school was well supported by affluent members of the Indian community with a number of Muslim boys having their fees paid by notable families such as the Kadoories and the Arcullis (White 2004, p. 213). In 1916 the Hong Kong government took over the control and running of this 'important Indian school' (p. 212). The school has gone through a number of incarnations on Hong Kong Island and also in Kowloon. There are presently primary and secondary streams with English as the medium of instruction for all lessons (p. 212). The school remains government-assisted and has preserved its close connection with South Asian students. However, its association with the Indian community has transformed. Now it is more generally recognised as a school for Hong Kong's ethnic minorities. Many Indians and Pakistanis attend the Sir Ellis Kadoorie School as they traditionally have, but so do Nepalese, Filipinos, Thai, and countless other nationalities. For many of Hong Kong's working-class ethnic minorities, the Sir Ellis Kadoorie School performs an important function by providing English-language education. This is often the preference of the parents who do not want their children struggling with Chinese language and writing. That being said government policy streams ethnic minorities into assisted English-medium schools unless they are shown to have an existing ability in and commitment to learning Chinese. Even with the desire to be educated at a local Chinese-language school, ethnic minorities are often put off and obstructed by entry demands and bureaucracy. The Hong Kong government is, however, instigating change in this area, and as always debate about the language of instruction for school children in the territory is a contentious subject. Estimates suggest that within the

South Asian community there are over 10,000 school-age children (Wong and Lo 2011). While many attend fee-paying private schools many others compete to gain a place in one of the seven secondary schools that accommodate ethnic minority students. With limited places many children have to wait several months before they are allocated a school place in a school such as the Sir Ellis Kadoorie School. It is common for students to have to travel some distance to their school, many crossing the harbour from Hong Kong to Kowloon or vice versa.

Modern Hong Kong has a school system that encompasses a wide range of needs for individuals throughout the territory. Local government run schools teach either in Cantonese, English, or Putonghua. The three-language system in Hong Kong is a primary concern among educators as there are vastly differing opinions as to which language gives Hong Kong children the best academic and career options. At different levels the government aids particular specialist schools such as Delia Broadway and English Schools Foundation (ESF). They are, however, at different points on a continuum. The Direct Subsidy Scheme which funds schools earmarked to cater to ethnic minority children is associated with working-class ethnic minorities and represents the aid given to Delia Broadway, for example. The ESF in contrast charges parents fees and also receives a considerable slice of its funding from the government. This group of schools is part of a colonial heritage in which the government supported the English language and UK curriculum education of the children of government workers. Much of its student body are now local Hong Kong Chinese and thus the ESF is itself going through a significant transformation. There are also international schools, which are essentially independent from the Hong Kong government and generally have the most expensive fees within the territory. They educate pupils in a variety of languages and exist as a way for expatriate or internationally focussed families to access an international-style (English, French, German, Australian, etc.) education for their children.

The diversity of Hong Kong's education system is a reflection of the populace. In the years since 1997 the school system has been in constant flux and education for ethnic minority children from families with low salaries (earning around HK$5,000 a month) has been a prominent concern within the Islamic community. The UMAH International School in the New Territories is an independent school with low cost fees of HK$4,800 a year. Its purpose is to provide inexpensive Islamic schooling. Throughout the territory there are four Islamic kindergartens, three Islamic primary schools and one Islamic secondary school. The Chinese Islamic secondary school is also a part of the government's Direct Subsidy Scheme.

Among the Indian community the ESF is a popular choice for children of professionals. Therefore, the local education system is commonly used by families unable or unwilling to pay the fees of the ESF (Kwok and Narain 2003, pp. 136–138). In recent years, substantial rises in ESF fees has increased the number of ethnic minority children seeking local education. A paradox has emerged in which the expatriate workers who would have typically been the customers of the ESF are now being priced out of the ESF market. Alternatively, many Europeans who regard Hong Kong as their permanent home are also pursuing Chinese-language education for their children. Thus the end of colonial Hong Kong has also seen a value shift where many expatriates have decided to send their children to local rather than ESF or international schools. This dynamic is also noted by Kwok and Narain (2003) who observe that Indian parents prioritise a local education at Chinese-language schools because it enables Indian students to engage with the cultural diversity of Hong Kong. The English-language medium of international schools is in some eyes a non-local influence and does not work for the interests of non-Chinese families settled permanently in Hong Kong (p. 137). The complexity of language education has therefore increased and there are many different and conflicting attitudes and demands regarding schooling.

With regard to the language of instruction there are two sets of concerns that are important to Muslim families. Many parents prize the English-language education that is available in the territory. They feel that a good education is provided and that their children are also offered a language skill useful for international business and travel. Alternatively, there is what appears to be a growing group following the handover who recognise Hong Kong as their permanent home and accordingly they desire the means for their children to be included in the spectrum of opportunities available to local Hong Kong Chinese. This desire is fundamentally centred on the acquisition of Chinese-language skills.

For the older generation of Indians in the territory there is a recognition that Cantonese is becoming less prevalent within their community. Some have argued that this is due to the fact that Indian families used to employ

Chinese *amahs* as childminders. Over the last thirty years these traditional *amahs* have been replaced with Filipina and Indonesian foreign domestic workers. As a result, Cantonese acquisition has become less common for a certain section of non-Chinese Hong Kong society (Kwok and Narain 2003, p. 238).

In recent years, parents have lobbied the government for their children to be provided with Chinese-language education. Unison Hong Kong, a non-governmental organisation that represents ethnic minorities in the territory, has complained about the insensitivity of education bureaucrats towards ethnic minorities. This insensitivity was demonstrated in the release of a consultation paper that discusses the development of an education policy to teach ethnic minorities Chinese. The paper was only made available in Chinese and was therefore unreadable by the majority of the students and parents that it was supposedly striving to include (Hong Kong Unison Limited 2008, p. 6). For ethnic minorities in Hong Kong, language education policy illustrates that ethnic minorities are considered foreign even if their families have lived in Hong Kong for generations. It is a peculiar situation that minorities encounter in which they will always be considered foreign, despite being the second, third, or fourth generation who are Hong Kong-born.

The plight of ethnic minorities in Hong Kong has seen an intensifying of the debate regarding racism. The 2008 introduction of the RDO (Racial Discrimination Ordinance) was a landmark in the fight. However, the fact that this law is based on the 1976 UK Race Relations Act means that there are a number of contemporary race issues that are overlooked in the RDO. In particular, the wording of the RDO makes it difficult to bring a case to court in issues of indirect discrimination, which has particular relevance to Hong Kong. In combination with problems such as these, the Hong Kong government has also worded the RDO so that government bodies cannot be held accountable or prosecuted under the bill.

Among ethnic minorities in Hong Kong there has been a sense of dismay that the RDO has failed to address one of their key concerns, the education of their children. The Hong Kong government exercises a policy of equal treatment in education and allows ethnic minority children an equal footing to compete in public education or the private sector. They promote a diversity of choice. As Carmichael observes, 'diversity of choice is apparently only for those who can afford to pay for a private education'

(2009, p. 33). Many of Hong Kong's ethnic minorities do access international schools where they can shop around for education in their mother tongue, English or Chinese. However, for the bulk of working-class ethnic minorities, there is often a feeling that there are few choices available to them. Many children are thus streamed into the selection of specially earmarked schools which have been funded to educate ethnic minority children. These schools are often considered the least desirable by Hong Kong Chinese parents as they produce low grades in examinations and are the least competitive. Only a small percentage of ethnic minority students enter the sixth form. Many never take the HKCE (Hong Kong Certificate of Education) examinations. In 2008, 316 minority students took the HKCE and of these 124 met the minimum criteria for sixth form study. Those that go on to complete their higher examinations find an additional hurdle in accessing university. In 2008 only 10 of the 24 ethnic minority students who sat the Hong Kong Advanced Level examinations actually received offers from universities (Carmichael 2009, p. 19).

So what are the reasons behind the problems faced by minority students in Hong Kong's public education system? One of the simplest answers is access to Chinese-language education. The highly competitive nature of public education in Hong Kong means that while minority youth have, in a nominal sense, access to education, very few are able to keep up with the pace of this education. The process of learning to read and write Chinese is where there are key complaints. Ethnic minority parents tend not to read and write Chinese and have a limited capacity to help their children with homework. Similarly, they have limited funds to employ tutors or enrol their children in extra-curricula classes. This is compounded by the issue that culturally, ethnic minority youth are not immersed in the Chinese language in the same way as their local Hong Kong Chinese peers.

In many Western nations, immigrants have a special curriculum tailored towards helping them acquire the language in which they are to be taught. This is intended to bridge the gap between them and the abilities of their indigenous peers. It is also intended to counter some of the problems faced by students trying to learn a language that is seldom, if at all, spoken in their home. As minority youth rise through the education system, their efforts to integrate and access the best of public education are curtailed. Access to English-language-medium secondary schools is also dependent on students having good grades in Chinese. Those fortunate enough to have prospered in this environment may be barred access to good secondary schools even if they have the requisite grades. Schools are under no statutory obligation to reveal their admission criteria and they are therefore discreetly able to practise discrimination. This is clearly an issue for schools wishing to protect their social and academic reputation. This is a notable concern as there is an association in the minds of some Hong Kong Chinese that the higher the number of ethnic minority pupils at a school, particularly those who are South Asian, the lower the calibre of the school.

The Hong Kong government has repeatedly dismissed calls to bring in a special Chinese curriculum for minority students. Their justification rests on the premise that they offer an education policy of equality. The Education Bureau (EDB) promotes early immersion in Chinese for minority students, yet schools are not given aid in adapting the curriculum to these students. Minority students are thus bombarded with a challenging situation at an early age, for which they are given little or no support. In such circumstances, ethnic minorities run the risk of academic failure early in their schooling and can develop poor self-esteem with regard to their abilities. It is not uncommon for ethnic minority students to have to repeat academic years at school.

Some schools have received extra funding for ethnic minority students, though there is no transparent allocation process as to who gets these extra funds or guidelines as to how the monies are to be spent. The Faculty of Education at the University of Hong Kong (HKU) has established a project to help some students after school with Chinese tuition. This is essentially an excellent idea and responds to some of the demands that parents and teachers have been making. The problem with this project is that it involves teachers from HKU coming to some of the special Direct Subsidy Schools that educate many minority children. Some teachers at the receiving schools feel that these HKU teachers tend not to know the strengths and abilities of the students very well. One teacher stated that this project would be more effective if it funded existing teachers to develop special curriculum aids, or gave teachers release time to develop such projects. It seems that despite a number of efforts from the government and EDB, the ultimate goal of addressing the needs of minority students continues to fall short.

In July 2011 Hong Kong's Equal Opportunities Commission (EOC) released a report that called upon the EDB to open access to Chinese-language education for minority students in Hong Kong. A concern of the report is that ethnic minorities in Hong Kong leave school at 15 or 16 unable to read and write Chinese and unable to competitively access the job market. It also noted that the designated schools for ethnic minorities work to place a barrier between them and the larger Hong Kong Chinese population. Ethnic minorities live throughout the territory, yet they have to travel long distances to a handful of schools that provide an education that many feel is unsuitable or irrelevant for them as Hong Kong citizens (Wong and Lo 2011). Another aspect that the report highlighted is that English-medium schools available to ethnic minorities through the Direct Subsidy Scheme do not only perform poorly in Chinese language but also in other subjects. Ethnic minority students are therefore at a considerable disadvantage.

It is also important to add that some of the academic challenges which Muslim youth face are unrelated to the dynamics existing in Hong Kong's education system. For some Muslim families the priority to learn the Qur'an comes at the expense of the children's schoolwork. Some families place a cultural priority on Islam that is not reflected in schooling. I would suggest that this is mostly a subtle and unintentional signal from the home, where the study at the mosque is the priority that parents insist upon. In addition, schoolwork and homework in particular may be little understood by their parents, many of whom have never been educated in English or Chinese themselves. They know little of their children's schoolwork and some have a limited capacity to aid them. This does not mean that parents do not value or prioritise schoolwork. It is simply that in some cases their lack of familiarity with the style of schooling, and the languages used in education, place such parents in a position where they can only offer limited support for their children's academic endeavours.

In my conversations with Muslim youth, I found that many individuals had aspirations to spend their lives in Hong Kong and to contribute to society. One young woman told me that she was encouraged by her parents to do her best and to make Hong Kong her home. She hoped that she might be able to become a doctor. Another boy told me how he wanted to be a teacher, and another wanted to join the PLA. Some of them recognised that even if they do well in their exams, it is hard to excel in Hong Kong. Yet many wanted to do well in Chinese and were keen to learn more. A study found that 78% of South Asian school students would like to learn Chinese in school (Ku, Chan, and Sandhu 2005, p. 47). This is notable given that the vast majority are educated in English. Their interest in Chinese-language education is compelling; only 47% said that they wanted to be educated in their mother tongue (2005, p. 49). This, I believe, shows how many ethnic minority youth wish to be part of Hong Kong and indeed recognise that a Chinese-language education is key to achieving a future in Hong Kong. This same study found that both South Asian students and their parents held high aspirations for their academic success. Increasingly, it seems that parents, some of whom objected to Chinese-language education prior to the handover, recognise its increased importance since 1997.

The remainder of this chapter deals with the existing patterns of language integration among Muslim youth in Hong Kong. This will show how a great many of the respondents are able to speak good Cantonese and use this language in their everyday lives. Different people access different languages in Hong Kong and use them in a variety of situations. Especially in relation to local media and language, many young Muslims share the interests and pastimes of their Hong Kong Chinese peers. In my opinion, this is a further compelling argument to underline just how important Chinese-language education is for ethnic minorities in Hong Kong. This chapter shows that unlike a large percentage of the expatriate community that passes through Hong Kong, many working-class ethnic minority families are actually invested in Hong Kong; it is their permanent home. The discussion starts by examining the many different ways in which young Muslims mix language in their everyday lives.

Many languages, many mixtures

Language is one of the most contentious issues in post-colonial Hong Kong society. Three major languages compete for dominance among the Hong Kong population. Cantonese, Putonghua, and English all relate to different priorities, local, regional, or international, all of which are unavoidable spheres of life in Hong Kong society. Identifying which of these languages are spoken by the participants indicates in which sociocultural sphere they are most engaged. The scope of languages used by the individuals in this research provides some insight into the multilingual character of Hong Kong. Every respondent speaks a minimum of two languages and one speaks a total of six languages.

Among the 37 key respondents 17 different languages are spoken. They are: Arabic, Cantonese, English, French, Ghanaian, Hindi, Hindko, Indonesian, Malayalam, Nepali, Pashto, Punjabi, Putonghua, Sinhalese, Somali, Tamil, and Urdu. As can be seen, South Asian languages are strongly represented. In some cases, the responses are a little vague as to how well the individuals speak the languages they claim. In general, all speak English, 20 speak Cantonese, and 21 speak Urdu. The Indonesian foreign domestic workers speak the least English, but all of them speak Cantonese. Alternatively, some Pakistani school students said that they did not speak Cantonese, yet confessed to following Cantonese television shows and speaking the language when travelling around Hong Kong.

In Hong Kong, the elite status of English is connected to a colonial past of domination. In addition, it is also related to contemporary pressures upon the territory to remain international and competitive in business (particularly in terms of trade, tourism, and accessibility to expatriates). While most areas of the territory are signposted in both Chinese and English, and popular businesses and brand names in English are visible everywhere, there are many places and circumstances in which speaking solely English is a disadvantage in Hong Kong. These situations are predominantly at street level involving perfunctory practices of travel, eating, and shopping. The status of English is tacitly indicated by the services and businesses that are primarily English-speaking, or at least effortlessly and competently bilingual. Such businesses, for example in the central area of Hong Kong Island, are restaurants catering to Western tastes (in décor and ambience), hotels, bars, and shopping malls. Stereotypically, many of these Westernised establishments cater to what Sassen (1996, pp. 220–221) describes as the 'new business elites'; they are costly and are to the tastes of a prosperous niche.

Speaking solely English in Hong Kong, or more precisely having no ability in speaking Cantonese, can therefore be understood as a class and economic marker. Just as Ang (2001, p. 188) comments that being white in Australia 'signifies a position of power and respectability', speaking only English in Hong Kong similarly portrays an individual as both wealthy and of a non-local or international disposition. The issue of whiteness and race is important because language is often displaced in these discussions. For example, Kalra, Kaur and Hutnyk (2005, pp. 111–112) acknowledge that white diasporas are the ones termed expatriate, and cosmopolitan. Non-white expatriates are more typically referred to in the vocabulary of diaspora, migration, and transnationalism. However, this model disguises the phenomenon that the privilege of English, as the lexicon of modernity and globalisation (Tomlinson 1999, p. 78) is power-laden as well. It is not that speaking English in Hong Kong can be directly traced to wealth and privilege, but that speaking English and not Chinese (and specifically Cantonese) in Hong Kong can be a powerful indicator of an international, cosmopolitan disposition. It is, however, only one of many class indicators, as English use in Hong Kong is diffused throughout many communities and cannot simply be allotted to an elite.

This confusion over the meaning of language is well defined by the case of African asylum seekers, many of whom are well-educated and middle class in their origins. However, as asylum seekers, and as black people in Hong Kong they are identified as being particularly underprivileged. The many that I have spoken to have excellent English-language skills and very little opportunity to learn Cantonese.

Although all the respondents speak English, it is for many a marginal language. The intonation in which their English is spoken gives further insight into the cultural mix and daily life of the participants. Three different Pakistani girls indicate these differences: speaking English with Chinese (Pari), American (Elisha), and English (Aseelah) accents. By contrast, Insaf, a 15-year-old male from Indonesia, had at the time of interview been living in Hong Kong and speaking English for just one year. His status is that of a middle-class cosmopolitan expatriate child, the son of a diplomat. Insaf's situation contains a counter-intuitive paradox and at the same time provides a unique example of everyday hybridity in the Hong Kong context. It is paradoxical because Insaf only began to learn English in Hong Kong, a Chinese territory. He is an expatriate child yet he attends an English-speaking government school that caters to locally-born ethnic minorities, and in recent years a small proportion of local Chinese youth. The government policy and colonial legacy towards non-Chinese-speaking minorities is that they should be schooled in English, not Chinese. Recent policy on language has confirmed a commitment to diversity and equality in language education, but because of other dynamics in public education it is still the case that the majority of ethnic minorities are educated in English. This has inevitably resulted in a basic education for local ethnic minorities that provides them with limited opportunities for employment in the territory. Insaf is a profound example of a plethora of cultural convergences and class contradictions: an expatriate Indonesian, learning English at a government school in Hong Kong, servicing working class, locally-born ethnic minorities. Similarly, Iftikhar commented that many Somalians arrive in Hong Kong unable to speak English or Cantonese, yet within a few months they can speak English well, and in a year fluently. To him, it was bizarre that they arrive in a part of China and learn to speak English, not Chinese.

The use of English by the participants is related to their schooling, their consumption of media and their use of information technologies. For some (Qaaria, Inas, Elisha, and increasingly Insaf), English is also a social language and one that they use in their daily lives navigating Hong Kong space. The vast array of other languages that are spoken and encountered by the respondents on a daily basis tends to be linked to specific contexts. Urdu, for example, is used by the majority of Pakistanis as a social language and a family language; for some like Waqi, it is even the language that is essential in his part-time job. The more minor languages of Hindko, Tamil, Pashto, and Malayalam are of direct relevance to Muslim youth as languages to communicate with family members, particularly when travelling to Pakistan or India. In the case of 20-year-old Hadaf from Pakistan, Hong Kong provides him with a rich opportunity to learn other languages and engage with other cultures. His Nepalese friends taught him how to speak Nepali, a language that he only uses when socialising with them. The learning and use of Nepali and English in Hong Kong by Hadaf and Insaf illustrate how any conception of an essential relation between language and place is redundant in multicultural contexts.

One of the key themes that emerged in testimonies of many of the respondents was that of language mix and switching. This is similarly a notable feature of Hong Kong society itself. No new dialect or distinct local tongue has emerged from the mixture of languages used daily in the territory, though language mix is diffuse. A monolingual person could easily be ignorant of the mixing of languages as a daily feature of Hong Kong life. A minor familiarity with languages such as English, Cantonese,

Urdu, Hindi, Japanese, Bahasa Indonesia, and Tagalog, would allow one to notice the way in which daily interactions can regularly include switching between these languages. The situations are particularly notable on Hong Kong Island and visible in street-level interactions and on public transport. Someone asking directions may use a number of languages to explain them and again may get a reply made up of words or phrases from one or more languages. This is a theme that is acknowledged by Huang (2004, p. 39) in her discussion of Wong's film *Chungking Express* (1994). She discusses how, during one scene, an off-duty police detective asks a mysterious woman at a bar a question in four different languages, in an attempt to find the right language to communicate with her. The example shows how multilingual Hong Kong is and similarly how ambiguous appearance can be with regard to language. Such interactions, although quite common, should not be confused with representations of creole language; they are more appropriately instances of opportunistic and spontaneous linguistic negotiations that are sentient both of the need to communicate and to represent oneself. This pattern is also shown by Mathews, an American professor of anthropology, who spent an evening conversing in Japanese with a Bangladeshi and Cameroonian in Chungking Mansions (2011, pp. 97–98).

Some examples of language use by respondents provide distinct juxtapositions to the ways in which multiculturalism is often understood. Aseelah, for example, is a Hong Kong-born Pakistani girl who has two Pakistani friends who attend a local Chinese-language school. When she socialises with them in the evenings, they all speak Cantonese together even though they are all also fluent in Urdu, the language spoken by all of them at home. On the surface, it is easy to present this as an example of exotic hybridity, one that is unusual: an oddity. It is, however, representative of the cultural mix of Aseelah's life, the culture in which she is immersed. This is revealed when she discusses her groups of friends.

> **Aseelah:** At school I've got two Pakistani friends and I've got three Indian friends. Indians and Pakistanis are different. Pakistanis don't smoke or drink and Indians do, that is the difference between us. But we have the same kind of relationship, the same things happen with us. My friends outside of school study in a Chinese school, not in the English school.
>
> **Paul:** Are they Chinese friends?

> **Aseelah:** Two of them are Pakistanis, and they study in the Chinese school so we talk in Chinese. The friends in my school they don't really know Chinese.

In the possession of fluent Cantonese, Aseelah provides a tangible example of cultural mix. She explains that she learnt Cantonese from a girl who was originally racist to her. They eventually became best friends and she picked up Cantonese playing with her in their local playground. Overcoming prejudice and making friends with someone who appears different is part of the reality of a multicultural life. It also provides a hopeful account of how facile racist behaviour can be overcome and softens the uneasiness of 'togetherness in difference' (Ang 2001, p. 200).

Although Aseelah goes to an English-language school, she lives in an area of Hong Kong which is largely occupied by local Chinese. Her family is transnational and working class. Aseelah's father, who is a taxi-driver in Britain, financially supports them. For many Pakistani men in Britain, taxi-driving has become a popular occupation as factory work in the Midlands and northern England has disappeared (Kalra 2000). He considers that work is better for him in Britain, while the family are best suited to living and schooling in Hong Kong. For Aseelah, Cantonese is the prime language of communication both for daily necessities and social life. Proficiency in Cantonese provides her with access to local Hong Kong Chinese culture.

Aseelah's English proficiency is remarkable and quite different from many of the other participants interviewed. I questioned Aseelah on the way she spoke and I commented that she seemed more like British South Asians I knew in England. She was very surprised by this and assured me that it was untrue as she did not wear 'mini-skirts'. She did go on to explain that the majority of her family live in Britain and that more of her relatives live in the English city of Birmingham than in Pakistan. Aseelah also notes that her family hold different attitudes to fasting and wearing the *hijab* in comparison with many other Pakistanis in Hong Kong. The reasons for this became more apparent when I asked about how life was different for her parents when they were young. This conversation reveals that the connection with Britain was influential in her mother's upbringing.

> **Aseelah:** My mum's life wasn't very hard. Most of my mom's cousins lived in England and then they were Westernised.

I wish also to draw attention to the way Aseelah refers to her mother as both 'mom' and 'mum'. This switching of emphasis and use of different terms was typical of much of her speech and provides another indication of the liquid nature of both language and culture. Although Aseelah is fluent in English, the way she speaks represents a mix of influences and it is not predictable or uniform. However, Aseelah's English-language skills, and to me quite recognisable English enunciation, seemed to be of limited use in her day-to-day interactions beyond her school education. This appears to be a common scenario among many working-class South Asian Muslims born or raised in Hong Kong.

In a Hong Kong study of language use by Indian adolescents at a local English-language government school, Jasbir Pannu (1998, p. 229) notes that nearly 40% of all conversations involve the mixing of languages. She highlights that pure Cantonese is the language spoken most often, followed by pure Punjabi. Pure English conversation accounts for only 9.2% of all interactions. Cantonese and Punjabi spoken together as a mix is more common than interactions in pure English. This demonstrates a truth about street-level cultural mix in Hong Kong. It is a place where not only are many languages spoken but also a place where many languages are mixed. As de Certeau (1997, pp. 46–54) acknowledges, languages exist organically in a relationship with the past and the present, and their use identifies a cultural point of view. In the context of Hong Kong, the perpetual rate of change prevents any single language dominating all aspects of life in the territory, so in contrast many languages become representative of Hong Kong culture and they are mixed in a fashion that mirrors the hybridity that exists in society. The absence of English as a central language in the mixes which Pannu discusses highlights its peripheral status in Hong Kong everyday life. Pannu (1998, p. 236) concludes in her study that within Hong Kong, Cantonese is a functional language concerned with daily interactions for the core of society, while English is an elite language related to business and a wealthy niche in society.

Hong Kong's working-class ethnic minorities are thus largely educated in an elite language that is of little use to them in helping to forge a future life in the territory. Without access to Chinese-language education defined as the ability to speak, read, and write in Chinese, opportunities for good academic grades or even access to vocational training are curtailed.

Young Muslims and ethnic minorities at government schools, as a majority working-class group, would surely benefit from the opportunity to learn the Chinese language at school and pursue the realistic goal of passing local exams and continuing with further education. It is paradoxical that minorities in Hong Kong are not educated in the language of the dominant cultural group: Cantonese. However, there are many parents who feel that their children would suffer from a Cantonese-language education. Certainly, those with aspirations to return to countries such as Pakistan and Indonesia would find it beneficial to be taught in English as this potentially provides them with more work, business, and travel options. At the same time, there is a large group of ethnic minority parents who are confident in their local ties and wish to extend this to the education of their children in Hong Kong's most widely spoken language. For these parents Cantonese, and written Chinese, provides an investment in their future lives in Hong Kong.

Cantonese-language Korean TV, *Dae Jang Geum*

Local Cantonese-language television programmes provide a prism through which we can use a different angle to consider the language use of young Muslims. It is a topic that shows just how keenly involved many young Muslims and their families are in the everyday interests of Hong Kong people. Unlike language itself, media consumption is not a particularly distinct indicator of culture. Listening to hip hop music, eating Indian food, and having a tattoo of a Chinese ideogram are all activities that borrow from cultures in a shallow way. Language is something that is clearly entwined with culture and cultural exchange, watching television is less so. However, if individuals are watching television programmes in a second language, then intercultural communication is occurring, or being primed. Referring to a shallow cultural practice such as watching a television programme in another language opens up ways in which we can consider the cultural hybridity of young Muslims in Hong Kong and their engagement with Hong Kong Chinese culture.

In May 2005, the final episode of a long-running Korean television drama series *Dae Jang Geum* aired in Hong Kong and was watched by more than 3 million people (Chow 2005b). The closing instalments of the television show were shown in many of the city's shopping malls and restaurants, providing a means for fans to enjoy the popular drama en masse, while encouraging them to continue to spend money in an evening time slot that was becoming increasingly slow for businesses (Chow 2005a). *Dae Jang Geum* became hugely popular throughout Southeast Asia and its popularity is apparent in the success of the theme park in South Korea that has been developed out of the drama's original set (IMBC 2005).

A number of the respondents commented on the huge popularity of this Korean television series that was shown on the local TVB television network dubbed in Cantonese. Waqi, a 17-year-old who moved to Hong Kong from Pakistan at the age of seven, stated that he really enjoyed the series and that his father was particularly fond of it, too. Similarly Hadaf, who has lived in Hong Kong for the last ten years, also responded enthusiastically to the show. He mentioned how he enjoyed speaking to his teachers about it as they were also avid fans. Half of all the youth interviewed said that they watched local Cantonese-language television to some extent, mostly enjoying television dramas. Zainab, a 19-year-old Pakistani girl, watches Cantonese television every night with her parents. Her family enjoys these shows and they discuss them together.

> **Zainab**: I talk to my parents at home in Urdu, and we watch Chinese television dramas together. We like them as they are similar to the Indian dramas we watch, like love stories or scary shows.

Zainab is interesting because she arrived in Hong Kong at the age of six. This would mean that she would have missed kindergarten, a key time when many Chinese children lay a strong foundation in writing Chinese characters. However, she has gone on to become very settled in Hong Kong and enjoys local entertainment. She does, however, possesses a language paradox. She watches Cantonese-language television, speaks Urdu at home, and is educated in English at school. A specialised Chinese curriculum for ethnic minority students would benefit individuals like Zainab. Throughout the territory there are many young Muslims who, despite understanding and speaking Cantonese, have no ability in reading or writing Chinese.

The majority of those who watch Chinese television dramas view them, like Zainab, with their family in the evening. The example of *Dae Jang Geum* highlights not only the familiarity with and understanding of

Cantonese by many of the respondents, but also how they share some of the key interests and fads of a large proportion of the majority Chinese population. It shows that language provides access to cultural products, pastimes, and practices.

What is also interesting to note regarding local Hong Kong media, is that Muslims are represented in a particular way. In some senses they are absent from many types of television shows. Period dramas and entertainment programmes do not tend to showcase Hong Kong's ethnic minorities. Television shows, comedies, dramas, and films set in contemporary Hong Kong do occasionally have Muslim, or South Asian characters. In my experience of watching these shows, these individuals are often represented as Cantonese speakers, often working class. In one television programme, a group of local Hong Kong Chinese boys played with a Pakistani boy. The young Pakistani boy spoke fluent Cantonese and in one scene got chased out of a public playground with his friends for playing cricket. There is no real focus on Islam and similarly, from what I have seen, it is not represented as an issue of conflict in contrast to what has been reported in the British media (Hopkins 2009, p. 36).

Young Muslims, largely of Pakistani descent, watching a Korean television drama dubbed in Cantonese highlights a complex cultural nexus that is typical of the globalised era. The layers of cultural information that are compacted into this practice are vast, not simply because of the reception of language, but also because of the form and content of the historical drama, and the communal enjoyment of this show with others during its broadcast. A similar pattern may be observable in the consumption of English media between countries such as Australia, America, Britain, and even English-speaking communities in Asian and African territories. The cultural referents in these products and broadcasts carry information that becomes part of the culturally hybrid experience of its viewers.

Hear Chinese, speak Chinese, read no Chinese

Language is a fascinating part of Hong Kong. The topic of language and ethnic minorities in the territory is certainly worthy of a book in itself. This very brief overview clearly corresponds with a growing realisation in Hong Kong that ethnic minorities would benefit from greater integration into society and that one way in which this could occur is via the opening of access to Chinese-language education. During the colonial period, the English-language abilities of minorities enabled them to perform a set of specific duties as intermediaries. Social and political change in Hong Kong means that this is no longer a valid way to consider minority groups. As many Muslim families in the territory understand themselves to be Hong Kong people, it is important for the Hong Kong government to recognise this. Just as the colonial government used Muslims as a resource in the police and prison services, the government of Hong Kong SAR could also use ethnic minorities as a resource.

While the issue of racial discrimination in Hong Kong has a variety of ambiguities (as we shall see in Chapter 10), education of ethnic minorities is an issue treated in less ambivalent terms. Young Muslims as a notable part of Hong Kong's ethnic minority population are often involved in local culture, speaking a variety of languages within which Cantonese is popularly included. The cultural connections of language suggest that Muslim youth live a culturally-mixed existence in Hong Kong and are able to navigate a variety of linguistic and social spheres in their daily lives. It is therefore important to recognise these language abilities that have arisen in spite of broad education policies that have tended to work towards the obstruction of ethnic minorities integrating with local Hong Kong Chinese culture. It is therefore my hope that future policy changes will include the development of a curriculum that enables ethnic minorities to engage with Chinese-language education. The primary concern should be to equip school leavers with a standard of Chinese comprehension that allows access to vocational training and allows them to deal with everyday administration using Chinese-language materials. The ultimate goal should be to give those ethnic minorities wishing to do so a realistic chance of accessing further and higher education. This would enable them in their turn to contribute to both the territory and their communities via the broader opportunities for business that this would engender.

9
Chinese/not Chinese

Our first encounters with people are often dictated by a broad set of essential associations, of previous experiences and simple stereotypes. Chapter 1 briefly highlighted how pervasive stereotypes of Muslims are. The debate in this chapter will challenge popular representations of Muslims even further. The discussion on language has already shown how complex the cultural intersections are in the lives of some of Hong Kong's young Muslims, and also how mundane and quotidian they are. In this chapter I present an in-depth exploration of two characters from my research. Pari and Fazeelah, from whom we have already heard a little in previous chapters, are now closely considered. These two individuals provide a way to understand the significance of the earlier discussion on language with regard to the embodied experience of a culturally-mixed life. While a perspective that promotes a link between mixing of languages in everyday life and hybridity has already been articulated, I have not fleshed out the actors involved in these processes. What do the lives of these individuals encompass? What is proposed here is that the daily lives of these two individuals provide an enunciation of everyday hybridity. Language is directly relevant in the following accounts as both subjects are bilingual, but here the focus is on their daily lives and experiences of living in Hong Kong.

Pari is a Pakistani girl who considers herself Chinese, and Fazeelah is a local *Hui* woman who reveals the dynamics involved with being Hong Kong Chinese and also a Muslim. They provide a challenge to assumptions regarding what it means to be Chinese or Muslim but at the same time they reveal their participation in Hong Kong's complex cultural hybridity as something commonplace and unremarkable. The challenges and conflicts their mixed culture presents to them are no greater than the opportunities it provides. Their responses raise crucial questions regarding Hong Kong, culture, and race and articulate examples of cultural mix that are overlooked when themes of style and identity, or policy, dominate analysis.

Pari

Pari, a 14-year-old girl of Pakistani descent born in Hong Kong, presented a very aloof demeanour in our interviews. After just a few minutes of talking with her, it became clear that she was concerned how she was perceived and also wished to control other people's assumptions about her. To begin with, she expressed difficulty in stating either her nationality or ethnicity. Being particularly uncomfortable describing herself as Pakistani and influenced, I believe, by the fact that the research looked at young Muslims, she finally decided to refer to herself as Muslim, though as our conversation progressed this is noted similarly as a problematic term.

> **Pari:** ... I feel like I'm Chinese not Muslim.
>
> **Paul:** Really?
>
> **Pari:** Yes, but then when I go home, then I feel I am Muslim again.

Her comments show that in her own mind being Muslim and being Chinese are mutually exclusive and are, in part, exercised by being in different spaces. When I questioned her further about why she should feel so divided, arguing that there are many *Hui* or Chinese Muslims in Hong Kong, she responded bluntly that this is irrelevant to her because she does not know any. It is a powerful response to make as it clarifies how rigid conceptual boundaries can be even for someone like Pari whose *everyday* is mixed with Islamic, Pakistani, Western, and Chinese culture.

While the pastimes of many of the participants are influenced by Western or English-language recreational pursuits, Pari's free time is spent mostly in a Hong Kong Chinese context. She spends her free time outside of school with Chinese peers and speaks Cantonese with them. She is one of the few participants who regularly eats Chinese food and approaches her halal diet with the simple edict: not to eat pork. She wears the same fashions as her Chinese friends and at their request leaves her *dupatta* at home. The reason for the omission of the headscarf comes from her prioritising of the Chinese principle of 'keeping face', saving the face of her friends, above the Qur'anic decree of modesty that is particularly important in Pakistani culture.

Pari watches Hong Kong movies in the cinema and locally-produced television dramas at home. She also visits internet and video games rooms with her friends. Much of her free time is spent hanging out in public spaces and city parks. Pari is reflexive in the way she manages her identity and at times reveals this in the arresting process of 'self-othering'. A method by which a person engages with the knowledge that they are perceived as 'other', a minority, or simply different. By identifying as 'other' she then uses that knowledge to present a more complex expression of who she is. Pari's way of expressing herself comes in the form of a preterition. This is a rhetorical device that uses omission as a way to present information. More simply put, Pari omits that she is Pakistani when she talks about Pakistanis.

> **Pari:** I hang around wherever my friends want, but I don't tend to go off of Hong Kong Island.
>
> **Paul:** Not off of Hong Kong Island?
>
> **Pari:** Especially I don't go to Wanchai or Tsim Sha Tsui, too many Pakis.

Pari's disassociation of herself from other Pakistanis is made through her own appropriation of the ridicule of them. Pari often speaks of Pakistanis in derogatory terms, as being not loyal, or troublesome to hang out with because of their religious and cultural ties. She feels that they place her, and by default her family, under scrutiny and judgement as she does not conform to their expectations. Even though being Pakistani is an unavoidable aspect of her identity, it is also something that she can transgress by identifying herself as Chinese. It is an identity that is backed up by her engagement and performance in Hong Kong Chinese culture, actually speaking, eating and dressing Chinese while among Chinese friends. It is only on the subject of musical preference that she expresses any engagement with South Asian popular culture. Rather ambiguously she indicates that she likes all music, but when I asked what her favourite song was at the time of the interview, she explained that it was a song from a Bollywood movie.

Preteritions in other works on multicultural youth (Jacobson 1998, p. 63; Noble, Poynting, and Tabar 1999, p. 39; Werbner 2002, p. 201; Yon 2000, p. 148) similarly highlight a desire to distance oneself from an aspect of one's culture and ethnicity. In terms of the ambivalence that Bhabha

(1994) discusses as a characteristic of hybridity, preteritions manage this ambiguity and steer it in a particular direction. Pari tries to reorient and manage my perception of her by showing that she does not consider herself a typical Pakistani. Rather than discuss the complexity of her identity the use of a preterition provides an unmistakeable challenge to stereotyping and shows that she wants people to be aware of the ambiguity of her identity. The same process is enacted by a Canadian-Italian girl in Yon's (2001, p. 148) study who intentionally speaks to Italians in her community store only in English. The managing of ambivalence through these preteritions demonstrates an overt use of cultural plurality. This indicates that while Pari's cultural hybridity might be complex, she is no less interested than other youth in controlling and manipulating the image and identity that she presents of herself. Everyday hybridity is therefore something that can be used tactically; it represents both a challenge and an opportunity.

The fact that the fusion of cultures is so distinct in Pari's account also raises a further question: What would become of an individual such as her outside of Hong Kong? If she were to move to Pakistan or Australia, she would be read physically in racial terms as a South Asian. Her platform to present and align herself as Chinese would be lost. Pari provides a profound contrast to Ang's (2001) discussion on the complexity of being Chinese but not speaking Chinese. As Pari both speaks the language and lives the culture, the question becomes: In what capacity is she not Chinese? Ang (2001, pp. 40–41) refers to Tu's (1994) discussion of 'cultural China', a term which he extends to all Chinese people regardless of their country of origin, religion, and language. The Chinese diaspora is a greater cultural China inclusive of Westernised Chinese who speak only English. De Certeau's comment about French being a global language predicates a 'cultural France' that decentres the French nation as the sole authority of French language and culture (1997, p. 54). Pari's example becomes an interesting facet within the concept. The argument that language is entwined with culture suggests that Pari (along with Aseelah, Hadaf, and Waqi) is also a member of cultural China, like countless other non-Chinese Chinese speakers in Hong Kong, Taiwan, Singapore and the 56 recognised ethnic minorities of China itself (China Government 2006).

Fazeelah

Fazeelah, a 30-year-old administrator in the education field, offers another Muslim account of life in Hong Kong but one that is in a variety of ways opposite to that of Pari. As a *Hui* in Hong Kong she is a subject of contrast to the numerous accounts of Muslims as political minorities in the West. She is one of only five respondents who speak only two languages, English and Cantonese. She is also the only respondent in the research, with the exception of Amisha, not to have learnt to read Qur'anic Arabic. Her everyday life is entwined with her commitment to Islam which takes up much of her free time, her full-time employment, and university studies. She sees her time as being divided among four spheres: her home life, her daily work, her part-time studies at university, and the voluntary work she does for the mosque as an active member of the Islamic Youth Association. As a local Chinese person her Muslim identity, and more specifically her difference, is hidden unless she chooses to wear the *hijab*. This is a liberty that most Muslims do not have in Hong Kong. All Muslims, and in a larger sense all non-Chinese, are seen as different because of race. When Fazeelah does don the *hijab*, she then experiences the paradox that she is deferred to as a foreigner. The way she is challenged about her ethnicity is always benevolent, and occurs in the daily routines of travelling around the city, shopping, and eating.

> **Fazeelah:** ... Nowadays they will just ask me, 'Are you from Indonesia or Phillipines?' or something like that. I say, 'Sorry, I am Hong Kong people, I am from Hong Kong.' They say, 'Wah! Hong Kong,' that's it.

Fazeelah's example represents the occurrence of what Gladney (2004, p. 77) has termed 'oriental orientalism'. This phrase acknowledges that Asian society also stereotypes and exoticises 'others'. In particular, Gladney (2004, p. 58) notes how images of China's ethnic minorities are almost wholly represented by smiling young females. This highlights an orientalism often seen only in European representations of the other, that females are less threatening and more appealing than males. Gladney reveals a power relation in which the exotic is seen as more base, sensual, and simple. The exotic is thus understood at some level as inferior.

White people are rarely discussed as exotic, but their conversion to Islam creates such an opportunity. The white man as exotic is discussed by Nederveen Pieterse (2007, p. 144) specifically in the context of museum exhibitions. He details a handful of examples where Europeans are the objects of an exotic gaze. An aspect of such reversed orientalism is noted by Franks (2000) when discussing white female converts to Islam in Britain. The orientalism that exists in both Hong Kong and British society is one that they share in the perception that Muslims are neither white, nor Chinese. But for Fazeelah the issue is more complex and leads to the contradictions that a Chinese Muslim in Hong Kong embodies. She and her family are local Muslims, yet like over half of the Hong Kong populace she comes from a family of migrants. The family's Islamic origins date back several generations, yet she grew up as her parents did with only a tentative understanding of Islam. As migrants from the Mainland where Islamic culture has been through various eras of political suppression, the family has become adept at keeping their Islamic identities private. Paradoxically, in Hong Kong the necessity to keep Islam underground, at least politically, is obsolete, yet it is something that prevails and is perhaps most evident with *Hui* youth.

A theme that characterises the *Hui* culture in Hong Kong is the reluctance to be either particularly visible or vocal. February 2006 saw Muslims in Hong Kong rallying against the caricatures of the prophet Muhammad that had been printed in a Danish newspaper, and subsequently across the world. Throughout this public debate, the *Hui* community in Hong Kong kept a low profile and stated in the media that Hong Kong was a peaceful place and there was no need to protest (Crawford 2006). Ibrahim Yeung, secretary for the Chinese Muslim Cultural and Fraternal Association, is quoted in this report as saying that, 'protesting on the streets isn't the way in Hong Kong. We keep a low profile. The government doesn't like protests.' He also stated that, 'many Muslims are successful in business. Their business is very important and they concentrate on business rather than … things happening elsewhere.' Eventually, a number of protests did take place but Chinese Muslims were absent from the demonstrations. This issue illuminates the differences among the Muslim communities of Hong Kong, particularly highlighting the Chinese Muslim, or *Hui*, preference not to be involved in protests and not to make a fuss in public. The dynamics of the Chinese Muslim community are different from other Muslim minority groups in Hong Kong and in the West, because they are a local and hidden community of Muslims.

Fazeelah discusses how she was able to keep her Islamic identity secret from all of her friends while she was at school. Only the headmaster at the Christian school she attended was aware that she and her brother were Muslim. She reports that in her workplace some colleagues are aware that she is a Muslim, but it is not widely known. Her boss asks her to pray at home stating that prayer at work in the day is not convenient because of space and the needs of other staff. Fazeelah provides strong support for the opinions of her boss and is in agreement with his sentiments.

> **Fazeelah:** The hours you work are on shift. You have lunch on shift, you have your tea break on shift. Actually you cannot get the time for your prayers. My boss told me that he felt very sad about this. But he wants me to understand the situation now. He said, 'Not just for you only. You need to think for the whole of society in your work.'

Fazeelah states that within the Chinese Muslim community, events and functions are well attended by older people and young children, teenagers and young adults are more absent. This is similarly apparent in research on *Hui* in Mainland China. Gillette (2001, p. 216) notes how among *Hui* in Xi'an there is an attitude that youth represents a time for study and work and that religion should be focussed on in later life. In contrast, Gladney (2004, p. 273) comments that for some *Hui* parents Islamic education can also be considered a resource, enabling their children to earn money as Imams, or become translators in Arabic and Persian.

This same model of prioritising work and academic success is part of what Fazeelah describes as the reasons why so few *Hui* youth in Hong Kong participate in Islamic education and activities at the mosque. According to Fazeelah, this was a reason why the Chinese Islamic school, which is a band three school (schools are ranked by the government in three tiers, one representing the most desirable schools with the best examination results and the highest performing students, and three the least desirable and with the poorest standards and results), is attended by more Pakistani students than Chinese. *Hui* parents are therefore more interested in children securing a position in a school with higher academic standards than attending one that provides Islamic guidance. Fazeelah suggests that parents in Hong Kong want their children to do well at school and get a good job, and then by being rich they will be happy (a theme acknowledged by Lui 2004, pp. 36–37). She also recognises that this is in opposition to the principles espoused in Islam which value learning good habits, and that the other aspects of life (work, material gain, and happiness) follow from this central and grounding behaviour. In light of such discussions, it is possible to see Fazeelah as being in a liminal position between local Hong Kong Chinese culture and Islamic culture. In many ways this might not just be representative of *Hui* in Hong Kong, but also, as literature has shown, of *Hui* in general (Pillsbury 1975; Pillsbury 1978; Gillette 2000; Gladney 2004).

Other aspects of Fazeelah's daily life demonstrate her negotiation between leading an Islamic life and at the same time striving to fit in with her work colleagues and non-Muslim peers. For example, she states that she checks details about television programmes and films on the internet so she can join in with conversations when her colleagues discuss these things. This is the most strategic and overt example of cultural navigation that I encountered. It highlights a very contemporary aspect of cultural communication and how Fazeelah is able to remain informed while not participating. She could simply not take part in these discussions or alternatively watch the shows; instead, she chooses to keep her Islamic principles of not watching television yet hides this from her colleagues and reads the synopsis of shows online so she can participate in their discussion. This is a questionable practice, a deceit, but one that Fazeelah seems to believe is morally justifiable. These actions provide a valuable contrast to the discussion of *Dae Jang Guem* which shows that many young Muslims enjoy local Hong Kong television with their families in the evening. The everyday hybridity that both Fazeelah and Pari represent are strikingly different, yet in some cases they are related to the same cultural referents and experiences, Cantonese, Islam, and Hong Kong everyday life.

The fact that Fazeelah's Chinese identity is contested by other Chinese when she is dressed with the *hijab* highlights how Islam is perceived to be an external facet of Hong Kong life, alien to the Chinese sphere. Her testimony, like Pari's, disarms the orientalism and cultural imperialism in theories of hybridity, cosmopolitanism and multiculturalism; it challenges essential and monolithic ideas of culture and race. Tactically, Fazeelah denies her cultural mix as shown in the way that she strategically kept her Muslim identity private while attending school, or by the fact that she tells colleagues she is a vegetarian in order to avoid having to explain to them her halal diet and the fact that she is a Muslim.

The denial of Fazeelah's Islamic culture and identity is the reverse of Pari's preteritions. Fazeelah avoids topics and situations that would identify her as a Muslim to her non-Muslim friends and colleagues. She even proactively researches television programmes that she does not watch in order to strike a balance between her Islamic principles and sociability. In some respects this situation appears to represent the troubled 'between two cultures' identity. For Fazeelah, however, this is just the way she chooses to manage the complexity of her culturally hybrid self. In conversation she is pragmatic about these strategies, shown also by the way she divides her life into four sections. She gives the impression that if tensions and anxiety exist between her cultural worlds, she has methods to alleviate them. Islam clearly has provided her with a great deal of support in her life enabling her to understand a heritage that is little understood among her family members. It has also given her status as a volunteer at the mosque. Islam was also a resource when she was a teenager, giving her access to academic skills that were not available in her home or at school. Fazeelah's everyday hybridity, if it can be captured or understood as a quality or possession, is mundane; there is little to celebrate or exoticise culture in her day-to-day routine. Fazeelah's cultural identity is also something that we can quite clearly understand as mobile and incomplete as she continues to learn about Islam and her Chinese culture on a daily basis.

Chinese festivals are another site of conflict for Fazeelah where she has to balance her Chinese culture and her religious beliefs. She normally celebrates the Mid-Autumn Festival at home. Her mother traditionally prepares homemade mooncakes for the family to eat at this time. The Mid-Autumn Festival is generally an outdoors celebration where families gather in parks and on beaches to display decorative lanterns and eat mooncakes while admiring the full moon throughout the night. Many of the Pakistani respondents enjoy celebrating this festival with their parents or friends by going to Victoria Park or other venues. It is curious then that Fazeelah's family celebrate this festival at home. Two other Chinese festivals, Ching Ming (清明節) and Chung Yeung (重陽節), sometimes called the grave-sweeping festivals, are celebrations focussing on filial piety. For Chinese Muslims this creates a conflict as Muslims believe that one should not celebrate the dead. So, during these festivals, Fazeelah does not visit relatives' graves. She also tells family members who want to visit graves that she will accompany them on another day. Many of her family know little about Islam and Fazeelah appears to, respectfully and subtly, educate her family about the religion.

The tension between Islamic norms of not glorifying the dead and Chinese traditions of filial piety is one of the key sites where a Chinese Islam can be noticed. The anthropology of Gillette (2000, p. 52) highlights the importance given to local graves within the *Hui* community and how they act as a history and genealogy of the Muslim sector of the city of Xian. In discussion with some elder Hong Kong Chinese Muslims at the Wanchai mosque, I was also introduced to the importance of local graves in the Muslim cemetery. Again, these are discussed as a wonderful resource to understand Hong Kong's Muslim history. It is likely that any discussion with *Hui* in Hong Kong may lead to an acknowledgement of the importance of the Muslim cemetery. One gentleman, Benny, related that he had a written genealogy of his Muslim ancestors going back many generations that charted an historic path from scattered origins across the southern mainland to Shanghai. Fazeelah's family had a similar document that in recent years has become lost.

Challenging authenticity

The examples of Pari and Fazeelah illuminate some very different themes. However, they are alike in the sense that each one is identifying more strongly with issues that the other one is less engaged with. For example, Pari has been raised a Muslim, has been taught how to pray, and read the Qur'an in Arabic, yet it is this she distances herself from. She tries not to wear her headscarf and she cares little about halal food other than not eating pork. In contrast, Fazeelah was not raised with much understanding of Islam despite the fact that her parents are *Hui*. She began to learn for herself as a teenager in response to an advert at the mosque, offering free help to Muslim students with their homework. Learning about Islam as a teenager has meant that Fazeelah has never learnt Arabic and is one of only two respondents not to have studied the Qur'an in Arabic. Muslims are meant to read the Qur'an in Arabic as they believe that this is the language in which it was revealed to the prophet Muhammad and is thus the word of God. Understanding and following the authenticity of these words is considered a crucial aspect of following Islam. Just as Pari can be challenged for not being Chinese, Fazeelah can also be challenged for not being Muslim on these grounds. But a challenge can also be placed on the authenticity of Pari as a Pakistani and Fazeelah as Chinese, particularly from their peers who at times may consider their behaviour unusual and quaint. Rather than focussing on the authenticity of such identities, what I have been striving to highlight above is a lived account of being a culturally-hybrid citizen in Hong Kong, and specifically being Muslim.

Pari and Fazeelah's testimonies present a timely departure from the concerns of Muslim youth often recycled as subversive, fundamentalist, and oppressed. We see in contrast that both Pari and Fazeelah are mostly concerned with how they are understood by their Muslim peers, friends, family, and work colleagues. What is palpable in their responses is the fact that Hong Kong is a city of cultural mix and fusion, one in which a variety of cultures intersect and combine. While it seems to be the case that difference stands out in Hong Kong, it also seems to be that difference does not incite the violent and antagonistic racism that is often reported in the West. Racism is, however, an important and timely issue in post-colonial Hong Kong society and one that we shall explore in the next chapter.

10
Racism versus freedom

Towards the end of my research I attended a conference on multiculturalism in Melbourne. The event had a broad scope dealing with issues of citizenship, migration, work and ethnicity. In the concluding forum provided by the keynote speakers, two comments were raised that are key to the issues covered in this chapter. One professor commented that while he had enjoyed the papers that were presented, he wished that there was a deeper engagement with the everyday experiences of the topics that were covered; particularly, he suggested with Muslim communities. I could not help but agree with the timely need to address the everyday lived experiences of individuals in our complex societies. The second comment I found more troubling. The director of the department hosting the conference asked while introducing a new publication from his department, 'It is the twenty-first century. Why are we still talking about racism in Australia?' My initial response was that of cynicism. Racism is always going to exist; it is a feature of human history, human weakness. But then I thought of my own research and the time that I had lived in Hong Kong, and I understood that I had come to think quite differently of racism in comparison with when I lived in England.

This chapter provides my answer to why I felt uneasy about the concern, or surprise, that racism persists. An undercurrent to what is discussed here is the issue of hope. Beyond racism, what are the real issues, what are societies aspiring to, what are we heading towards? In a conversation with Mary Zournazi, the Australian sociologist Ghassan Hage argues that 'because of the way capitalism is developing, the difficulties and miseries that people are encountering in life because of their class position have become so much more important than the miseries of identity and misrepresentation—or, even in a more complex way, they emerge within the miseries of identity and misrepresentation' (Zournazi 2002, p. 158). Identity politics are no longer simply an issue of inequality.

Hage distinguishes a spectrum of people from different cultures, of different ages, in disparate societies who are faced with very similar threats of social exclusion, poverty, and the cycle of deprivation. He does note, however, that these inequalities are often overlapping with issues of identity politics.

This need for recognition, however basic, recurs in Hage's (2003, pp. 144–146) discussion of the pedestrian crossing. He recounts the story of a new emigrant to Australia and the empowerment and sense of recognition the migrant receives when cars stop for him at a road crossing. Despite feeling isolated and marginalised in this new Australian home, the pedestrian crossing is an aspect of culture in Australia that gives him an important sense of humanity that had been lost during the traumas of the Lebanese civil war. Hage posits the civic notion of the pedestrian crossing as a 'social gift'. Noble and Poynting (2010, p. 491) describe this as a gift 'both from and to society' that rests on recognition. The account of the pedestrian crossing shows in one sense how the conventions of a public space can hold meaning for individuals that extend beyond their intended purpose. The anecdote articulates a common misconception, that multiculturalism as a concept and project is actually representative of the lifestyles and needs of the people it claims to address. In Hage's example, inclusion and recognition are achieved in circumstances unrelated to policy initiatives and the concerns of public debate. As Nederveen Pieterse suggests, '*actual* street-level cultural diversity, is miles ahead of multiculturalism—and represents circumstances that policy is yet to address' (2007, p. 98). The pedestrian crossing is therefore a metaphor for those aspects of daily life that give us solace, recognition, humanity, and hope. It is a key aspect of everyday hybridity, that the multiculture is sustained and strengthened not by the platitudes of tolerance advocated in the project of multiculturalism, but more prosaically by the attitudes and values of everyday people in real scenarios of exchange and encounter (Wise 2005).

The accounts given in this chapter provide an important contrast to others of young Muslims in the post-9/11 era. In this discussion of racism and prejudice, there is a notable absence of the religious prejudice and violence towards Islam that is commonly reported in the West (Amin 2002; Cainkar and Maira 2005; Fekte 2004, Poynting 2004; Poynting and Mason 2006). The analysis challenges popular representations of minority

Muslim youth as both problems and victims. The young people in this study are aware of the challenges of being a Muslim in the West, and despite prevalent racism and limited opportunities in Hong Kong, they are mostly positive about the territory, their future within it, and the benefits they have by living in it.

Their willingness to dismiss the prejudice they encounter is fundamentally a sign of acculturation. Prejudice, for many of the respondents, is not regarded as a 'big deal'. In light of the fondness that many of the participants express for Hong Kong, are they accepting institutional racism and marginalisation in return for the safety, freedom, and religious tolerance that young Muslims enjoy in the territory?

Hong Kong and everyday racism

The issue of racial prejudice and discrimination provides a strong insight into what life is like in Hong Kong as an ethnic minority. In an intriguing look into the notorious Chungking Mansions in Tsim Sha Tsui, Wong and Mathews (1997) detail the popular racism that permeates daily interaction. They note how one incident of miscommunication results in a racist outburst by a Chinese lady that is promptly dismissed by the South Asian man at which it is directed. It reminds us that prejudice is pervasive in Hong Kong society.

Recent political events have sought to redress the everyday racism encountered within the city. The introduction of the Racial Discrimination Ordinance discussed in Chapter 3 is, of course, relevant to this chapter, but it actually works as a background element. None of the accounts in this chapter deals with specific incidents of racism in which recourse to the law has been sought. Rather, what we explore in this chapter are the experiences of everyday racism and how they are understood. Perhaps the most significant issue regarding the Racial Discrimination Ordinance is that it provides a social landmark regarding racism in Hong Kong. Racism now has political recognition and warrants legislation.

Hong Kong's popular racism has many parallels with the 'everyday racism' that Velayutham identifies in Singapore (Velayutham 2009). In the Hong Kong context, there is a similar dynamic in which elements of the Chinese majority make jest and refer to the physical features and skin colour of others in a tactless manner. Hong Kong's everyday racism, which occurs in passing comments and gestures, is not violent or confrontational and is often presented as normal and harmless (Essed 1991, p. 50). One aspect of the popular racism experienced in Hong Kong and Singapore is that the inhabitants of these cities have not been conditioned to feel any restrictions with regard to racial comments. Essed feels that within Britain white people have become anxious in expressing or having any negative views of people of other ethnicities (Essed 1991, p. 40). What the discussion below shows is that within Hong Kong there is a very straightforward and brash way of talking about difference, and despite efforts to curtail discriminatory practices, these ways of talking are the norm. Not all acknowledgements of physical traits and difference are meant or received negatively. One Nigerian Muslim asylum seeker told me proudly that Chinese people love his large nose. They often tell him that it is attractive and lucky. However, these same sorts of comments would not be very welcome in multicultural London or Los Angeles and would be read as a racial jibe. Such comments would be regarded as incredibly ignorant. There is thus a considerable difference regarding the sense of propriety surrounding discussions of race between different national contexts and the cultural groups within them. That is to say, there are quite different circumstances and meanings associated with, for example, being Lebanese in Sydney and being Lebanese in London, and accordingly the conventions of interethnic behaviour in these places.

An example of local attitudes is provided by Hong Kong cartoonist Larry Feign who focuses on the day-to-day absurdities of cross-cultural communication and exchange in the territory. In one of his Lily Wong cartoons, Feign shows how discrimination towards a Filipina foreign domestic worker is enacted in a sign written in only Chinese and Tagalog, forbidding Filipinas to use the lift. Her boss, who is outraged, questions why the sign is not presented in English. The Chinese security guard responds by saying that if it were in English they would get complaints from Western foreigners. The suggestion is that it is only Westerners with their liberal sensibilities who are really concerned about racism. The cartoon forms part of a larger story regarding the segregation of the lift. In one of the final instalments Erma, the domestic helper, is encouraged by her Western boss to make a stand and use the lift, to act like Rosa Parks. In the end, the Filipina rebukes her boss arguing that Parks never made a penny out of her political stance, and the boss responds in defeat, 'you have been in Hong Kong too long.' The cartoons succinctly describe the type of racism and prejudice that is an everyday feature in Hong Kong and suggests that making money, or living well, is more important to many people than equality. While the comic strip is over 15 years old, it is fair to say that these attitudes still exist. Younger generations are, however, challenging and redefining some of these values. Attitudes to public space, racism, education, and the environment among what have been termed 'the post-80s generation' are being renegotiated; nonetheless, popular racism is still quite evident.

The concern that Hong Kong people are far from politically correct is expounded by Williams declaring that 'people in Hong Kong drink too much, stay out too late, are mean to helpless animals, use racial slurs in polite conversation, and worst of all have no sense of shame' (cited in Law 2000, p. 201). Such a brash and candid attitude to difference is perhaps idiomatic to those living in Hong Kong. Being confronted with a complex array of different types of people requires a prompt and perfunctory method to work out (paraphrasing Gilroy 1991) 'where you are from', and 'where you are at'. The complexities of difference tend to be reduced to the darkness of skin, an issue that moves beyond benign curiosity and often becomes one of discrimination. Highlighting the type of racism popular in the territory and the general resignation towards it, an opinion column in a local English newspaper humorously discussed incidents of racism and summed them up simply with the headline 'Afraid of the dark' (Wolfendale 2002, p. 19).

Among the individuals to whom I spoke, there was a common recognition of these types of popular racism. For some these encounters are trivial, but for others they are an intense irritation. Ashja, a 15-year-old Indian boy who has lived in Hong Kong since he was two years old, expressed great unhappiness with racism in Hong Kong. His everyday encounters with racism are numerous and he describes them as both a burden and an obstacle in his day-to-day routine.

> **Ashja:** I have seen many people in the lift … they cover up their nose trying to say that … they don't want us here. Like we are not suitable to be in Hong Kong. They say bad words also. Sometimes big guys also say these things.

This response echoes those which Velayutham reports. There is often no direct confrontation just simply a reaction of disgust, projecting the idea of uncleanliness and contamination. Remarkably Ashja, while not the only participant to report racism was, aside from Franky, the only one who appeared to be seriously troubled by it. Aseelah demonstrates a more common attitude among the participants, a dismissal of the relevance of racism. In our interview, she argued that everyone talks about everyone else and she reminded me of my minority status by saying that even I, as a *gweilo*, will get talked about all the time. The term *gweilo* is a Cantonese phrase for a foreigner. Its translation varies but refers to Caucasians as ghosts or devils, i.e. ghost man, or foreign devil. It is extensively used and is common even as a means for non-Chinese to refer to themselves. However, many people, both Chinese and non-Chinese, find the term offensive. In identifying me as a *gweilo*, Aseelah intended to show that there is no special treatment for anybody; everyone is considered by their traits and differences and that, for her, is not really a problem. Aseelah sees this attitude as an egalitarian element in daily exchanges; everyone is equal in their freedom to speak candidly about and to one another. Her perspective is that if everyone is treated similarly and no one makes a fuss, who gets hurt? One account of discrimination that she provides that I touched upon earlier in our discussion of language highlights the dynamic of accepting racism.

> **Aseelah:** When I was new to this building … I think that we were the first Pakistani family that lived here. There were two kids. I didn't even know how to speak Chinese at all at that time … These two kids, whenever they saw me, they would cover their mouth and nose with their hands … Later on one of the kids, she became my best friend. She was the one who taught me Chinese. We talked together and then played together and now I know Chinese.

The residential elevator and the offensive behaviour encountered in that space signify the beginning of a process of familiarity. This evolved into accommodation and acknowledgement and eventually a cross-cultural friendship and the learning of a new language. Aseelah's willingness to compromise or accept the racism she encountered, and her friend's ability to overcome her stereotype of Pakistanis, both facilitate the hopeful outcome of their rather negative first encounter. It appears that because the prejudice was not focussed on as a social transgression, or perceived as unduly offensive by Aseelah, it could be overcome and ultimately an attitude could be changed. In contrast to the work of Velayutham's where it is reported that a thoughtless remark prevented a girl from wearing a swimsuit for twenty years (2009, p. 265), Aseelah's testimony is remarkably positive and trivialises the racism encountered. While it is crucial not to underplay the power dynamics of racism, Aseelah's account, with its blasé acceptance of racism, is not unique among the respondents. There is much that can be learnt from this example in terms of the conventions of multicultural youth.

Another 15-year-old Hong-Kong-born Pakistani girl, Elisha, spoke of prejudice she had received in the street. One day as she was walking home, a group of boys made fun of her *shalwar kameez*. They ridiculed the clothes as silly and ugly-looking; this upset Elisha enormously. However, the following day the boys waited for her on her return home and apologised. Elisha, like Aseelah and a number of others, explained that experiences of discrimination were often overcome. Arif also explained that among the workers at Chungking Mansions various conflicts occurred. They are however 'humdrum', and people move on. He said that quite simply, 'Grudges aren't held.' Elisha replicated these comments in saying that while peers could do hurtful things in Hong Kong, they often put them right and such efforts made much of the prejudice she encountered appear trivial.

When Franky spoke about the racism he experiences as an African asylum seeker in Chapter 4, it was clear that it was a huge obstacle for him in his daily life. For many of the Muslims born or raised in Hong Kong there is a more comical approach to the everyday racism they encounter. Murtaza, a 13-year-old Pakistani boy, presented me with an anecdote about racism during a focus group discussion with 11 other peers. He stated that the day after Osama Bin Laden was killed, he left for school as usual in the morning. On his way out the door, a Chinese neighbour called to him and said, 'Hey, I hear they killed your dad.' When Murtaza spoke these words during the interview, the whole focus group burst out laughing. The comment and association was simply absurd, and to the entire group, amusing. Comments like this, though at times less comical and frequently more irritating, are often regarded as harmless in comparison with the more challenging slights presented from peers within the same ethnic community.

Pari, who was discussed in the previous chapter, says that the discrimination she experiences with regard to her headscarf come from both her Chinese friends and the Pakistani community. When hanging out with her friends in the evenings and weekends at public parks or games arcades, they ask her not to wear the headscarf as they dislike the curiosity it arouses in others. Interestingly Pari is far more aggravated by other Pakistanis who, when seeing her without her headscarf, criticise her family. There is a renegotiation of the power relations of prejudice in this account. Even as a minority in a Chinese city, Pari is most bothered by the prejudices within her own Pakistani community, not those of her Chinese peers. This undoubtedly plays a strong part in her identification as Chinese rather than Pakistani. Her account is a distinct example of acculturation. It is common to hear of young Muslims in Britain becoming 'too Westernised' for the tastes of their parents; in the Hong Kong model we can recognise the same processes. For Asad, a 16-year-old Pakistani boy, there is a very simple premise; his parents know nothing of Hong Kong.

> **Asad:** I was born here, and my parents were born in Pakistan. They don't understand much about the life in Hong Kong … My father doesn't understand much of the daily life. He works in Tsim Sha Tsui as a tailor. I know the Chinese culture. The teacher teaches us, my parents have never learnt, they don't know the history of Hong Kong and I don't really know anything about Pakistan.

As Asad is conversant with Hong Kong culture, he feels he is more able to accept the issues of everyday prejudice that he encounters. Some Muslim youth identify strongly with local Chinese culture and accordingly behave like their Hong Kong Chinese peers. For example, Pari is the most relaxed among all the participants regarding halal food. Her attitude to eating food with her friends is quite unique among the sample. She cares very little about halal food and feels that as long as she does not eat pork, she can do as she pleases. Even her vigilance towards pork appears questionable, as she eats with her local Chinese friends regularly. Pari accepts the prejudices of her Chinese friends and peers and is confident among them as she shares their language, leisure interests, and much of their culture.

These brief accounts are quite remarkable from a Western perspective on Muslim minorities because they show an absence of prejudice towards Islam. The idea of Islam as a contentious political and ideological issue is absent even in accounts of prejudice regarding dress. In general, there is a disinterested attitude towards racial discrimination contrasted with pride regarding the fact that Islam is respected, or at least tolerated. One truly universal finding in my fieldwork was the absence of religious prejudice. Regardless of participants' ages or ethnicity, the same answers came back. Prejudice is not related to religion just to race and ethnicity. Ashja, who was the most vocal and distressed about racism in Hong Kong, clarified that Islam is not an issue of discrimination.

> **Ashja:** If you talk about Islam in Hong Kong, most people respect Islam in Hong Kong. Not all of them but ... because in Hong Kong many people don't have religion for themselves.

Ashja identifies a truth that Chinese religious traditions in Hong Kong are not from the same Judeo-Christian traditions as Islam (Ballard 1996). His comments also suggest that the local Chinese do attribute respect to religion even if it is foreign and not understood. Kiran noted how her Chinese school friends were very curious about Islam as a religion and Waqi commented that he discussed religious practices in passing with Chinese workers in neighbouring shops at his part-time job. Aseelah's closest Chinese friend even liked to try and fast with her during Ramadan.

International politics, wars, and events on the global stage have raised awareness of Islam within the territory over the last decade. In the post-9/11 era, Muslims in Hong Kong have been sensitive regarding pejorative stereotyping and were prompt to complain at a police anti-terrorism exercise that specifically labelled the terrorists in the drill as Middle Eastern (Law 2002). Despite such incidents, all of the individuals were keen to point out that prejudice in Hong Kong was not really concerned with Islam. Hadaf is emphatic and quite proud that prejudice is on the grounds of race and not Islam, 'never, never' he urges. His pride regarding this fact is another example of how racial discrimination is tacitly accepted.

Modood suggests that 'an oppressed group feels its oppression' most strongly when it challenges the principles that they value the most (2005, p. 104). He suggests that the Rushdie affair in Britain was so volatile and misunderstood because it attacked Islam, the key element of British Pakistani identity. The Hong Kong setting is a contrast as it provides a scenario where all religions are given a basic level of respect and this appears to contribute to the quality of life for Muslims in Hong Kong. The issue of religious respect in Hong Kong has been voiced by a number of scholars including Vaid (1972), Weiss (1991), White (1994), and Bouma and Singleton (2004). White adds that between religious groups there is a great deal of mutual respect and accommodation (1994, p. 147). She recounts that before the Hindu temple was built in Happy Valley, Hindus would pray at the Sikh Gurdwara. In Hong Kong it is common for Hindus, Muslims, Sikhs, and Christians to meet and socialise together in situations they would not in India. Attitudes to religion in Hong Kong are one way in which hybridity and a nascent multiculturalism are innately fostered as Hong Kong's cultural mix and history have not privileged one religion.

One further reason for this religious dynamic is that no single religion dominates and influences secular law and administration in Hong Kong. In such a setting, Muslims benefit from not being perceived in terms of an oppositional ideology. There is a tendency to consider multiculturalism through the framework of identity, culture, ideology, and policy, and to overlook the national and historic context in which these elements exist. It is quite clear in the accounts above that Hong Kong's attitudes to Islam, or organised religion in general, greatly influence the everyday experiences of its ethnic minorities. For example, Filipino workers in Dubai encounter certain obstacles by being nominally Roman Catholic that they do not encounter in Spain. The Christian cultural heritage of the West may similarly be considered a source of cultural friction for its Muslim minorities (Ballard 1996). Commenting on the Rushdie affair in Britain, Ahmed (2004, p. 176) notes that the burning of Rushdie's novel by British Muslim protestors was a deeply ill-advised publicity stunt to pull on Western Europe. He argues that those scenes broadcast across national television were reminiscent of fascist oppression by Nazis in World War II. It is unlikely that such protests in Southeast Asia would evoke the same associations and in turn generate more friction and mistrust between majority and minority communities. It is therefore necessary to consider how the subtleties of circumstance and context influence the experiences of ethnic and religious minorities.

Religion is also not a focus of prejudice due in part to the way racism is constructed in Hong Kong. In a conversation with a Hong Kong Chinese convert to Islam, I was told that racism was about materialism. In Hong Kong, people associate dark-skinned people with poor countries and thus look down upon them. This is similar to the findings of Wong and Mathews's (1997) research that light skin is associated with wealth and modernism in Hong Kong. Within this paradigm Japanese and Koreans are considered honorary whites.

The fact that racism and discrimination for Muslims in Hong Kong is largely unrelated to Islam does not detract from the issue that racism is an everyday reality for ethnic minorities in Hong Kong. The dismissal of the relevance of racism is a form of compromise that many Muslims may accept in exchange for the perceived benefits to life in the territory. The respect shown for Islam as a religion is undoubtedly a part of these benefits. However, a more general sense of freedom appears to be a fundamental way in which the young people feel acknowledged, safe, and comfortable as religious and ethnic minorities in Hong Kong.

Freedom

How can we equate racism and freedom? It is rather strange to link the two together and contrast ideas of freedom with accounts of popular racism. Freedom is, however, a term used by the respondents in a variety of ways to refer to their experience of living in Hong Kong. For some, it is quite simply the freedom of movement that they enjoy in the city, but other themes are also related to this, such as safety, religious tolerance, and even the public transport infrastructure. The recognition of freedom by the participants is also dependent on the understanding that they are unlikely to have the same liberties in other countries. One key way in which this understanding is garnered, is from contact with family and friends in other countries and over the internet. At the same time, Muslim youth are aware that the circumstances that contribute to the freedom and safety they enjoy in Hong Kong are, in part, connected to a broader social attitude of distance, individuality, and non-involvement. This is a nuance to the dynamic that Aseelah and Fazeelah noted, by which everyone is free to talk about difference. The pervasive indifference that also exists in the territory is arguably connected to Chinese Confucian attitudes of keeping face, conformity, and social hierarchy (Eoyang 1998, pp. 21–23). As a result, relationships outside of family and work, such as street-level everyday interactions, can be impersonal, abrupt, and self-centred.

All of the individuals to whom I spoke reflected on the unique freedoms they enjoyed in Hong Kong in some capacity. The popularity of freedom in various guises was something that initially surprised me during the research. Many noted that freedom was their most valued element of daily life in Hong Kong. Waqi, a 17-year-old male Pakistani, who has lived in Hong Kong for 13 years, was emphatic in this declaration.

> **Paul:** So what do you enjoy most about living in Hong Kong?
>
> **Waqi:** The thing I enjoy the most about living in Hong Kong is that we have freedom. Whatever I like to do, I can do. This is my favourite thing, because in other countries it is not the same. I heard that in England after five or six in the evening you cannot go out. In Hong Kong even at three o'clock in the morning you can go out or come home safely. Whatever you like to do, you can do it.

What is immediately striking about this response is that it is an account not just of freedom, but also of urban safety. This freedom of movement and safety is a distinct feature of everyday life in Hong Kong and it is one that youth of both genders utilise (Lee 2000, Ma 2002). While the design and commerce of modern cities tend to promote a sense of freedom, mobility, and independence, it is seldom the case that such safety and freedom of movement (particularly in such a densely-populated metropolis as Hong Kong) is actually achieved. In contrast, cities have increasingly become a site of fear and anxiety particularly with regard to youth and ethnic minorities (Sandercock 2003, pp. 108–125; Bauman 2008, p. 65). This issue becomes even more urgent with reference to Muslim youth. A body of literature identifies that young Muslims in the West are consistently the targets of victimisation and attacks (Amin 2002; Cainkar and Maira 2005; Fekte 2004; Poynting 2004; Poynting and Mason 2006). The youth riots in England during August of 2011 highlight how tensions can spill out into urban space in an alarming and volatile manner. The freedom and feeling of safety that Waqi describes is therefore at odds with many of the accounts that young Muslims have given in the West in the post-9/11 era. Sandercock states that 'when public space is perceived as too dangerous to venture into, then the principle of open access, of a civic culture, is destroyed' (2003, p. 125). Feeling intimidated and unsafe is an enormous threat to multiculturalism and the simple social workings of urban life. In the language of business and consumption favoured by Hong Kong, feeling unsafe becomes a threat to internationalism and the title of 'world city' and, fundamentally, wealth. It undermines the general sense of ease in which everyday encounters and civility flourish. In Hong Kong racism, although common, is not threatening or intimidating; people like the ethnic minority youth in this research still tend to feel safe. The sense of liberty and security in Hong Kong can be considered another example of a pedestrian crossing, a sign of co-operation and adherence to social obligation. There are however, as we shall see below, other elements to this dynamic that renege on such social obligations.

If we consider once more the comments of Waqi above, it is notable that he, and many others, compare their freedom in Hong Kong to the experiences of family and friends living either in the West, or in other Islamic countries. Kanwal, for example, a 14-year-old Pakistani girl, commented that her cousins in London were allowed to go out but they were simply too scared to go out independently or in the evening. Such concerns about 'staying in' are a notable aspect of life for Muslim youth in Western societies in the post-9/11 era (Noble and Poynting 2010, pp. 497–498). In contrast, Kanwal feels that Hong Kong is an attractive place to live because in Pakistan girls are not allowed out; they have to stay in and cannot get an education. In Hong Kong, Kanwal is free to study. She presents Hong Kong as a tangibly hybrid place where the cultural practices and values of ethnic minorities endure and significantly adapt.

The Pakistani girls in this book are considerably less spatially free than their male Pakistani and non-Pakistani female Muslim peers. This however, does not detract from their recognition and enjoyment of Hong Kong's freedoms. Jumana, for instance, cherishes the religious freedom that she has in Hong Kong. This, she declares, is because in Hong Kong she has a choice to wear the headscarf unlike in Pakistan and Turkey where headscarves are either mandatory or forbidden. Her words demonstrate how important this is to her, 'It is a freedom that I can wear the scarf, it's like I'm free.' The topic of religious freedom dovetails with the absence of religious prejudice that the participants earlier revealed.

The freedoms discussed relate in some way to physically embodying public space. This is evident in the numerous examples the youth provide, be it the ability to stay out late and safely as described by Waqi or the freedom to wear religious dress as noted by Jumana. One girl, Qaaria from Sri Lanka, relates freedom to the public transport system of Hong Kong. Her claim is that it is cheap, efficient, safe and immediately accessible. She draws an international comparison in claiming that public transport in Sri Lanka is unreliable, dirty, and has poor infrastructure. This, she argued, was the opposite of Hong Kong. Inas, a 14-year-old Indonesian girl identifies her freedom in the social recreation she enjoys in frequenting Hong Kong malls and cinemas. These varied descriptions of freedom emerged through the conversations on the research topics, of everyday life, education, religious practice, halal food, and use of space.

The fact that freedom was an issue that all participants chose to independently talk about is extraordinary. Their experiences represent the fundamentals of what freedom should encompass in the physical experience of living in a city, riding on a tram, for instance, or simply feeling safe. The fact that these everyday practices are perceived and valued as expressions of freedom is clearly important to acknowledge in order to understand young Muslims in Hong Kong. For many of these individuals it must be understood that freedom is generally expressed as a perceived potential; the youth recognise that they 'can' stay out late, and dress or travel freely. This does not mean, however, that they exercise this freedom. Their gender, culture, family, and community responsibilities often create circumstances and obligations that mean they are not as free as the society in which they live. Despite this, the more general ambience of freedom in the territory appears to have a qualitative impact on their everyday lives. Therefore, the perception of their environment as one in which they are safe and free influences the quality of their lives.

Freedom is something that Dil articulates quite simply: 'My favourite thing about living in Hong Kong is that every single person here minds their own business and doesn't interfere in other's lives.' Discussing prejudice, she goes on to reveal her disinterest: she does not get involved. 'I think if they want to discriminate, let them discriminate. I am not concerned with their business.' Remarkably, Dil believes that the discrimination that she encounters presents no hindrance to her life; it can be simply shrugged off. Ashja articulates these sentiments in a very different manner of humility and concern.

> **Ashja:** According to my point of view Hong Kong is a peaceful place to live, but I don't think I could say it is a pleasant place to live.

He explains that he had a recent encounter where a man was involved in an accident and he came across him injured and lying in the street. People continued to pass the man by, as if to ignore his presence. Ashja, alone, aided the man and called an ambulance.

> **Ashja:** It's just according to my own point of view, but many people think Hong Kong is a better place to live. Hong Kong is a nice place but the people are not nice. That's the point; people don't really care about each other. They mind their own business like the whole country does.

The unique safety and freedom of urban Hong Kong are described by Ashja as coming at a price, the cost being that of social distance and uninvolvement. The juxtaposition between Dil's fondness for the Hong Kong way of 'minding your own business' and Ashja's contempt of it illustrates the considerable gulf between the different lives of young Muslims and their experiences of Hong Kong. However, they do converge on the truth that social distance is a notable feature of everyday life in the territory. This is remarkable, considering that Hong Kong has some of the most densely populated urban space in the world.

An expensive freedom

The social conventions of the pedestrian crossing in Hage's (2003) work provide a metaphor for the lived experience of multiculturalism and everyday hybridity. In the discussion above a very different public space occurs again and again; it is that of the residential lift where the minutiae of intercultural encounter is considered. The lift provides an analogy for Hong Kong, recognisable as a cramped shared space. Feign's cartoon and the accounts of Ashja and Aseelah show that the lift is a space where prejudice surfaces and unalike strangers are brought together for brief and impersonal journeys. The lift, for many Hong Kong citizens, is a necessary part of everyday life, required by residents, workers, and consumers to get where they are going. Whatever discomforts the experience brings, be it prejudice, unsavoury foreigners, or invasion of personal space, they are suffered because once the doors open, freedom and individuality can be regained. Similarly the prejudice, racism, and social distance described in Hong Kong are unpleasant everyday factors that are often accepted in exchange for the many varied freedoms that the territory can deliver.

This chapter shows that racism for young Muslims in Hong Kong is a reality, but also that it is generally related to 'difference' rather than to Islam itself. This poses a striking contrast when considering the experience of Muslims in Britain, Australia, France, and the United States that needs to be addressed. Furthermore, the participants regard this popular prejudice and discrimination in an ambivalent way, recognising and sometimes accepting it as a characteristic of Hong Kong life. In contrast, other factors that are considered unique or typical to Hong Kong such as freedom, safety, and religious tolerance are valued as positive aspects of everyday life in the territory.

Freedom is something that can also be considered as important to adult Muslims. This is touched upon by So (2010) in her research on Pakistani women in Hong Kong. She acknowledges that freedom is an important aspect of life for these women, despite the fact that they encounter prejudice and do not have a high standard of living in the territory. One woman exercises her freedom by subscribing to the Playboy cable television channel. She feels that she is able to express her sexuality in a more liberal way domestically while living in Hong Kong. She rarely has other Pakistani visitors at her home in contrast to Pakistan where neighbours and friends visit her home on a casual, everyday basis. She would never dream of having such a channel in Pakistan where it would soon become public knowledge to her neighbours and she would be judged among her community. Hong Kong's freedom, in this case a domestic and erotic freedom, can therefore be experienced and expressed in numerous ways.

The tendency for Muslims to trivialise the everyday racism they encounter is an important issue to reflect upon. While a number of participants identify racism as their least favourite thing about living in the territory, it is more common to listen to complaints about halal food, peers, or other issues. This is in contrast to Velayutham's (2009) work on Singapore in which racism is seen as a burden, humiliation, and obstacle in daily life. This difference may in some sense relate to Hong Kong culture itself, but also to the ages and socio-economic class of the respondents. As the majority of the participants in this study are working class, they are arguably both more acculturated to the working-class prejudices of Hong Kong people and similarly less influenced by middle-class, and Western, race politics. Certainly a number of reports (Yang Memorial 2000; Ku, Chan, and Sandhu 2005) regarding working-class ethnic minorities in Hong Kong demonstrate that they are marginalised yet often unwilling to demand more in terms of rights, help, and information. Institutional racism is, however, a real issue in Hong Kong and language policy in education is a determining factor that limits the further education and employment of ethnic minorities in the territory. In contrast with Britain and Australia where ethnic minorities are encouraged to learn English, the majority language, in order to assimilate, government policy in Hong Kong is to teach all non-Chinese in English, a minority language. Local-born working-class ethnic minorities are also considerably obstructed in terms of their job opportunities beyond menial work as they are not taught to speak, read, and write Chinese. Language education policy in Hong Kong illustrates the fact that ethnic minorities are considered foreign even if their families have lived in Hong Kong for generations.

There is a very frank attitude to race in Hong Kong. Non-Chinese are simply understood as foreigners. With this comes a sense of liberty in that many people deal with self-evident difference in a very immediate and straightforward way. While it is refreshing to see people discuss important issues in a direct manner, this does not preclude the reality that many will take offence at the terms being used and the questions asked. Becoming accustomed to this way of talking about racial and cultural difference, accepting and tolerating it, eventually means being complicit in it. This is something I noted personally when I was cynical about the fact that racism is still an issue in the twenty-first century. I have previously suggested that this indifference to racism is an aspect of acculturation to the conventions of difference exercised in the territory. How can we come to understand the fact that so many of the participants shrugged off popular racism? In one sense Hong Kong's racism is almost comical. Feign's cartoon reminds us of this, as does Murtaza's anecdote about Bin Laden's death. Hong Kong's racism can be amusing because of its blatant ignorance and brashness. It is not menacing or violent, yet this is neither a reason to tolerate nor condone it. In the Australian context, Noble and Poynting (2010, p. 497) highlight the normalisation of hostile prejudice towards young Muslims. Numerous encounters with anti-Muslim aggression leave many young people reluctant to complain to authorities because of a disillusionment with Australian attitudes towards Islam and the willingness of government institutions to support the needs and concerns of Muslims. The situation is summed up in another context by Back's (2007) account of a young British Sikh living in England who is constantly stopped and harassed by police and security guards because of his Indian ethnicity. He comments that 'I just laugh about it but I realize it's not really funny' (2007, p. 146). This is indeed a crucial issue for minorities in Hong Kong who are perhaps reluctant to complain too bitterly about their marginalisation because of the relative opportunities and freedoms accessible in the territory. If we acquiesce to these inequalities because they do not cause too much discomfort, then what is to become of minority communities when economic and political circumstances change, as they are prone to do? Without real inclusion in Hong Kong society in terms of educational opportunities, without the support of anti-racism legislation that is contemporary and has the power to make government bodies accountable, and without the rejection of ignorant and naïve racist attitudes of the general public, ethnic minorities run the risk that their 'imagined' foreign status will one day be used against them and their families with dire effects. This argument is made more distinct by the fatal shooting of an unarmed homeless Nepalese man by a Hong Kong police officer in March 2009 (Tsang and So 2009). Too often, Hong Kong's everyday and institutional racism is disregarded and perceived as harmless, and while it is refreshing to see youth managing difference on their own terms, this must be supported by legislation and policy that delivers equal rights.

A point that can become lost in concluding this chapter is perhaps the most important one to address in the light of the subject of this book and the way in which it is framed. Racism is undoubtedly a burden to ethnic minorities in Hong Kong. Dark-skinned minorities are perceived to be lowly and unclean by many in Hong Kong. As these people come from countries which are considered backward economically and impoverished, they seem to be at odds with Hong Kong's rapacious capitalism and business spirit. For Muslims in Hong Kong racism is not too much of a burden because Islam is treated as a religion on equal terms with others. Islam is not the focus of prejudice and discrimination in Hong Kong. Despite the fact that many young Muslims are humiliated, frustrated, and angered by the popular racism of the territory, there is a sense of ease that they are free as Muslims. Their accounts portray quite clearly that in countries like Pakistan and Britain there is an enormous responsibility connected to a Muslim identity. Therefore, the dynamic of racism versus freedom is particularly important to Muslims in Hong Kong as opposed to other ethnic minorities.

As local attitudes to race are slowly being challenged by new legislation, the open and inclusive attitude towards religion in Hong Kong is something that should be both commended and studied. Seldom does a contemporary work on ethnic minority Muslim youth find that Islam is such a neutral subject, not contentious, marginalised, or repressed. It would be fair to say that while Muslims in Hong Kong encounter numerous everyday experiences of prejudice and discrimination, and that in some cases this impinges on their religious practices or commitments, Islam is remote and unthreatening to Hong Kong Chinese culture and tends not to be a motivation for prejudice or discrimination.

11
Use of space

> Social space thus remains the space of society, of social life. Man does not live by words alone; all 'subjects' are situated in a space in which they must either recognize themselves or lose themselves, a space which they may both enjoy and modify. In order to accede to this space, individuals (children, adolescents) who are, paradoxically, already within it, must pass tests. This has the effect of setting up reserved spaces, such as places of initiation, within social space.
> (Lefebvre 1991, p. 35)

All everyday activities are linked in some way to the use of space; they occur within a physical space and can have an impact on and influence over multiple spaces. As humans, we physically occupy space and thus all discussions about society are in a variety of ways connected to geography, architecture and space. Youth have a special relationship with space because they are limited in terms of the places they may access and the freedom they have to come and go in spaces that are of legitimate use for them. Urban space such as street benches, bus stops, playgrounds, and storefronts share much in common conceptually with adolescents. They are in-between spaces, places often of mundane use as people go about their everyday affairs. The liminal status of such spaces make them prime for appropriation, for the use of youth who are similarly in-between, not fully children in the social sense and not legally adult.

Young people have the ability to transform everyday spaces and give them new meanings. For example, a group of ethnic minority youth using an urban street corner as a gathering space are performing just one facet of their daily lives but in turn they influence how other people, both young and old, use and navigate that particular area (Back 2007; Dolby 2001; Keith 2005; Nayak 2003; Räthzel 2008; Sandercock 2003; Watt and Stenson 1998). Such recognition of youth and geography is well-explored, but in addition to these physical spaces technology has altered how people meet, converse, and interact. Young people chatting online or using SMS texting on their phones extend their physically occupied space in dialogue with, sometimes potentially unlimited, others (Kelly and Pomerantz 2006; Nunes 2006; Souza e Silva 2006). Similarly cultural norms, religious rules, government legislation, and regulations for public spaces influence what sort of people are allowed or facilitated to participate in activities in particular zones and places. In terms of hybridity, space is important to address as it is the stage on which intercultural mix and encounter is performed.

The use of urban space by ethnic minority youth, however banal, reveals and demonstrates what the social norms, etiquette, status, and systems of daily life are for the communities they live within. The emerging concept of everyday multiculturalism, that has many parallels to the paradigm of everyday hybridity, utilises the concept of space centrally in its discussions. As Harris (2009, pp. 191–192) explains, everyday multiculturalism 'is concerned with the sites and competencies that especially shape and define youth culture and identity: everyday neighbourhood locales and micro-publics of compulsory intercultural negotiations, a capacity for vernacular rather than formal intercultural literacies, and the context of global flows of popular culture.' The limited spaces which youth are able to access work to develop their capacity to deal with the other people they encounter in these spaces, to negotiate their differences and cohabitate in a particular social realm (Harris 2010, p. 581). Observing the way different spaces are used and understood is thus a fundamental way to understand youth cultures and their dynamics. Cultural hybridity becomes one of the elements that such a focus highlights. One of the reasons I believe the use of space is so valuable to observe is because when people are asked about multiculturalism, identity, race, and religion during research projects, they invariably speak from an internalised and personal perspective. We tend to hear less about how these issues are played out in real terms, or the circumstances in which they occur. Minority youth are valuable to research because their social experiences are ones where intercultural exchange is something that they take for granted, it is their norm (Harris 2009, p. 194). By understanding how they use space, we end up researching their everyday hybridity, the lived reality of encounter and cultural mix rather than its considered articulation.

When thinking of space, one of the key places we associate with Muslims is the mosque. However, little work on Muslim youth engages with young people's experiences of the mosque. Work by Lewis (1997), Abusharaf (1998), and Werbner (2002) all offer rich detail about the significance of the mosque in the Muslim communities in Britain or America, but omit the day-to-day use of this important space. The significance of the mosque for young Muslims is manifold; it is a place of prayer, festivity, socialising, and education. Understanding how this space is utilised and accessed as a specific minority religious place can offer important insights into Hong Kong's Muslim community.

Whist orthodox religious space is crucial to address, the exchanges that occur beyond them are also key. Van Vliet (1983) proposes that studies of youth are primarily engaged with observing them in typical and predictable spaces such as the home, school, and the local playground. Arguing that youth spend much of their time away from these zones, he presents a paradigm of a 'fourth space' in youth culture where young people are in spaces not scrutinised or controlled by adults, utilising in-between spaces to modify and enjoy for their own recreation. Van Vliet finds that gender and class relate to the distances and amount of time youth travel and spend in the fourth space. Influenced by Van Vliet, Matthews and Limb (1998) observe that teenagers come to use and navigate space independently. Youth assess particular places as dangerous, private, or safe and make their own decisions about how they are to be used. These social dangers are recognised either as ones subscribed to due to the influence of parents and society, such as 'don't go in the woods alone', or ones formed through personal and peer experience like avoiding a bench in a particular street because of the crowd that hangs out there.

These dynamics are also represented by Back (2007, pp. 60–68). He illustrates how youth in London use public space in a variety of ways in order to gain safety, privacy, and freedom. In one account, a group of girls use a residential stairway to congregate and spend time with each other. This space is described as an 'interstitial' space between home and street. The girls are able to avoid their parents and local gangs in this space. Interstitial space is therefore another way to consider what Van Vliet discusses: the use and forging of unique individual spaces beyond the realms of authority, security, and intimidation. For young Muslims, the surrounding environment and placement of mosques are worthy of note because it is within these spaces that youth may gather and socialise independently of parents and teachers. By focussing on these somewhat banal quotidian spaces the significance of style and consumption, dominant in other works on multicultural youth, can be examined in actual practice.

Again, the accounts presented in this chapter describe Hong Kong as a place of hybridity where mix is an ingrained element of the city's image and appearance, but also of the spaces that youth encounter and the activities they perform. The participants demonstrate, and often recognise for themselves, that Hong Kong is a place of mix, that it creates certain situations and circumstances that are unique and valuable.

Within this discussion of Hong Kong space there are parallels to other debates on ethnicity and multiculturalism in urban communities. Ang (2001), Amin (2002), and Sandercock (2003) have all discussed how ethnicity and cultural mix are considered volatile issues for contemporary cities. These arguments are particularly relevant to this chapter because they recognise that young Muslims are frequently among the most socially and economically marginalised of youth, and both the most feared and intimidated in urban spaces. Sandercock (2003, p. 122) notes this by arguing that Muslims are perceived as being in opposition to the liberal norms of Western societies, while Amin (2002, p. 961) describes the economic deprivation, ethnic segregation, and new youth politics of young Muslims in British cities as contributing factors to the urban ethnic unrest experienced in England throughout 2001. The accounts presented in this chapter provide a valuable contrast to concerns about multicultural harmony and volatile Muslim communities in Western cities. The participants challenge some of the assumptions made about Muslim youth, demonstrating their lived intercultural experience.

This chapter begins with some of the perceptions that were voiced about Hong Kong as a culturally mixed place. These feed into a discussion on the youth micro-geographies of some of the participants. The spaces they frequent in their free time reveal different dynamics of class, gender, and ethnicity. Many of the encounters they describe demonstrate mundane and banal intercultural transactions. One crucial issue that the analysis of this chapter reveals is that cultural diversity is a normal and necessary part of daily life in Hong Kong; it is mostly accepted and dealt with in prosaic ways. The testimonies show how daily encounters make youth *learners* and *educators* of culture in spaces where intercultural contact is both rudimentary and commonplace.

Hong Kong space

> **Hadaf:** Oh, it was amazing, I come to Hong Kong and I had never seen these kind of buildings. I had never seen Chinese people or the clothes that they were wearing, different clothes from us. So I thought where have I come? What is it; it is too different for me.

Hadaf is speaking here of his arrival in Hong Kong at age ten. It is a visceral account and describes the impact of the buildings and the new people he sees. It details his experience of encountering the space of a different culture. It reminds us that mundane, everyday life can, at times, also be fantastic and exhilarating, and that even the quotidian has its extraordinary moments. The initial awe of Hadaf as a young boy from Islamabad encountering the Chinese city where he is to grow up and work is still present in his description of his current understanding of the ethnically mixed area of Tsim Sha Tsui.

> **Hadaf:** It feels very mixed when you are here. In Hong Kong there are people from many different countries. People from everywhere they all stay in Hong Kong. If you go to Tsim Sha Tsui, around any road, you can find so many people from other countries.

The asylum seekers to whom I spoke at Chungking Mansions offer similar responses to Hong Kong's mix. For these young men who have spent at most only a few years in Hong Kong, the city, and particularly Tsim Sha Tsui seems incredibly multicultural. For Iftikhar who has come from the notoriously troubled city of Mogadishu, Hong Kong is distinctly Westernised and the people distinctly Chinese. This is a mix which he and a number of his fellow African asylum seekers agree upon and one that they feel makes Hong Kong a world city. Kiran, a 14-year-old Pakistani girl, whose father works as a security guard, acknowledges how the Hong Kong cityscape carries connotations of power and place.

> **Kiran:** Hong Kong is not like other parts of China, it's more like New York. Hong Kong is like those countries, the things here are all different, Western people made these things so I think it's more like the West.

For Kiran, Hong Kong is more Western than Chinese despite the fact that the only other Chinese city she has visited is Shanghai and that she has never been to any Western country. During the research I encountered no consensus on how to conceive of Hong Kong as a place. It was described as Chinese, Asian, Western, and as a mix. Qaaria describes Hong Kong as a mix but Chinese at the street level. Dil, who has lived in Hong Kong her whole life, argues that it is specifically the mix of cultures that makes Hong Kong a multicultural and diverse place.

> **Dil:** Hong Kong is a very mixed cultural place. Hong Kong doesn't have a special culture. In Pakistan most people are Muslim, in India they are Indian, but in Hong Kong the people are mixed.

Although the participants never use the terms multicultural, cosmopolitan, or hybrid, their responses do portray Hong Kong in these ways, as a heterogeneous space. There is a more general understanding that Hong Kong is a hybrid place with spaces of deep diversity. This may simply be a more common perspective of ethnic minorities; certainly many Hong Kong Chinese do not regard Hong Kong as a multicultural place. They are, however, more likely to regard Hong Kong as cosmopolitan, international, and Westernised. This is a distinction that they use in differentiating themselves from the Mainland Chinese who they can regard as backward and uncouth. Unlike London and New York which are widely regarded as cosmopolitan and multicultural, Hong Kong's identity is more ambiguous; the absence of a strong national identity, a history of colonialism, and renewed Chinese sovereignty are factors tangible at street level. It is these factors that are arguably the most influential in understanding the particular type of multiculturalism that exists in Hong Kong and the hybridity that emerges from it.

Female space

Many examples of how youth use space highlight class and gender issues that underscore a number of distinct differences between their lifestyles. For example, free time for youth, which I discuss using Van Vliet's (1983) term 'the fourth space' to signify time away from parents and teachers and institutions, is spent in a variety of different ways. Each participant identified a group of friends and a locale, or settings in which they socialised. For Qaaria, who is one of the most Westernised of the group, the mall is the focus of her leisure time.

> **Qaaria:** If we are not in school we go shopping or to the movies. We like to come into Times Square, or Pacific Place shopping malls. There is usually a group of five of us, sometimes more.

Malls in Hong Kong are a big part of social and community life. This was noted in the account of how *Dae Jang Guem* was shared en masse in shopping malls, in part due to efforts made by concerned shopkeepers regarding the absence of consumers. Consumption is very much the ethos of Hong Kong in terms of both recreation and lifestyle. It is not uncommon for couples to go shopping together as a date. What has been apparent in this work is that shopping malls are quite peripheral to the majority of young Muslims. Working-class ethnic minorities, and particularly Muslims, do not have a culture of hanging out in shopping malls like Western or Hong Kong Chinese youth. Only Inas and Qaaria described shopping malls as a focus of their free time. Murtaza did mention he liked to window-shop for sports goods, but this was localised to the shops near his home and not the grand shopping malls that Qaaria describes.

Qaaria is typical of the other youth in the malls she mentions as she displays her contemporary girlhood in typically Western ways, wearing slip-on shoes, mini-skirt and singlet top. She is a perfect example of the unproblematic absorption of Islamic culture into Western mainstream hegemony; she consumes, dresses in Western contemporary fashion rather than in an Islamic style, attends the correct venues and keeps her religious obligations mostly personal and separate from interactions with friends and peers. The fact that she occupies these opulent urban commercial spaces with her Westernised cosmopolitan friends does not detract from the fact that she is a Hong Kong-raised, bilingual Sri-Lankan and a practising Muslim.

Similarly, Inas spends much of her leisure time going to the cinema and visiting the same malls as Qaaria. She also has a number of Muslim friends while Qaaria's social circle includes no Muslim peers. At the weekends, Inas occasionally goes cycling and likes to 'party'. A number of these pastimes are somewhat different to the lifestyle she had when living in Indonesia, where she acknowledges that she was more religious than she is now. She feels the Hong Kong environment has made her more Western and believes that the same changes would happen to her friends in Indonesia if they were to arrive and live in Hong Kong. This is an interesting insight to contrast with the transformations Indonesian foreign domestic workers experience in Hong Kong. Inas comes from a wealthy family; her father works for the Indonesian consulate, yet she experiences Hong Kong as a place where she does not have to be too religious. Inas expresses awareness that her own behaviour and lifestyle have been altered by living in Hong Kong. The change she notes is that of becoming more Westernised which may be counterintuitive to a Western gaze that sees Hong Kong as primarily a Chinese city. It confirms once more that despite the fact that the territory does not possess officially sanctioned multiculturalism, Hong Kong is a place of multiculture, of cultural mix and fusion that operates at a variety of intersecting levels. Particularly with Inas, we see how a certain level of wealth combined with non-Chinese ethnicity determines an experience of Hong Kong that is Westernised and free of the national and cultural constraints that may exist elsewhere.

It would seem that for the majority of Pakistani girls in Hong Kong the fourth space is not one of recreation or socialising; it represents time travelling home or to school, or doing family chores. These girls are also quite clearly working class, with fathers working as night watchmen or drivers, and their mothers domestically situated as housewives. Dil, Sahira, Jumana, Kanwal, Kiran and many others interviewed, all return directly home after they leave school and there they remain, rarely or never venturing out in the evenings to meet with friends for entertainment and activities. When Kiran does meet up with friends she normally goes to the library to study with them, or plays badminton in the local park. It therefore appears that Pakistani girls are not allowed to access the fourth space very often. While we might be accustomed to adolescents curating their own specific styles of recreation, Pakistani girls have a limited type of social and spatial freedom which means that their recreational pursuits tend to be focussed on domestic and family activities. Dil provides an example of this dynamic.

> **Paul:** What sort of things, if you are not at home, what do you do with your friends?
>
> **Dil:** Actually I never go out with my friends, I always go out with my family.
>
> **Paul:** Really? So you don't ever hang out with your friends? You don't go shopping or anything like that?
>
> **Dil:** No never.

Dil appears to have a large group of friends at school who are of both genders. She also appears to be popular among her peers. Even so, she is quite happy her social life is limited to school. She enjoys family activities such as visiting the cinema with her siblings, and experimenting with Italian cookery at home. She is close to her siblings and enjoys listening to the various music choices of her elder brothers. Being with family is clearly not just something that is an obligation for Dil: it is something she really enjoys. Other Pakistani girls report how much of their free time is spent at home with their family. Kanwal likes to spend her free time listening to a variety of pop music when she is at home and states that her favourite artist is Britney Spears. She is happy to pursue other recreational activities at home like watching TV and chatting online, but finds the domestic responsibilities that accompany this space tedious. One of Kanwal's major and frequent responsibilities is minding her 3-year-old niece. She describes this as a duty that is both boring and a burden.

What can be drawn from the observation of these girls is that their behaviour is regulated in different ways in comparison with the more middle-class Qaaria and Inas who are entrusted into the open spaces of Western capitalism. For working-class Pakistani girls, home and family are the focus of much of their free time. Their intercultural encounters in the fourth space appear to be somewhat limited (though this does not mean they are not engaged in intercultural social activities in other spaces). These girls may well be educated in a multicultural environment and live in a Chinese city, but their free time is mostly experienced domestically. The fourth space for these girls is tightly regulated and generally their time beyond family scrutiny is brief, involving a walk to school or a trip to the local store for groceries. It also appears that this control of space reinforces the cultural specificity of being a Pakistani woman. The home, of course, is also the place where teenage Pakistani girls receive further religious instruction from their mothers and other female relatives. These girls are fluent in Urdu and in some cases other regional dialects important to the family; they are involved in the running of the household (childcare, grocery shopping) and most of them are learning to cook their mother's recipes.

In terms of space these young Muslim girls conform to the pattern suggested by Van Vliet (1983, p. 572) that youth, and particularly females, from lower income backgrounds have a shorter spatial range in their use of the fourth space. However, their situation is different to that noted by Van Vliet and also Nayak (2003, pp. 75–101) in that these girls are largely restricted to the home, not just the local area. Gender norms of Pakistani culture, in addition to class, appear to be influential in the ways young female Muslims use and access space.

Virtual space

There is, however, another aspect of space which broadens our understanding of these working-class Pakistani girls. While their free time is mostly limited to the home, within the home they are able to access a much broader and unregulated space when they, as all of them do, go online. In a focus group discussion with 11 South Asian Muslim school students all but one confirmed that they regularly used Facebook. Eighteen-year-old Qatadah has over 300 friends on the site, many of course his Pakistani female peers. Some of these girls have profile pictures of themselves modestly dressed with their headscarves; others have glamorous photos in which they are wearing makeup, and again others have pictures of cute cartoon animals or a prayer written in Arabic. Fatin, a 14-year-old Pakistani girl, commonly uses Facebook as part of her day-to-day domestic life.

> **Fatin:** After school I mostly go home, and then I study. I read Qur'an at the weekend at home ... I like to use the computer. I go on to Facebook. Not everyday, but most days.

Fatin and many of her classmates from various different ethnicities use Facebook. At the end of the day, they go home and many will go online to talk about the events of the day with their friends. Similarly, they use Facebook to keep in contact with friends that they have at other schools and also their extended family.

Arnett (2000, p. 474) has stated that young Americans between the ages of 19–29 spend more time alone than any other group except the elderly. It is quite feasible to consider that a good deal of this time is spent online, and also arguable that within this space they are not alone as they may well be chatting and interacting with other users. I argue that the physicality of the tools of online communications engenders a personal space as personified by the term PC (personal computer). Although users of laptop computers, mobile phones, PDAs, iPads and the like, may be very public in their use, the emphasis is generally on a single user for a single interface. Online chatting and social networking sites such as Facebook and Twitter have grown enormously in popularity in recent years (Bauman 2007b, pp. 1–6). The use of these sites has also been a means by which youth can try out identities, and display themselves for scrutiny and approval (Harris 2004, p. 129, Kelly, Pomerantz and Currie, 2006). The private but very public nature of this space, which may be best termed here as the 'fifth space' for youth, is frequently a cause of concern, perhaps simply because it has few boundaries and it is problematic for adults to supervise. Furthermore, youth tend to covet their own spaces, so while Facebook remains popular, other sites tend to be made successful via the rapidity with which youth flock to and utilise them. Facebook may now be a place where your mother or relatives have profiles, but a micro blog on Tumblr or Bebo can be used more personally with just a group of friends.

Pakistani girls in Hong Kong are therefore able to access a new level of spatial freedom via lives online. Many participants talked about how they go online not just for social communications, but also for entertainment. Elisha likes to look for recipes, while Kiran spends time looking for news and pictures about her favourite Bollywood actress, Kareena Kapoor. In this capacity, and because of the unregulated nature of internet sites, we can imagine these girls as being more worldly and knowledgeable about the 'outside world' even if their freedom to participate in it is restricted to virtual exploration rather than physical embodiment. In the virtual world these girls are able to try out new identities, chat with boys, and explore more about Islam.

Online news sites and blogs were certainly popular sources of information regarding the death of Osama Bin Laden. During one focus group, the issue of Bin Laden animated even the quietest of Pakistani girls. One 17-year-old Pakistani girl Uma told me how she had been keenly reading up information online about the assassination of Bin Laden. She was very cross about the way the Americans had handled the affair. Much of her searching online was to find a reliable picture of the dead Bin Laden so she could verify that he had really been killed. Her thirst for this picture and outrage at the handling of the incident provided a unique insight into this otherwise quiet girl. It also highlighted how her engagement with virtual space delivered her the freedom to pursue her personal interests and curiosities.

Strategic space

Pari, as another working-class Pakistani female, presents a distinct contrast in her use of space in comparison with the other Pakistani girls. She is one of four siblings supported by her father's driving job. In contrast to her Pakistani peers she spends her recreational time outside school hours with a group of Chinese friends with whom she speaks Cantonese. They move about the city and hang out in parks, get food, and play Japanese video games in arcades. Pari is unlikely to be seen walking the marbled floors of the opulent Westernised shopping malls, but neither is she confined to her home and domestic chores. As a result, her non-conforming use of space is subject to scrutiny by others. She says that other Pakistanis make comments if they see her hanging out in the local park with her friends.

> **Pari:** Sometimes Muslims talk about our family like. They say the parents don't teach their daughter to stay at home.

This scrutiny has led to Pari zoning her use of the fourth space, identifying specific areas where she does not go. As mentioned previously, she avoids Wanchai and Tsim Sha Tsui where many Pakistani and South Asian businesses are situated and families live. The Wanchai area of Hong Kong and Tsim Sha Tsui on the Kowloon peninsula are distinct multicultural areas of the territory. This diversity is something that Smith (2003) describes as the historical character of the Wanchai district. The variety of different communities that have lived and worked in Wanchai leaves Smith with the feeling that this particular area of Hong Kong is continually in search of an identity. But for Pari the association is clear; Wanchai, like Tsim Sha Tsui, simply has too many Pakistanis in it for her to feel comfortable in that space. Pari's avoidance of these areas is related to her dislike of many of the Pakistani traits from which she feels separate. This dislike is also evident when she elaborates upon why she feels Pakistanis, though framed as Muslims, are no fun to hang out with, and why she prefers Chinese friends.

> **Pari:** ... I don't like to stay with all of those Muslims. They are always caring about their house and have to go home. If they hang out with us they will just say, 'Oh, I have to go home, my mum will need me.' So boring, yes? If you hang out with someone, you should stay with that person, right? But then if you run away, what am I going to do (*laughing*)?

Paul: Okay I get it, I get it.

Pari: The Chinese, they don't care, they call up their mum and say they're still hanging around with friends, and its okay. But the Muslims, they are always rushing home.

Pari's responses are quite exceptional and while other girls share some similarities with her, she stands as an extreme example of a particularly spatially free and Chinese-influenced Pakistani Muslim. Her deviance from the norms for Pakistani girls is also demonstrated by the fact that she discusses the gender of her Chinese friends with a guarded ambiguity. Pari appears less concerned about socialising with boys than her female Pakistani peers. She avoids Pakistani zones of the city and she socialises with both boys and girls. She is clearly aware of different cultural spaces and that her behaviour is culturally inappropriate to some Pakistanis who understand her only in ethnic terms as a Pakistani, not in local terms as a product of the mix of the city.

Another aspect of city zoning is that some South Asian women feel uncomfortable in Tsim Sha Tsui with its large number of South Asian men. Chungking Mansions is described as an intimidating place by a number of South Asian female friends and acquaintances to whom I have spoken. In conversation with a youth worker who provides counselling and guidance to a number of government schools with ethnic minorities, I was alerted to the fact that some Pakistani girls are cautious about travelling on the MTR at the Tsim Sha Tsui station as some of them have been harassed or molested by South Asian men there. Such comments suggest again that some of the major issues that Pakistani girls encounter regarding space are connected to places that other Pakistanis, or South Asians, occupy. A personal example of such conflict occurred once when I was travelling on a tram to Happy Valley. A Pakistani man was opposite me and three Indian women dressed in opulent jewellery and richly coloured saris sat further away to my left. I believe the women, probably Sindhi, were on their way to the Hindu temple. The man muttered to himself in Urdu for much of the journey, appearing quite disgusted. As we neared Happy Valley, he leant towards me and said, 'I don't mind your type, it's them I don't like.' Such inter-ethnic minority tensions remind us that there is no reason to believe in unity in difference during everyday exchanges. Minorities may well find a voice together against the mainstream on particular issues at certain times, but in the day-to-day sharing of space, frictions do exist even in free and safe Hong Kong.

In general, the majority of girls in this research engage with Hong Kong space in particular zones. For the majority of Pakistani girls, the home is a strong focus and activities in spaces outside of the home are mostly undertaken with family members. Their fourth space is limited; however, their school life, home life and even their online virtual life expose them to a variety of different cultures and an array of values and lifestyles.

Young men and appropriated space

The use of space by young male Muslims in Hong Kong provides a distinct contrast to that of the majority of the girls. Generally, all the boys in the study have a good deal of autonomy to move around the city. This freedom is only curtailed by demands such as schoolwork, mosque study, and employment.

In contrast to the regulation of female movement, the males interviewed are well-occupied after school hours. Both Hadaf and Sharif spend every afternoon at the mosque for three hours or more, while Waqi works in a shop from five to ten each evening. Ashja also has a fairly busy routine. He does part-time work as a web designer and regularly attends Taekwondo training. He also plays basketball and football. He spends most evenings studying and then plays football, which is his greatest passion. He joins in games with local Hong Kong Chinese players for one to two hours until ten o'clock when the lights are turned out on the pitch. Only Insaf has a less regimented routine; his free time is spent playing sports with friends and as the drummer in his band. Much of his recreation at home is focussed on music.

Two of the eldest school boys that I spoke to gave rich examples of how they use and feel about space in Hong Kong. Their testimonies detail some of the intercultural encounters that they routinely have. Waqi spoke at length about his busy daily itinerary that includes school work as a prefect, praying, and part-time work in a Pakistani food supplies store. These commitments require considerable amounts of daily travel between different settings. Waqi also plays cricket for an under-18s team, representing Hong Kong. His passion for cricket is pursued in his free time and he plays games with friends whenever he can. It is this desire to play cricket whenever he wishes that represents his only frustration about living in Hong Kong.

> **Waqi:** One thing I dislike about Hong Kong is that whenever we play cricket, there are very few places we can go in Hong Kong. If we go to the football ground and we play, the guards come and say, 'Oh, you can't play here, it's a football ground.' This is the thing that I don't like.

This comment gives an insight into a crucial theme for Pakistani boys. Their love of cricket is obstructed by rules governing the use of space in Hong Kong. The majority of public parks provide football pitches, playgrounds, and basketball courts for Hong Kong youth, but never cricket grounds. Cricket grounds are normally owned by cricket or social and sporting clubs where membership is limited to a wealthy elite. Lefebvre (1991, p. 165) argues that any natural space which has been 'modified in order to serve the needs and possibilities of a group' can be understood as appropriated space. The appropriation of space is a theme apparent in works on youth, sub-culture, and ethnic minorities (Massey 1998; Matthews and Limb 1998; Borden 2001; Nayak 2003; Keith 2005; de Souza e Silva 2006; Back 2007). This social appropriation is relevant to how youth make their own social spaces through the colonisation and tactical use of public spaces. Borden (2001, p. 54) takes this theme and applies it to the colonisation of urban locations by skateboarders. He notes how skateboarders perceive space as possessing potential for their own explicit uses. Similarly, Waqi's frustration at being moved off an empty football pitch relates to this identification of the potential of space and shows the adaptability of these young Muslims to persist in playing cricket despite a lack of provisions. I have often seen groups of Pakistanis boys playing cricket in a basketball court near the Wanchai Mosque In all my conversations with South Asian Muslims, cricket and public space have become a recurring theme. Often, young men are stopped from playing cricket and are made to feel peripheral and subversive as they try to appropriate spaces for their own use. These youth see potential in a variety of unused spaces where they can practise bowling and batting. However, these activities are often opportunistic and short-lived, as security guards, pedestrians, and residents protest that the spaces are being wrongly used, or complain of the noise the young men create. Ashja told me that sometimes cultural differences were a factor in these complaints. Some Chinese simply objected to the behaviour of South Asians. He suggested that they dislike the way the young men play as it is seen as rowdy and

Figure 9 South Asian young men playing cricket in a basketball court near the Wanchai mosque (photo by Sarah O'Connor)

chaotic and at odds with the Hong Kong Chinese norms about the use of recreational space.

I have witnessed the negotiated transference of a basketball court cricket match to a basketball game. The example I saw involved the court being split in two, cricket at one end and basketball at the other. Only when enough basketball players arrived for a full game did the cricket players acquiesce to the prescribed function of the court. Despite the fact that they were there first, it was the recognition of the legitimacy of the space as a basketball court that ultimately dictated that the cricket game should cease. The cricket players were all South Asian and the majority of the basketball players were Chinese. The change in use was a pedestrian process between the two groups, neither confrontational nor jovial; it just happened. This example shows how the use of space relates to cultural practices and it also raises the question of how cultural spaces need to be facilitated in multicultural settings. While Wanchai and Tsim Sha Tsui are clearly culturally diverse spaces their legitimate functional space for the mix of cultures they house is limited. Cricket is one example of an everyday pastime and priority for many of the Muslim young men in the territory.

Waqi's anecdote above, like the findings of Law (2000) and Borden (2001), indicates that youth are engaged in a de Certeau-like circumventing of the provisions, rationality, and order that has been imposed upon the urban landscape in order to indulge in their own particular recreation. A Pakistani playing cricket in a Wanchai basketball court is an exhibition of Hong Kong's hybridity, an example of how culture endures in settings that are geared towards other needs. The comments of Waqi, Hadaf, Sharif, and Ashja all identify cricket as an important cultural, social and leisure practice for South Asian young men. It is therefore important to consider the relevance of this. For example, there are a number of studies that indicate that youth in Hong Kong are at risk. Many are socially excluded, bored, and involved in anti-social behaviours (Law 2000; Lee 2005; Tang 2006). Within such research and media reports space is often highlighted as an important aspect in understanding the experiences of these young people. The fact that cricket is such a passion among South Asian young men is important for policy makers concerned with creating an inclusive array of facilities for Hong Kong's diverse communities. Waqi's example provides a different way of interpreting youth at risk and demonstrates how youth are marginalised by pursuing recreational activities that are not catered for in public space.

Most importantly, this example reveals the embodied practice of lived hybridity. The key element I would like to identify in my account of how the basketball court changes from a place for Pakistani boys to play cricket to a place where mostly Chinese youth play basketball, is that it occurs without confrontation. In addition to this rather benign intercultural transaction is the fact that two different cultural groups did meet. Unlike the segregation that Amin (2002, p. 962) identifies as a barrier to multiculturalism in Britain, Hong Kong's mixed residential areas and urban density mean that different cultures have little choice but to deal with each other. However, in line with Amin's findings (2002, p. 968), it is often working-class youth that does most of this mixing simply because they are more prone to use public space in these ways. Hong Kong space provides a stage where negotiations between different cultures are unavoidable. They have to occur; they are necessary. As a result, observation of Hong Kong's urban space becomes an observation of Hong Kong's everyday hybridity.

Young male Muslims appear to have a different form of regulation in their use of the fourth space in comparison with their female peers. On the whole, it is fair to say that the young men are all more spatially free.

However, they are limited by the need to attend to studies, both academic and religious, and also, in the case of Waqi, employment and commitment to his cricket team. The movements of all these boys with the exception of the more ambiguous Insaf, relate to a fourth space use that sees consumption as peripheral or of very shallow importance, indicating that in everyday scenarios these young men do not spend a great deal of money and when they do it is tied to cultural products and services. For example, many respondents reported eating at Pakistani restaurants. The fourth space for young men is also related to those areas where mosques and halal restaurants are available, often Wanchai and Tsim Sha Tsui.

Hong Kong space provides a way to understand the everyday life of young Muslims in the territory. The use of space between the respondents is diverse though some similarities relate to gender, class, and ethnicity. Space provides the stage where prosaic negotiations between cultures actually occur and are necessary. Space is key because its observation and analysis allows one to recognise the need youth have to engage in cultural activities with peers and also the need for an arena to perform for others. This is important, as the performance of hobbies and interests is a crucial way in which young people can learn and become motivated about their abilities and skills (Gustavson 2007, pp. 18–19).

Appropriating space to play cricket games, for example, allows youth to overcome isolation and marginalisation; in addition, it can be seen as a way to make a claim for citizenship, ownership and involvement in the public sphere. This observation of the everyday uses of space provides a new understanding of the everyday lives of young Muslims in Hong Kong. It presents an opportunity to observe and engage with a representation of Muslim youth that speaks of their day-to-day exchanges and concerns. It is a timely departure from work that addresses post-9/11 themes of subversion, religious extremism, and Islamophobia. The presentation of these accounts responds to the concerns raised by Phillips (2009) and Hopkins (2009) by showing Muslims in the spaces of their prosaic everyday transactions. It therefore contributes to the project of recognising that Muslims 'face many of the same issues as other groups' (Phillips 2009, p. 2). Instead of addressing Muslim individuals and communities in a simply positive light, discussions such as this provide a context to understand Muslims beyond their binary representations (Hopkins 2009, p. 28). Everyday hybridity circumvents 'positive versus negative' representations of

Muslim youth and instead captures instances of daily life that provide texture and context for our understanding of these individuals.

The issue of recreational cricket games represents one way in which Pakistani males are spatially excluded in everyday Hong Kong life. Public parks and sports grounds generally cater to the interests and pastimes of the dominant Hong Kong Chinese population. Therefore Tai Chi gardens, basketball courts, boating ponds, foot massage paths, sitting out areas, and exercise apparatus are common. Wise (2005) highlights how mundane interactions are central to understanding multi-ethnic communities and shows how the most perfunctory of inclusions can foster greater community ties. It is therefore feasible to consider that if the Hong Kong government were to facilitate the use of recreational areas for cricket matches, they might in turn alleviate some of the stresses, frustrations, and marginalisation that young South Asians experience in Hong Kong. This suggestion is sensitive to how young Muslims like to spend their free time and how it can be obstructed by a lack of provisions in public space.

However, I would add a note of caution that while the inclusion of facilities for cricket games is a rather benign way to open up public space to ethnic minorities, it risks a type of thinking that sees cultures as separate, occupying different spaces and could foster divisions than at present do not exist in Hong Kong society. Asad, for example, said that once their games of cricket are stopped, they play basketball instead. By not having a legitimate 'cricket' space, these young men alter their behaviour. They would prefer to play cricket, but in the end they do what is allowed in Hong Kong, and participate in Hong Kong culture by playing basketball. Similarly, Franky from Ghana often picks up games of basketball in Tsim Sha Tsui Park. He notes that despite the fact that most Hong Kong Chinese avoid him because he is black, the tables turn when he is on the basketball court. The associated prowess of black basketball players means that he is a valuable asset in a game; even if he plays badly (which he assures me he never does) he is an imposing member of the team. It is arguable that Hong Kong society is relatively harmonious because recreational and cultural divisions have not been fostered by public provisions. It is something of a dilemma; how can facilities be improved without altering the valuable harmony that exists? Perhaps public recreational spaces could be created that are multifunctional and thus accessible for a variety of uses and activities. This could provide young South Asian young men with a valid space to play cricket while not creating segregation or obstructing intercultural dialogue and negotiations.

The topic of social space in Hong Kong is fascinating. Even this exploration of Muslim youth and space skims the surface of some complex interlinking issues. I have not discussed the very relevant appropriation of space by Indonesian foreign domestic workers in this chapter. Sunday mornings at Victoria Park are clearly also relevant for our understanding of Muslims in Hong Kong. We see that as there are no specific ethnic locales in the city, or more correctly there are no residential zones that are occupied en masse by minorities, public space becomes one of the key areas in which we see working-class ethnic minorities pursuing their social affairs.

In this chapter, I have explored a variety of issues. The gendered use of space is a very important perspective that enables us to recognise the considerable differences in Pakistani culture surrounding males and females. Tactics and appropriated space present a very vibrant engagement with the everyday lives of the respondents. The issue of virtual space is compelling, showing us a different level of social interaction and engagement with a form of popular space that is a recent development. This is all the more important in the discussion because it is youth who are the pioneers of social networking developing the social mores of virtual space. This final chapter also shows that the topic of Muslims and ethnic minorities in Hong Kong is a fruitful one for further academic scrutiny and discussion.

12
Conclusion: Thoughts on an anonymous letter

During the very beginning of my research I was passed an anonymous letter via a friend. What I read challenged some of my perceptions of Islam in the territory, about the international school community, and Hong Kong itself. It was donated as a contribution to the voices of young Muslims in Hong Kong. All I know about the girl that wrote to me is that she is from a wealthy South Asian Muslim family, she excels in her studies, she attended an international school in Hong Kong, and at the time she was planning to go to university in the United States. The letter was originally drafted as a confessional essay that would form part of her university application. Here is an excerpt from the text.

Desert Flower by Waris Dirie was shoved under my nose by my mother, in an attempt to keep me entertained while she conversed with the librarian. Sighing, I flopped down into a chair and began to read.

Six hours later, I closed the back cover. My head was spinning as I tried to comprehend the magnitude of what I had just read. Waris Dirie, the daughter of a Somalian goatherd, fled an arranged marriage at the age of twelve wearing nothing but a scarf draped around her. She is now a Special Ambassador for the United Nations as well as a supermodel. It was a story that traversed continents and oceans, spanned worlds of human pain, and inspired me to take what I had learned and make an attempt at putting things right.

This book affected me so profoundly because Waris Dirie reminded me of myself. At the age of five, Waris Dirie underwent the process of female genital mutilation (FGM). This is the term used to refer to the removal of part, or all, of the female genitalia. It is practiced by Muslims all over the world. An estimated two million girls every year are at risk of being mutilated, this works out to 6000 a day. 135 million of the world's girls and women have already undergone this horrific procedure. I am one of them.

As I am writing this, I honestly can't believe that this has happened to me. When I remember the procedure; I remember being oblivious to fear, numb to pain and unconcerned whether I would live or die, I feel like I'm talking about someone else. I was butchered with my parent's permission and I can't help but feel bewildered, yet outraged that this could happen to a girl as young as six.

There was absolutely nothing I could do, and there is nothing I can do now to put it right. This feeling of powerlessness has since haunted me and will continue to haunt me for years to come. Initially, I blamed my parents, but realized that my parents were victims of their upbringing, following cultural practices that have remained unchanged for centuries. They know that women in our community who have not been circumcised are considered to be 'like men' and are ostracized by society.

The author's very tender expression, that balances coming to terms with what happened to her, loving her culture and parents, and her desire to educate others in order to stop the practice is most touching. Nothing in my subsequent research contrasted with this account. Her story is the only one of female circumcision, or female genital mutilation (FGM) in Hong Kong that I have ever encountered. The subject, which is very much a taboo in Western culture, is seldom discussed in reference to Muslims beyond sub-Saharan Africa. Among South Asians the practice is very rare occurring within a very small group of sects. I must stress that there is little information on this subject available and it is thus both difficult and irresponsible to make generalisations. In Western multicultural societies FGM tests the very boundaries of acceptable multiculturalism (Shweder 2000; Boyle, McMorris, and Gómez 2002). The greatest challenge is that often the women who have undergone FGM are those who are central in sustaining the cultural practice for their own daughters. This tension, between cultural tradition and family is given a very human context in the letter.

The story that this young woman presents is another remarkable account of Hong Kong's everyday hybridity. It reminds us that along with the mundane and the workaday, the everyday includes the most challenging of issues. This young woman was living the typical life of a 6-year-old, attending school, engaging in extra-curricular activities, and at the same time enduring a deeply controversial rite of passage. Her account reminds us that through the celebration of ethnic foods and

Conclusion: Thoughts on an anonymous letter

cultural fashions, hybridity is often misrepresented. Sharing and celebrating cultural diversity and difference is merely the recasting of the recognition of difference; it has little to do with understanding and living with cultural difference. The processes of coming to terms with FGM, of learning and speaking another language, of religious practices and a whole host of lived issues, speak of the reality of living as a minority in a culturally hybrid environment.

One of the reasons that I have chosen to discuss this letter in conclusion is out of respect to the brave young woman who was able to express this complex issue so maturely and who was so willing to contribute her story to this research project. It serves to acknowledge that there are many experiences of Islam in Hong Kong and that even wealthy internationally educated Muslims experience a complex hybridity in their daily lives that may not be representative of the 'street', but speaks a truth of everyday life for a particular social niche. This story is also included to show that while a great many issues have been covered in this book, there are many more to pursue and investigate. Hong Kong has a vibrant society that is worthy and important to study. Be it Muslim youth, ethnic minorities, migrants, or the local Chinese experience of 'others', these issues are all informative to Hong Kong studies and international sociology.

This young lady's letter captures a gendered experience of growing up as a Muslim in Hong Kong. The accounts of the participants in this study have also included the voices of many young women and identified issues particular to them. These are so important as it is young women who represent the *zeitgeist* of Hong Kong's Muslim majority. We see this most urgently in acknowledging the recent social transformations surrounding the rise in numbers of Indonesian foreign domestic workers in the territory. These young women are now the largest single group of Muslims in Hong Kong.

Young Muslim men face quite different challenges in present-day Hong Kong. For young *Hui* men, commitment to work and study appear to be more urgent and taxing than religious duties. As such, they are involved in the demanding and competitive career pursuits typical of Hong Kong Chinese youth in the territory. By contrast, South Asians no longer have the privileged position of colonial intermediaries with the local Chinese, guarding, protecting and policing. Instead, many locally-born and raised South Asian Muslims find themselves with limited employment prospects due to the way in which ethnic minorities are educated in the territory and also the prejudice they endure. Racial prejudice is certainly a central concern for many Hong Kong residents. Particularly we see this in the case of African Muslim asylum seekers. Unable to work in the territory and seldom proven to be in legitimate political or physical danger they remain in limbo in Hong Kong and are often deeply marginalised (Mathews 2011). Criminal activities are one option available to them and some South Asian asylum seekers are recruited as drug dealers by Chinese triad gangs. Many locally-born South Asians are also part of these gangs as they feel poor employment prospects and racism provide them with no other choice (Carney 2010). This is again one area in which work on ethnic minorities in Hong Kong begs for further development and support.

This book has importantly addressed Muslim youth in Hong Kong and in the process looked at Islam and the lived experience of multiculturalism in the territory. One of my aims was to provide a contrast with work on Muslims and Islam in the West. By simply venturing into the topic of Islam in Hong Kong a comparative association has been made. What is contained within the research lends itself to further analysis also. This work extends beyond its key features, Islam, youth, and Hong Kong. It responds to bigger issues about the everyday experiences of ethnic and religious minorities in urban multicultural settings. We see themes such as language, food, religious education, freedom, and the use of space as valuable foci to explore the experience of being Muslim in Hong Kong. When combined, they give us a rich account of Muslim youth, Hong Kong, and everyday hybridity.

In aiding a comparative analysis this work has shown Muslims in both a Western and Chinese context. Particularly in reference to halal food we come to understand some of the idiosyncrasies of being Muslim in a Chinese cultural climate. These extend beyond the experiences of the *Hui* and Uyghur that have been covered in many other works (Israeli 2002; Gladney 2004) and instead encompass those of South Asians and Indonesians in a Chinese city. At the same time, it is apparent that Hong Kong is not simply a Chinese city; the Western influence upon Hong Kong's hybridity is tangible even if it is often tacit. Some individuals speak of their free time in shopping malls, of their education, and of the television and music that they watch and listen to. The insights that these provide are clearly useful to contrast with other work on Muslim minorities.

Conclusion: Thoughts on an anonymous letter

By being open to the possibilities within the experiences of daily life, as researchers, we open ourselves up to a dense array of information. Everyday hybridity has enabled me to respond to what the participants have revealed rather than pursuing them for key details that I presume to be the most relevant parts of their experience. This sort of research is concerned therefore with being able to listen (Back 2007) and being open to other research possibilities (Stoller 1997). Similarly Highmore (2007, p. 178) argues that the sort of analysis and methods of enquiry that the everyday life social theorist Michel de Certeau demonstrates, are attractive to researchers who want to make enquires without knowing what the results will be. Therefore, the scrutiny of everyday life and its unrepresented and overlooked experiences is a way to ground theory and explore new ways of discussing culture and society.

I have tried for the most part to let the research and respondents speak for themselves and have not been particularly vocal about my political position on many of these issues. This is for good reason. Many of the classic works on everyday life social theory have pushed for the everyday to be understood as a site of change and revolution. In thoughtfully considering Muslims in Hong Kong, the most radical aspects of this work are those that reveal what currently exists.

Michel de Certeau argues that systemic change always results in radical politics becoming part of the system they strive to counter. In essence, he argues that the popular recognition of these new ideas actually seals their fate; they become entwined in the political system they are addressing. In his own words, 'every one of the movements that have attempted to make a statement through collective "consciousness-raising" ... has run up against the same barrier. From the moment when, through its own process, an action begins to change the balance of forces, it is interrupted by repression organized by the established powers' (de Certeau 1997, p. 120). This change to the 'balance of forces' is something of which I am particularly mindful. In de Certeau's argument, the pitfalls reside in the mode of representation. He sees language as flawed, so deeply interwoven with the culture and discourse of power that it is muted in its ability to challenge systems. The question then becomes: What is the most effective way to be heard and to express oneself? The introduction of the Racial Discrimination Ordinance is not something that I would ever wish to block. I am indeed pleased that this progress has taken place. However, I am concerned that the mode of thinking that instructs the Hong Kong population not to be racist may in turn damage much of the innate cultural harmony that does exist.

Multiculturalism in Australia, Canada, and Britain has faced enormous obstacles in its efforts to control the attitudes and opinions of people towards minority communities. Certainly within Britain we have seen racism morph from a colour-based prejudice to a culturally founded one (Modood 2005). As I finish writing these passages in August of 2011, the youth riots in Britain follow a similar model. The collective action, desperate and hysterical as it may seem, provokes only authoritarian reactions that strive to further suppress the disaffected. Consciousness-raising is quickly subsumed in the structural hegemony. Hong Kong is a different environment and imperfect policies and practices from other countries should not naively be transplanted into this setting. I make this argument in light of how many Muslims in Hong Kong enjoy religious freedom, feel safe, and shrug off popular racism. This is something woefully absent in the West despite efforts to nurture it. I believe that we need to consider the broader mechanisms involved in society; we should not simply ask what we want to change, but also what we want to preserve. What is valuable in the way Hong Kong deals with difference? What may be altered by policy changes?

It is in this light that I would like to see the everyday experiences of Muslims in Hong Kong read as a type of prefigurative politics. Understanding and observing how people live and what they value, contains a political message. Muslims in Hong Kong are not politicised; they are not striving to alter Hong Kong society. This is key. At the same time, their greatest marginalisation comes in the form of education. If local Muslims as ethnic minorities are unable to access appropriate education, which should enable them to integrate into Hong Kong society as active members, then anti-racism consciousness-raising is of little use as there will be few ethnic minorities ready and able to access the broader work environment. Similarly, much of Hong Kong's population will not encounter ethnic minorities in their everyday life; very little will change. As de Certeau suggests, the model will continue. Those most able to benefit from the anti-racism legislation may well be the ones that are already most able to succeed, namely those who were supported in their education financially so they can excel. The bulk of the working class will remain economically and socially marginalised.

Conclusion: Thoughts on an anonymous letter

Government policy that streams ethnic minorities into English-language-medium education serves to undermine the hybridity that the city breeds. While a number of families desire English language education it is also clear that large numbers feel themselves to be local in orientation and aspirations. A Chinese language curriculum for non-Chinese-speaking minorities would widen the participation of ethnic minorities academically and in all sectors of employment. In some respects, these policies reflect a pernicious racism, and at the same time they marginalise the position of local ethnic minorities to the detriment of Hong Kong itself. As Hong Kong matures as a post-colonial Chinese city and grows ever more confident with its unique international history, I believe it will recast these relationships in a more inclusive frame. In recent years, it has become clear that young people who have grown up amid the city's affluence have different concerns to the previous generations of Hong Kong people.

My belief is that the experiences of Muslims in Hong Kong are valuable because they show a minority not stigmatised because of Islam. Learning from the sense of freedom that young Muslims have here is something that can contribute to work on Muslim minorities in the West. More generally the freedom and safety of Hong Kong itself, as a world city, is worthy of contemplation. The territory is densely populated, polluted, and is lacking democracy, yet it possesses a unique multicultural ethos that many Western countries would trumpet. A key aspect of this lived rather than proscribed multiculturalism is that it is natural and uncontrived. Unlike the multiculturalism that de Finney (2010) describes in Canada, Hong Kong's everyday hybridity is not informed or structured by political manifestos. It is more correctly an organic type of hybridity. What does concern me, however, is that the minorities that live within Hong Kong, albeit marked often by racial and ethnic difference, are similarly treated as foreign subjects, despite the fact that many are born and raised here.

The very basic message that can be enunciated by the government directed at its Muslim population, and in a broader sense, at all ethnic minorities, is to open up the remit upon which local identity is founded. Embracing minorities involves so much more than a nod towards internationalism and anti-racism. Its very basic inclusion should be founded on communication. If Hong Kong was to become confident enough to push for its minorities to be conversant and literate in Chinese, then a great deal would change. After all, language is culture and by limiting the access minorities have to Cantonese, Hong Kong society also limits the integration of its minority communities. To me, this is the factor that is both most urgent and most able to redress the marginalisation of many ethnic minorities. All of my suggestions push towards the acknowledgement of Muslims as a local part of Hong Kong, as ethnic and religious minorities, as permanent residents, and as Hong Kong people rather than as foreigners. Hong Kong possesses a great many circumstances that facilitate a broadly harmonious society. There are no ethnic ghettos and religious difference is respected. There is therefore much to celebrate in Hong Kong.

There is so much about the topic of Islam in Hong Kong that I have not presented. There is much regarding the lives of expatriate Muslims that would be fascinating to explore, or the lives of elderly Muslims like that at the UMAH home for the elderly. I have also been asked by some Muslims to consider the need for Islamic finance in Hong Kong. This is an issue that has been seriously debated by the government since 1997 (Yiu 2011). Progress has been slow and many of Hong Kong's Muslims, immersed in a city that is a finance hub, wish to be able to invest in businesses in line with Islamic law. These issues are important but the focus of this book has centred upon what I have felt to be the greatest oversight to date, the accounts of young working-class Muslims. These individuals provide a real insight into everyday life in Hong Kong and the experience of being a Muslim. Islam is certainly a long-standing element of life in Hong Kong and one that has in recent years become of growing interest to Hong Kong residents (Lee 2003; Lam 2011).

My lasting impression from this research is that more needs to be asked about Hong Kong. This goes beyond supporting social progress and demanding more in terms of enquiry. Hong Kong needs to be listened to more, to be watched more, to be considered more. It seems trite as an academic to call yet again for further research. Yet in a most honest and earnest way, Hong Kong appears to be an intermediary place, and in being so it is a potent laboratory for social research. It promises to give us an alternative account. Its exotica are not too foreign or unfamiliar; it is relevant to all places as it is itself such a fusion. My anonymous letter confirms this again. Whatever conceptions people have of Hong Kong, they must always be prepared for them to be challenged.

Appendix: The key participants

Name	Age	Gender	Ethnicity	Years in Hong Kong
Aara	15	female	Indian	5
Amisha	31	female	Indonesian	4
Arif	42	male	Pakistani	22
Asad	16	male	Pakistani	15
Aseelah	15	female	Pakistani	since birth
Ashja	15	male	Indian	13
Benny	52	male	HK Chinese	since birth
Dil	14	female	Pakistani	since birth
Elisha	15	female	Pakistani	since birth
Fatin	14	female	Pakistani	since birth
Fazeelah	30	female	HK Chinese	since birth
Franky	32	male	Ghanaian	6
Gabir	25	female	Indonesian	6
Hadaf	20	male	Pakistani	10
Hina	16	female	Pakistani	since birth
Iftikhar	23	male	Somalian	4
Inas	14	female	Indonesian	2
Insaf	15	male	Indonesian	1
Jawa	28	female	Indonesian	4
Jumana	15	female	Pakistani	12
Kanwal	14	female	Pakistani	since birth
Kiran	14	female	Pakistani	9
Mahek	14	female	Pakistani	8
Mahmood	27	male	Somalian	1

Name	Age	Gender	Ethnicity	Years in Hong Kong
Muhammad	14	male	Pakistani	7
Murtaza	13	male	Pakistani	since birth
Pari	14	female	Pakistani	since birth
Qaaria	13	female	Sri Lankan	12
Qatadah	18	male	Pakistani	10
Riya	27	female	Indonesian	2
Sahira	13	female	Pakistani	12
Sharif	14	male	Pakistani	6.5
Shazeb	17	male	Pakistani	10
Suri	31	female	Indonesian	5
Uma	17	female	Pakistani	11
Waqi	17	male	Pakistani	13
Zainab	19	female	Pakistani	13

Bibliography

Abbas, Ackbar. 1997. *Hong Kong: Culture and the politics of disappearance*. Hong Kong: Hong Kong University Press.
———. 2000. 'Cosmopolitan de-scriptions: Shanghai and Hong Kong', *Public culture*, 12, pp. 769–786.
Abusharaf, Rogia Mustafa. 1998. 'Structural adaptations in an immigrant Muslim congregation in New York.' In *Gatherings in diaspora: Religious communities and the new immigration*, ed. by Stephen R. Warner and Judith G. Wittner, pp. 235–260. Philadelphia: Temple University Press.
Ahmed, Akbar S., 1994. *Postmodernism and Islam: Predicament and promise*. London: Routledge.
Amin, Ash. 2002. 'Ethnicity and the multicultural city: Living with diversity', *Environment and planning*, 34, pp. 959–980.
Ang, Ien. 2001. *On not speaking Chinese: Living between Asia and the West*. London: Routledge.
Arnett, Jeffrey Jensen. 2000. 'Emerging adulthood: A theory of development from the late teens through the twenties', *American Psychologist*, 55, pp. 469–480.
Asian Migrant Centre, Asian Domestic Workers Union, Forum of Filipino Reintegration and Saving Groups, Indonesian Migrant Workers Union, and Thai Women Association. 2001. *Baseline research on racial and gender discrimination towards Filipino, Indonesian and Thai Domestic helpers in Hong Kong*. Hong Kong: Asian Migrant Centre.
Back, Les. 2007. *The art of listening*. Oxford: Berg.
Ballard, Roger. 1996. 'Islam and the construction of Europe.' In *Muslims in the margin: Political responses to the presence of Islam in Western Europe*, ed. by W. A. R. Shahid and P. S. Van Konigsveld, pp. 15–51. Kampen: Netherlands Kok Pharos.
Basit, Tehmina N. 1997. *Eastern values; Western milieu: Identities and aspirations of adolescent British Muslim girls*. Aldershot: Ashgate Publishing Company.
Bauman, Gerd. 1996. *Contesting culture: Discourses of identity in multi-ethnic London*. New York: Cambridge University Press.
Bauman, Zygmunt. 2007a. *Liquid times: Living in an age of uncertainty*. Cambridge: Polity.
———. 2007b. *Consuming life*. Cambridge: Polity.

———. 2008. *Does ethics have a chance in a world of consumers?* London: Harvard University Press.
Benitez, Mary Ann. 'Number of foreign helpers falls by 17,000', *South China Morning Post*, 2 July. http://archive.scmp.com [accessed 23 July 2006].
Bhabha, Homi K. 1994. *The location of culture*. London: Routledge.
Borden, Iain. 2001. *Skateboarding, space and the city: Architecture and the body*. Oxford: Berg.
Boubekeur, Amel 2005. 'Cool and competitive: Muslim culture in the West', *ISIM Review*, 16, pp. 12–13.
Bouma, Gary D., Joan Daw, and Riffat Munawar. 2001. 'Muslims managing religious diversity.' In *Muslim communities in Australia*, ed. by Abdullah Saeed and Shahram Akbarzadeh, pp. 53–72. Sydney: University of New South Wales.
Bouma, Gary D., and Andrew Singleton. 2004. 'A comparative study of the successful management of religious diversity: Melbourne and Hong Kong', *International Sociology*, 19, pp. 5–24.
Boyle, Elizabeth Heger, Barbara J. McMorris, and Mayra Gómez. 2002. 'Local conformity to international norms: The case of female genital cutting', *International Sociology*, 17, pp. 5–33.
Cainkar, Louise, and Sunaina Maira. 2005. 'Targeting Arab/Muslim/South Asian Americans: Criminalization and cultural citizenship', *Amerasia Journal*, 31, pp. 1–27.
Carmichael, Sarah. 2009. 'Language rights and education: A study of Hong Kong's linguistic minorities', Centre for Comparative and Public Law, the Faculty of Law, the University of Hong Kong. http://www.law.hku.hk/ccpl/pub/occasionalpapers/index.html [accessed 25 February 2012].
Carney, John. 2011. 'Asylum seekers recruited as drug dealers', *South China Morning Post*, 8 May. http://archive.scmp.com [accessed 23 July 2011].
Certeau, Michel de. 1984. *The practice of everyday life*, trans. by Steven F. Rendell. Los Angeles: University of California Press.
———. 1997. *Culture in the plural*, trans. by Tom Conley. Minneapolis: University of Minnesota Press.
Certeau, Michel de, Luce Giard, and Pierre Mayol. 1998. *The practice of everyday life volume 2: Living and cooking*, trans by. Timothy J. Tomasik. Minneapolis: University of Minnesota Press.
Cheung, Esther M. K. 2004. 'Introduction: Cinema and the city at a moment of danger.' In *Between home and world: A reader in Hong Kong cinema*, ed. by Esther M. K. Cheung and Chu Yiu-wai, pp. 248–271. Oxford: Oxford University Press.
Cheung, Siu-keung. 2000. 'Speaking out: Days in the lives of three Hong Kong cage dwellers', *Positions*, 8, pp. 235–262.
China Government. 2006. 'Ethnic groups in China.' http://www.china.org.cn/e-groups/shaoshu/ [accessed 5 March 2006].

Choi, Christy. 2011. 'Trapped in misery by the lure of false dreams', *South China Morning Post*, 17 July. http://archive.scmp.com [accessed 6 August 2011].

Chow, Rey. 1998. *Ethics after idealism: Theory-culture-ethnicity-reading*. Indianapolis: Indiana University Press.

Chow, Vivienne. 2005a. 'In malls, restaurants and homes, a farewell to a love affair', *South China Morning Post*, 2 May. http://archive.scmp.com [accessed 23 July 2006].

———. 2005b. 'Finale puts biggest jewel in broadcaster's crown', *South China Morning Post*, 4 May. http://archive.scmp.com [accessed 23 July 2006].

Committee on the promotion of civic education. 1997. *The basic law of the Hong Kong Special Administrative Region of the People's Republic of China*. Hong Kong: Joint Publishing.

Constable, Nicole. 1997. 'Sexuality and discipline among Filipina domestic workers in Hong Kong', *American Ethnologist*, 24, pp. 539–558.

Constitution and Mainland Affairs Bureau 2006. 'Race discrimination bill.' http://www.cmab.gov.hk/doc/en/documents/policy_responsibilities/the_rights_of_the_individuals/race/RaceDiscriminationBill_e.pdf [accessed 28 December 2006].

Crawford, Barclay. 2006. 'Peace of the action', *South China Morning Post*, 10 February. http://archive.scmp.com [accessed 23 July 2010].

Detaramani, Champa, and Graham Lock. 2003. 'Multilingualism in decline: Language repertoire, use and shift in two Hong Kong Indian communities', *Journal of Multilingual and Multicultural Development*, 24, pp. 249–273.

Dolby, Nadine. 2001. *Constructing race: Youth identity and popular culture in South Africa*. New York: State University of New York Press.

Dwyer, Claire. 1998. 'Contested identities: Challenging dominant representations of young British Muslim women.' In *Cool places: Geographies of youth cultures*, ed. by Tracey Skelton, and Gill Valentine, pp. 50–65. London: Routledge.

Ellin, Nan. 2003. 'Fear and city building', *Hedgehog Review*, vol. 5, no. 3, pp. 43–61.

Eoyang, Eugene. 1998. 'The human trinity: Language, education, culture.' In *Teaching language and culture: Building Hong Kong on education*, ed. by Barry Asker, pp. 11–26. Hong Kong: Addison Wesley Longman.

Erni, John Nguyet. 2001. 'Like a postcolonial culture: Hong Kong re-imagined', *Cultural Studies*, 15, pp. 389–418.

Essed, Philomena. 1991. *Understanding everyday racism: An interdisciplinary theory*. London: Sage.

Fanon, Frantz. 2004. *The wretched of the earth*, trans. by Richard Philcox. New York: Grove Press.

Fekete, Liz. 2004. 'Anti-Muslim racism and the European security state', *Race and Class*, 46, pp. 3–29.

Fenn, Andrea. 2010. 'Indonesian maids in Hong Kong blur the borders', *Jakarta Globe*, 19 October. http://www.thejakartaglobe.com/lifeandtimes/indonesian-maids-in-hong-kong-blur-the-borders/402153 [accessed 14 July 2011].

Finney, Sandra de. 2010. '"We just don't know each other": Racialised girls negotiate mediated multiculturalism in a less diverse Canadian city', *Journal of Intercultural Studies*, 31, pp. 471–487.

Forman, Ross G. 2004. 'Projecting from Possession Point: Hong Kong, hybridity and the shifting grounds of imperialism in James Dalziel's turn-of-the-century fiction', *Criticism*, 46, pp. 533–574.

Franks, Myfanwy. 2000. 'Crossing the borders of whiteness? White Muslim women who wear the hijab in Britain today', *Ethnic and Racial Studies*, 23, pp. 917–929.

Gillespie, Marie. 1995. *Television, ethnicity and cultural change*. London: Routledge.

Gillette, Maris Boyd. 2000. *Between Mecca and Beijing: Modernization and consumption among urban Chinese Muslims*. Stanford: Stanford University Press.

Gilroy, Paul. 1991. '"It ain't where you're from, it's where you're at", the dialectics of diasporic identification', *Third Text*, 13, pp. 3–16.

Gladney, Dru, C. 2004. *Dislocating China: Muslims, minorities, and other subaltern subjects*. Chicago: University of Chicago Press.

Gustavson, Leif. 2007. *Youth learning on their own terms*. London: Routledge.

Haddad, Yvonne Yazbeck. 1991. *The Muslims of America*. New York: Oxford University Press.

Hage, Ghassan. 2003. *Against paranoid nationalism: Searching for hope in a shrinking society*. Annandale: Pluto Press.

———. 2007. 'At home in the entrails of the West: multiculturalism, ethnic food and migrant home-building.' In *Home/world: Space, community and marginality in Sydney's West*, ed. by H. Grace et al., pp. 99–153. Annandale: Pluto Press.

Halliday, Fred. 1996. *Islam and the myth of confrontation*. London: I.B. Tauris.

Harris, Anita. 2004. *Future girl: Young women in the twenty-first century*. London: Routledge.

———. 2009. 'Shifting the boundaries of cultural spaces: Young people and everyday multiculturalism', *Social Identities*, 15, pp. 187–205.

———. 2010. 'Young people, everyday civic life and the limits of social cohesion', *Journal of Intercultural Studies*, 31, pp. 573–589.

Hawwa, Sithi. 2000. 'From cross to crescent: Religious conversion of Filipina domestic helpers in Hong Kong', *Islam and Christian-Muslim Relations*, 11, pp. 347–367.

Highmore, Ben. 2004. *Everyday life and cultural theory: An introduction*. London: Routledge.

———. 2007. *Michel de Certeau: Analysing culture*. London: Continuum.

Ho, Wai-Yip. 2001. 'Historical analysis of Islamic community development in Hong Kong: Struggle for recognition in the post-colonial era', *Journal of Muslim Minority Affairs*, vol. 21, no. 1, pp. 63–77.

———. 2002. 'Contested mosques in Hong Kong', *ISIM Newsletter*, 10, p. 14.

Hong Kong Tourism Board. 2008. 'List of halal food outlets/vegetarian restaurants in HK for Muslim visitors', *Discover Hong Kong*, http://www.

discoverhongkong.com/eng/gourmet/dining/images/gp_pdf_hala.pdf [accessed 17 February 2008].
Hong Kong Vegetarian Society. 2008. '2008報告.' http://www.vegsochk.org/reports/ [accessed 10 August 2011].
Hong Kong Yearbook. 2009a. *The facts.* http://www.yearbook.gov.hk/2009/en/index.html [accessed 28 June 2011].
———. 2009b. *Religion and custom.* http://www.gov.hk/en/about/abouthk/factsheets/docs/religion.pdf [accessed 28 June 2011].
Hopkins, Peter. 2009. 'Muslims in the West: Deconstructing geographical binaries.' In *Muslim spaces of hope: Geographies of possibility in Britain and the West*, ed. by Richard Phillips, pp. 27–40. London: Zed Books.
Huang, Tsung-Yi Michelle. 2004. *Walking between slums and skyscrapers: Illusions of open space in Hong Kong, Tokyo, and Shanghai.* Hong Kong: Hong Kong University Press.
Hui, Polly, and Ravina Shamdasani. 2006. 'Race bill "no panacea for prejudice"', *South China Morning Post*, 3 December. http://archive.scmp.com [accessed 3 December 2006].
Huntington, Samuel P. 2003. 'The clash of civilisations?' *Foreign Affairs*, 72, pp. 22–49.
IMBC. 2005. *Dae Jang Geum Theme Park.* http://www.imbc.com/entertain/mbcticket/mbcplay/2004/daejanggumtheme_eng/ [accessed 1 November 2005].
Incorporated Trustees of the Islamic Community Fund. 1997. 'History of Muslim in Hong Kong.' http://www.islam.org.hk/eng/TrusteeHistory.asp [accessed 3 March 2008].
Ip, Iam-chong. 1998. 'The spectres of marginality and hybridity: "Hong Kong identity" in cultural criticism', *Chinese Sociology and Anthropology*, 30, pp. 45–64.
Islamic Union of Hong Kong 2007, 'Halal food in Hong Kong', *Islamic Union of Hong Kong.* http://www.iuhk.org/Eng/E_halalfood.htm [accessed 11 November 2007].
Israeli, Raphael. 2002. *Islam in China: Religion, ethnicity, culture, and politics.* Lanham: Lexington Books.
Jacobson, Jessica. 1998. *Islam in transition: Religion and identity among British Pakistani youth.* London: Routledge.
Kadison, Dan. 2009a. 'Can a street name be biased? Some think so', *South China Morning Post*, 4 October. http://archive.scmp.com [accessed 12 October 2009].
———. 2009b. 'Chinese street names to stay unless derogatory term sparks outcry', *South China Morning Post*, 11 October. http://archive.scmp.com [accessed 12 October 2009].
Kalra, Virinder S. 2000. *From textile mills to taxi ranks: Experience of migration, labour and social change.* Aldershot: Ashgate.
Kalra, Virinder S., Raminder Kaur, and John Hutnyk. 2005. *Diaspora and hybridity.* London: Sage.

Keith, Michael. 2005. *After the cosmopolitan: Multicultural cities and the future of racism*. London: Routledge.

Kelly, Deidre M., Shauna Pomerantz, and Dawn H. Currie. 2006. '"No boundaries"? Girls' interactive, online learning about femininities', *Youth and Society*, 38, pp. 3–28.

Ku, Hok-bun, Kam-wah Chan, Wai-ling Chan, and Wai-yee Lee. 2003. *A research report on the life experiences of Pakistanis in Hong Kong*. Hong Kong: Centre for Social Policy Studies, Department of Applied Social Sciences, the Hong Kong Polytechnic University; S. K. H. Lady MacLehose Centre.

Ku, Hok-bun, Kam-Wah Chan, and Karamji Kaur Sandhu. 2005. *A research report on the education of South Asian ethnic minority groups in Hong Kong*. Department of Applied Social Science, Hong Kong Polytechnic University and Hong Kong Unison. http://www.unison.org.hk/R_Research.htm [accessed 23 March 2011].

Kwok, Siu Tong, and Kirti Narain. 2003. *Co-prosperity in cross-culturalism: Indians in Hong Kong*. Hong Kong: Chinese University Press.

Lai, Ming-yan. 2010. 'Small dragon dance, or, tale of a migrant domestic worker's transnational morphing.' Association of Cultural Studies Crossroads Conference. 17 June 2010. Hong Kong: Lingnan University.

Lam, Lana. 2011. 'Growing Chinese interest in Islam', *South China Morning Post*, 31 July. http://archive.scmp.com [accessed 31 July 2011].

Law, Niki. 2002. 'Muslims accuse police of racial slur', *South China Morning Post*, 15 December. http://archive.scmp.com [accessed 23 July 2004].

Law, Wing-sang. 2000. 'Northbound colonialism: A politics of post-pc Hong Kong', *Positions*, 8, pp. 201–233.

Lee, Eliza W.Y. ed. 2003. *Gender and change in Hong Kong: Globalization, postcolonialism, and Chinese patriarchy*. Hong Kong: Hong Kong University Press.

Lee, Ella. 2001. 'Unholy row: Opposition to plans for a mosque is fuelling SAR Muslim's feelings of being discriminated against', *South China Morning Post*, 1 October. http://archive.scmp.com [accessed 3 August 2009].

Lee, Francis Wing-lin. 2000. 'Teens of the night: The young night drifters in Hong Kong', *Youth and Society*, 31, pp. 363–384.

Lee, Sherry. 2003. 'The call of Allah', *South China Morning Post*, 10 December. http://archive.scmp.com [accessed 2 April 2007].

Lefebvre, Henri. 1984. *Everyday life in the modern world*, trans. by Sacha Rabinovitch. New Brunswick: Transaction Publishers.

———. 1991. *The production of space*, trans. by Donald Nicholson-Smith. Oxford: Blackwell.

Lethbridge, Henry J. 2003. 'Cast, class and race in Hong Kong before the Japanese.' In *Hong Kong: A reader in social history*, ed. by David Faure, pp. 517–542. Oxford: Oxford University Press.

Leung, Lai-fun. 2004. 'Are Muslims in Hong Kong more marginalized after "September 11"?', Bachelor Thesis. Department of Applied Social Science,

City University Hong Kong. http://hdl.handle.net/2031/792 [accessed 1 October 2009].

Lewis, Philip. 2002. *Islamic Britain: Religion, politics and identity among British Muslims*. New York: I.B. Tauris.

———. 2007. *Young, British and Muslim*. London: Continuum.

Lin, Angel M. Y. 2005. 'Doing verbal play: Creative work of Cantonese working-class schoolboys in Hong Kong.' In *Internationalizing Cultural Studies: An anthology*, ed. by Ackbar Abbas and John Nguyet Erni, pp. 317–329. Oxford: Blackwell.

Lo, Alex. 2000. 'McDonald's fries in trouble over animal oil'. *South China Morning Post*, 3 July. http://archive.scmp.com [accessed 23 July 2004].

Louis, W. M. Roger. 1999. 'The dissolution of the British Empire.' In *The Oxford history of the British Empire: The twentieth century*, ed. by Judith M. Brown and W. M. Roger Louis, pp. 329–356. Oxford: Oxford University Press.

Lui, Tai-lok. 2004. 'Hong Kong.' In *Teen life in Asia*, ed. by Judith J. Slater, pp. 35–50. London: Greenwood Press.

Luk-Fong, Pattie Yuk-yee. 2006. 'Hybridity in a guidance curriculum in Hong Kong', *International Journal for the Advancement of Counseling*, 28, pp 331–342.

Ma, Eric. 2002. 'Emotions energy and sub-cultural politics: Alternative bands in post-1997 Hong Kong', *Inter-Asia Cultural Studies*, 3, pp. 187–200.

Maira, Sunaina. 2005. 'The intimate and the imperial: South Asian immigrant youth after 9/11.' In *Youthscapes: The popular, the national, the global*, ed. by Sunaina Maira and Elisabeth Soep, pp. 64–81. Philadelphia: University of Pennsylvania Press.

Marchetti, Gina. 2004. 'Transnational cinema, hybrid identities, and the films of Evans Chan.' In *Between home and world: A reader in Hong Kong Cinema*, ed. by Esther M. K. Cheung and Chu Yiu-wai, pp. 196–223. Oxford: Oxford University Press.

Massey, Doreen. 1998. 'The spatial construction of youth cultures.' In *Cool places: Geographies of youth cultures*, ed. by Tracey Skelton and Gill Valentine, pp. 121–129. London: Routledge.

Mathews, Gordon. 2011. *Ghetto at the center of the world: Chungking Mansions, Hong Kong*. Chicago: University of Chicago Press.

Matthews, Hugh, Melanie Limb, and Barry Percy-Smith. 1998. 'Changing worlds: The microgeographies of young teenagers', *Tijdschrift Vorr Economische en Socile Geografie*, 89, pp. 193–202.

Mayaram, S., 2009. 'Introduction rereading global cities: Topographies of an alternative cosmopolitanism in Asia.' In *The other global city*, ed. By Shail Mayaram, pp. 1–32. London: Routledge.

McDonald's Singapore. 2011. *Company info: Milestones*. http://www.mcdonalds.com.sg/companyinfo_milestones.html [accessed 2 August 2011].

Modood, Tariq. 1997. ' "Difference", cultural racism and anti-racism.' In *Debating cultural hybridity*, ed. by Tariq Modood and Pnina Werbner, pp 154–172. London: Zed Books.

———. 2005. *Multicultural politics: Racism, ethnicity, and Muslims in Britain*. Minneapolis: University of Minnesota Press.
Morris, Jan. 1997. *Hong Kong*. The final edition. London: Penguin.
Nayak, Anoop. 2003. *Race, place and globalization: Youth cultures in a changing world*. New York: Berg.
Nederveen Pieterse, 2007. *Ethnicities and global multiculture: Pants for an octopus*. Plymouth: Rowman & Littlefield Publishers.
Ng, Maggie. 2010. '24pc of South Asian Men can't find work', *South China Morning Post*, 11 January. http://archive.scmp.com [accessed 23 July 2004].
Noble, Greg, and Scott Poynting. 2010. 'White lines: The intercultural politics of everyday movement in social spaces', *Journal of Intercultural Studies*, 31, pp. 489–505.
Noble, Greg, Scott Poynting, and Paul Tabar. 1999. 'Youth ethnicity and the mapping of identities: Strategic essentialism and strategic hybridity among male Arabic-speaking youth in South-Western Sydney', *Communal/Plural*, 17, pp. 29–44.
Nunes, Mark. 2006. *Cyberspaces of everyday life*. Minneapolis: University of Minnesota Press.
O'Connor, Paul. 2010. 'Accepting prejudice and valuing freedom: Young Muslims and everyday multiculturalism in Hong Kong', *Journal of Intercultural Studies*, 31, pp. 525–539.
———. 2011. 'Everyday hybridity and Hong Kong's Muslim youth', *Visual Anthropology*, 24, pp. 203–225.
Pannu, Jasbir. 1998. 'Language choice and identity: The world of the Hong Kong Indian adolescent.' In *Language in Hong Kong at century's end*, ed. by Martha C. Pennington, pp. 219–242. Hong Kong: Hong Kong University Press.
Patri, Mrudula, and Pennington, Martha C. 1998. 'Acculturation to English by an ethnic minority: The language attitudes of Indian adolescents in a Hong Kong International School.' In *Language in Hong Kong at century's end*, ed. by Martha C. Pennington, pp. 339–362. Hong Kong: Hong Kong University Press.
Phillips, Richard. 2009. 'Muslim geographies: spaces of hope?' In *Muslim spaces of hope: Geographies of possibility in Britain and the West*, ed. by Richard Phillips, pp. 1–12. London: Zed Books.
Pillsbury, Barbara. 1975. 'Pig and policy: Maintenance of boundaries between Han and Muslim Chinese.' In *Minorities: A text with readings in intergroup relations*, ed. by B. Eugene Griessman, pp. 136–145. Hinsdale: Dryden Press.
———. 1978. 'Being female in a Muslim minority in China.' In *Women in the Muslim world*, ed. by Lois Beck and Nikki Keddie, pp. 651–673. Cambridge: Harvard University Press.
Plüss, Caroline. 1999. 'The social history of Hong Kong: A resource guide.' Occasional Paper No. 1. Hong Kong: The Jewish Historical Society.
———. 2000. 'Hong Kong's Muslim organisations: Creating and expressing collective identities', *China Perspectives*, 29, pp. 19–23.

Poynting, Scott. 2006. 'What caused the Cronulla riot?' *Race and Class*, 48, pp. 85–92.

Poynting, Scott, Greg Noble, and Paul Tabar. 2004. *Bin Laden in the suburbs: Criminalising the Arab other*. Sydney: Institute of Criminology.

Poynting, Scott, and Victoria Mason. 2006. '"Tolerance freedom, justice and peace"? Britain, Australia and anti-Muslim racism since 11 September 2001', *Journal of Intercultural Studies*, vol. 27, no. 4, pp. 365–391.

———. 2007. 'The resistible rise of Islamophobia: Anti-Muslim racism in the UK and Australia before 11 September 2001', *Journal of Sociology*, 43, pp. 61–86.

Räthzel, Nora. 2008. 'The local space of normality: Creating spaces of safety and spaces of danger introducing Altona and Bergedorf.' In *Finding the way home: Young people's stories of gender, ethnicity, class and places in Hamburg and London*, ed. by Nora Räthzel, pp. 41–72. Gottingen: V & R Unipress.

Said, Edward. 2003. *Orientalism*. New York: Vintage.

Sandercock, Leonie. 2003. *Cosmopolis II: Mongrel cities of the 21st century*. London: Continuum.

Sardar, Ziauddin. 2009. 'Spaces of hope: Interventions.' In *Muslim spaces of hope: Geographies of possibility in Britain and the West*, ed. by Richard Phillips, pp. 13–26. London: Zed Books.

Sassen, Saskia. 1994. *Cities in a world economy*. Thousand Oaks: Pine Forge Press.

Shweder, Richard A. 2000. 'What about "female genital mutilation"? And why understanding culture matters in the first place', *Daedalus*, 129, pp. 209–232.

Sim, Amy. 2009. 'The sexual economy of desire: Girlfriends, boyfriends and babies among Indonesian women migrants in Hong Kong', *Women's empowerment in Muslim contexts*. http://www.wemc.com.hk/web/publications.htm [accessed 21 July 2011].

Smith, Carl T. 2003. 'Wanchai: In search of an identity.' In *Hong Kong: A reader in social history*, ed. by David Faure, pp. 157–210. Oxford: Oxford University Press.

So, Fun-hang. 2010. 'Between two homes: On the lives and Identities of Pakistani women in Hong Kong and Pakistan.' A talk for Hong Kong Anthropological Society, Hong Kong Museum of History, 16 September 2010.

South China Morning Post. 1998. 'Local Muslims find their voice', *South China Morning Post*, 31 December. http://archive.scmp.com [accessed 11 November 2011].

———. 2006. 'Minority students will not get help to learn Chinese', *South China Morning Post*, 11 December. http://archive.scmp.com [accessed 13 December 2006].

Souza e Silva, Adriana de. 2006 'From cyber to hybrid: Mobile technologies as interfaces of hybrid spaces', *Space and Culture*, 9, pp. 261–278.

Stoller, Paul. 1997. *Sensuous scholarship*. Philadelphia: University of Philadelphia Press.

Tang, Kwong-leung, Hung Wong, and Chau-kiu Cheung. 2006. 'Study on the drug abuse situation among ethnic minorities in Hong Kong', *Hong Kong Government Narcotics Division*, June. http://www.nd.gov.hk/text/research/index.htm [accessed 23 February 2008].

Tomlinson, John. 1999. *Globalization and culture*. Cambridge: Polity Press.

Tsang, Phyllis. 2009. 'Anger over holding of inquest in Cantonese', *South China Morning Post*, 6 August. http://archive.scmp.com [accessed 13 March 2010].

———. 2011. 'Animated news of killing of Bin Laden "offensive"', *South China Morning Post*, 7 May. http://archive.scmp.com [accessed 3 August 2011].

Tsang, Phyllis, and Peter So. 2009. 'Brother appeals for fair probe of police shooting', *South China Morning Post*, 27 March. http://archive.scmp.com [accessed 13 March 2010].

Tu, Wei-ming. 1994. 'Cultural China: The periphery as the center.' In *The living tree*, ed. by Wei-ming Tu, pp. 1–34. Stanford: Stanford University Press.

———. 2001. '"Confucian" East Asia and modernity.' In *Identity, culture, and globalization*, ed. by Eliezer Ben-Rafael and Yitzak Sternberg, pp. 105–119. Leiden: Brill 2001.

Turner, Graeme. 2003. 'After hybridity: Muslim–Australians and the imagined community', *Continuum: Journal of Media and Cultural Studies*, 17, pp. 411–418.

Unison Hong Kong Limited. 2008. 'Response to the consultation paper on developing a supplementary guide to the Chinese language curriculum for non-Chinese speaking students', *Hong Kong Unison*, March. http://www.unison.org.hk/CSLresponseenglish.pdf [accessed 10 July 2008].

Vaid, K. N. 1972. *The overseas Indian community in Hong Kong*. Hong Kong: Centre of Asian Studies, the University Hong Kong.

Van Vliet, Willem. 1983. 'Exploring the fourth environment: An examination of the home range of city and suburban teenagers', *Environment and Behaviour*, 15, pp. 567–588.

Velayutham, Selvaraj. 2009. 'Everyday racism in Singapore.' In *Everyday multiculturalism*, ed. by Amanda Wise and Selvaraj Velayutham, pp. 255–273. London: Palgrave.

Wakeman, Frederick E. 1966. *Strangers at the gate: Social disorder in South China, 1839–1861*. Berkeley: University of California Press.

Wan, Cynthia. 2001. 'Saudis step in to Mecca date-palm battle', *South China Morning Post*, 14 April. http://archive.scmp.com [accessed 8 March 2004].

Watt, Paul, and Kevin Stenson. 1998. ' "It's a bit dodgy around there": Safety, danger, ethnicity and young people's use of public space.' In *Cool places: Geographies of youth cultures*, ed. by Tracey Skelton and Gill Valentine, pp. 249–265. London: Routledge.

Weiss, Anita M. 1991. 'South Asian Muslims in Hong Kong: Creation of a "Local Boy" identity', *Modern Asian Studies*, 25, pp. 417–453.

Welsh, Frank. 1993. *A History of Hong Kong*. London: Harper Collins.

Werbner, Pnina. 2002. *Imagined diasporas among Manchester Muslims*. Oxford: James Currey.
White, Barbara-Sue. 1994. *Turbans and traders: Hong Kong's Indian communities*. Hong Kong: Oxford University Press.
Williams, Linda. 1996. *HK Magazine*, 19 January.
Winkelmann, Marieke Jule. 2005. 'Informal links: A girl's madrasa and Tablighi Jamaat', *ISIM Review*, 17, pp. 46–47.
Wise, Amanda. 2005. 'Hope and belonging in a multicultural suburb', *Journal of Intercultural Studies*, 26, pp. 171–186.
Wise, Amanda, and Selvaraj Velayutham. 2009. 'Introduction: Multiculturalism and everyday life.' In *Everyday multiculturalism*, ed. by Amanda Wise and Selvaraj. Velayutham, pp. 1–17. London: Palgrave.
Wolfendale, Stuart. 2002. 'Afraid of the dark', *Standard*, 3 August.
Wong, Albert. 2008a. 'UN presses city over racism bill', *South China Morning Post*, 13 March. http://archive.scmp.com [accessed 13 March 2008].
———. 2008b. 'Lawmakers throw the future of anti-racial-bias bill into doubt', *South China Morning Post*, 10 July. http://archive.scmp.com [accessed 10 July 2008].
Wong, Eve F. Y., and Gordon Mathews. 1997. 'Foreign eyes on Hong Kong people: The view from Chungking Mansions', *The Hong Kong Anthropologist*, 10, pp. 32–37.
Wong, Martin, and Jennifer Lo. 2011. 'Bureau "is failing ethnic minorities"', *South China Morning Post*, 12 July. http://archive.scmp.com [accessed 16 July 2011].
Woodward, Mark Taylor. 1989. *Islam in Java: Normative piety and mysticism in the sultanate of Yogyakarta*. Tucson: University of Arizona Press.
Yang Memorial Methodist Social Service. 2000. *Educational needs and social adaptation of ethnic minority youth in Hong Kong*. Hong Kong: Yang Memorial Social Services.
———. 2002. *A study on outlets of the South Asian ethnic minority youth in Hong Kong*. Hong Kong: Yang Memorial Methodist Social Services.
Yiu, Enoch. 2011. 'No Islamic bonds despite 4-year push', *South China Morning Post*, 29 October. http://archive.scmp.com [accessed 20 November 2011].
Yon, Daniel. 2000. 'Urban portraits of identity: On the problem of knowing culture and identity in intercultural studies', *Journal of Intercultural Studies*, 21, pp. 143–157.
Yuval-Davis, Nira. 1997. 'Ethnicity, gender relations and multiculturalism.' In *debating cultural hybridity*, ed. by Pnina Werbner and Tariq Modood, pp. 193–208. London: Zed Books.
Zine, Jasmin. 2001. 'Muslim youth in Canadian schools: Education and the politics of religious identity', *Anthropology and Education Quarterly*, 32, pp. 399–423.
Zournazi, Mary. 2002. *Hope: New philosophies for change*. Annandale: Pluto Press.

Index

9/11, 13–15, 36, 37–38, 41, 61, 83, 152, 159, 162–163, 188

Abbas, Ackbar, 58, 65, 80
accents, 130
African Muslims, 32, 38, 44, 55–56, 61–64, 88, 89, 157, 175, 194
Al Qaida, 14
alcohol, 99, 107, 132, 155
ambiguity, 99, 142, 183; and halal food 97–113
America, 12–14, 37–38, 41–42, 55. 77, 130, 137, 166, 173, 180, 181, 191
Ang, Ien, 77, 99, 119, 129, 133, 142, 174
anti-racism law; *see* racism legislation
Apple Daily, 42
Arabic, 27, 32, 119, 129, 145, 180; learning 7, 70–71, 74, 76, 120, 143, 148
Arshad, Muhammad, 42
asylum seekers, 36, 53, 55, 61–63, 89, 92, 130, 154
Australia, 11, 14, 37, 77, 119–120, 129, 137, 142, 151–152, 166–167, 196
authenticity, 71, 78, 148–149

Back, Les, 15, 167, 171, 173, 185
basic law, 10
basketball, 184–189
Bauman, Gerd, 83, 93
Bauman, Zygmunt, 162, 181
between cultures, 14
bin Laden, Osama, 42, 157, 181
Bohra Muslims, 31–32

Britain 10, 29, 60, 137, 154, 167, 187, 196
British Muslims, 12–16, 77, 78, 105, 120, 133, 144, 158, 159, 160, 166, 168, 173
British National Overseas passport, 36
Buddhism, 37, 110

Calcutta, 23, 55
Cameron Road, 21
Canada, 11, 42, 196–197
Cantonese; food; 7, 109; language, 27, 32, 39, 44–45, 48, 60, 63, 110–112, 117–118, 120, 122–124, 128–138, 140, 143, 146, 156, 182; people, 11; schooling, 75, 135–138, 198
Chaand Raat, 94
Chief Executive, 10–11
Chinese Muslim Cultural and Fraternal Association, 31, 144
Chinese Muslims, *see* Hui and Uyghur
Chinese naturalisation, 36
Christianity, 13, 47, 75, 80–81, 89, 91, 104, 110, 145, 159, 160
Chungking Express, 58, 132
Chungking Mansions, 9, 22, 28, 36, 51, 55–66, 102, 106, 107, 132, 153, 157, 175, 183
conversion to Islam, 37, 69, 143
cricket 6, 74, 137, 184–190
cultural capital, 110
cultural China, 142

Dae Jang Geum, 135–138, 177
Danish cartoon protests, 36, 40–42, 144

de Certeau, Michel, 16–17, 85, 100, 186; and language, 134, 142; and prefigurative politics 17, 195–196
dim sum, 100, 101, 110–111, 174
Direct Subsidy Scheme (DSS), 122–123, 126–127
discrimination; *see* racism
drugs, 56, 99
dupatta, *see* headscarves

education; higher, 44, 118, 125, 138; religious, 69–83; schooling, 6, 9, 12, 44, 61, 75–82, 87–90, 117–138, 145–146, 159, 177–184; vocational, 44, 118, 134, 138
Eid, 46, 60, 90, 92, 94
elevator, 62, 154–156, 165
English language, 11, 32, 48, 51, 60, 63, 78–79, 90, 97, 117–138; schooling, 9, 12, 44, 75, 117–138
Equal Opportunities Commission (EOC), 42, 127
ethnicity, 5, 17, 71, 74, 81, 85, 89, 95, 139–149, 151, 159, 167, 174, 178, 188; of participants, 199
everyday hybridity; 16–17, 192–197; defined 64–66; food, 100; identity, 139, 142, 146–147; and language, 130; and multiculturalism, 152, 165, 172; reified, 109; and urban space, 187–188
expatriate, 27–29, 75, 79, 122–123, 128–130, 198
extremism, 12–14, 37–38, 74, 188

face, 41, 140, 161
Facebook, 180–181
fasting, 19, 60, 70, 80, 90–93, 95, 133; *see also* Ramadan
Female Genital Mutilation (FGM), 191–193
fieldwork, 8–10
Filipinos, 89, 121, 160; Filipina foreign domestic workers, 39, 50, 124, 154

football, 15, 184–185
Forman, Ross, 65–66
freedom, 12, 19, 25, 38, 47, 50–51, 61, 78, 83, 151–169, 194, 196–197; expensive freedom, 165; religious practice, 85, 163; spatial freedom, 171, 173, 175–190

gender, 53, 70, 82, 162–164, 173–174, 176–190; difference, 10, 100, 105; roles, 50–51
Ghana, 52, 62, 91, 189
ghettoisation, 11, 120, 198
Gillette, Maris Boyd, 98, 111, 145–146, 148
Gladney, Dru, 65, 143, 145–146, 194
globalisation, 18, 39, 59, 130
Guangzhou, 23, 26
gweilo, 156

hafiz, 6, 72–73, 82
Hage, Ghassan, 100, 110, 151–152, 165
hajj, 8, 37, 85, 90
halal, 7–8, 28, 49, 55, 61, 66, 85, 97–113, 140, 146, 148, 158, 164, 166, 188, 194, 204; and Qur'an, 111
handover, 18, 33, 35–37, 43, 117, 123, 128
Happy Valley, 5, 25, 30, 101, 160, 183
Hari Lebaran, 90
Harris, Anita, 75, 94, 102, 172, 181
headscarves, 7, 76–77, 79, 89, 133, 180; and discrimination, 49, 157–158; and freedom, 163; and identity, 143–146, and Indonesian foreign domestic workers, 45–46, 49, 51; omission of, 49, 140, 148
Highmore, Ben, 80, 195
hijab; *see* headscarves
Hinduism, 160, 183
Ho, Wai-yip, 30, 35
homosexuality, 46, 47, 50, 51, 53
Hong Kong 10–11, 65; colonial period, 10, 16, 18, 23–24, 27, 29, 30, 32, 35,

42, 45, 117, 122–123, 129–130, 138, 176, 193
Hong Kong Certificate of Education (HKCE), 125
Hopkins, Peter, 13–15, 69, 83, 137, 188
Hui, 4, 7, 19, 76, 80–82, 193–194; and Danish cartoon protests, 40–41; and halal food, 98–99, 101–102, 105, 111; history 23, 30–31, 37; identity 139–149
hybridity; 11, 58, 75–76, 78; exotic, 132; and Hong Kong, 64, 174, 176; and language, 132, 134, 135; *see also* everyday hybridity

identity, 12–14, 16–17, 71, 78–80. 83, 95–98, 139–149, 151–152, 159, 160, 168, 172, 176, 182, 197
immigration, 38, 43, 61
Incorporated Trustees of the Islamic Community Fund, 25, 31
Indians, 4, 8, 23–28, 30–31, 36, 45. 55, 99; frictions with Pakistanis, 59–60, 71, 82; and language use, 120–121, 123–124; 132–134, 136, 167, 176, 183; local Indians, 24, 27, 31
Indonesians, 3, 4, 8, 89, 129, 131, 164; and food, 49, 99, 108, 111, 112; foreign domestic workers, 6–7, 18, 22, 35, 36, 39, 45–54, 74–75, 82, 90, 124, 177–178, 190, 193–194; prayers, 86
internet, 42, 46, 86, 141, 146, 161, 171, 179–181, 184
Iraq, 41
Islamic Finance, 198
Islamic Youth Association, 9, 30, 38, 143
Islamophobia, 37, 188

Jamia Masjid, *see* Shelley Street Mosque

Japanese; ethnicity, 161; occupation, 27–28; language, 132; video games, 182
Jardine Matheson, 23
Judaism, 12, 85, 104
Jumu'ah prayers, 5, 23, 88–89

kindergarten, 5, 30, 60, 123, 136
Korean Television; *see Dae Jang Geum*
Kowloon Mosque, 3, 5, 21, 22, 45, 51, 52, 102; history, 25, 28, 30; lessons at, 72; proximity to Chungking Mansions, 55; Ramadan, 95

languages, 19, 66, 117–138, 143; and culture, 118–121; *see also* Cantonese language, English language, Urdu
Law, Wing-sang, 65, 155, 186–187
Lefebvre, Henri, 16, 99, 171, 185
Lewis, Philip, 15, 73, 83, 120, 173
local boys, 24, 27, 29, 31
London, 13, 41, 154, 163, 173, 176

Macau, 23, 31
Mainland China, 4, 7, 10, 11, 56, 62, 65, 117, 144, 145
Mainland Chinese, 43–44, 94, 176; giving birth in Hong Kong, 44
marriage, 24, 27, 29, 40; outside of faith, 8, 59–60
Masjid Ammar, 30; *see also* Wanchai Mosque, mosques
Mathews, Gordon, 52, 55–59, 63, 132–133, 160, 194
McDonald's, 100–109
Mecca, 8, 37; *see hajj*
media, 12–15, 37, 42, 44, 65, 83, 96, 118, 128, 131, 135–137, 144; *see also* television, internet
mini skirt, 91, 133, 177
Mo Lo, 45
mobile phones, 5, 46, 102, 172, 180

Modood, Tariq, 77, 159, 196
mooncaakes, 110–111
mosques, 5, 74, 101, 173, 188; history of 29–32; Sheung Shui, 37; *see also* Kowloon Mosque, and Wanchai Mosque
MTR, 21–22, 25, 183
Muhammad (the prophet), 13, 40, 86, 144, 148
multiculturalism, 12–16, 78, 146, 152, 192; everyday multiculturalism, 172; and freedom, 162, 165; and food, 110, in Hong Kong, 33, 160, 176, 178, 187, 194; and language, 132
Museum of Coastal Defence, 25
music, 46, 135, 141, 179, 184, 194
Muslim youth, 12–13, 16, 38, 70, 74–75, 83, 87, 93, 102, 112, 118–137, 149, 153, 158, 161–163, 169, 172–174, 188–190, 194
Muslims; elderly, 37, 98, 198; as minorities 12–15, 95, 160; police officers, 18, 24–29, 33, 138; population in Hong Kong, 3–4, 35; prison guards, 25, 28–30, 35, 138; representations of; 13, 15, 98; sailors, 23–24, 27, 33, 39

Nepalese, 26, 44, 121, 129, 131, 168

Oi Kwan Road, 4–8, 30, 101
Opium Wars, 4, 18
Orientalism, 13, 143–144, 146
Osman Ramju Saddick Islamic Centre 5, 30, 51; *see also* Wanchai Mosque

Pakistanis, 6, 8, 18, 60, 72–75, 78–79, 81–82, 89–99, 104–105, 108, 118, 120–121, 130–133, 156, 158, 182–183, 185; Chungking Mansions, 55, 59; freedom, 162–163, 166, 175–190; identity, 103, 133–134, 139–149; language, 129–137; Pakistani Association, 31; and police force, 25, 29; racism, 44, 71, 88–89, 141, 156–159; relationships with Indonesians, 46, 51; security guards, 3–4, 35; stores, 100, 101, 108
pedestrian crossings, 152, 163, 165
People's Republic of China, 4, 35, 36; *see also* Mainland China
pilgrimage, *see hajj*
Pillsbury, Barbara, 97–98, 146
Plüss, Caroline, 24, 31
police, 44, 62, 132, 159, 167, 168
pork, 24, 49, 97–99, 102–104, 107, 110–112, 140, 148, 158; *see also* halal
post-colonial, 12, 16, 27, 35, 39, 65, 128, 197
prayers, 4, 6, 19, 23, 31, 46, 49, 50–52, 62–63, 70, 73–74, 78, 81, 85–95, 145, 160, 173, 180, 184; and cultural difference, 76, 98; *see also Jumu'ah* prayers
preteritions, 141–142, 147
Putonghua, 11, 117, 120, 122, 128–129
pyjamas, 5, 58

Qur'an; 7, 46, 81, 90, 96, 102, 180; and headscarf, 140; learning of, 6, 60, 69–76, 82, 120, 127, 143, 148; and parents, 81, 93; prayer times, 86

riots, 162, 196
Rushdie, Salman, 159–160
racism, 13, 15, 19, 61, 62, 149, 151–169, 183, 194, 196–197; between Muslims, 89; everyday racism, 153; legislation, 36, 43–45, 124; opposition to new mosque, 37; and religion 152–153; in UK, 60
Ramadan, 19, 46, 60, 70, 73, 80, 85, 90–96, 159

Sandercock, Leonie, 162, 171, 174
San-yuan-li incident, 26

SARS (Severe Acute Respiratory Syndrome), 36, 38–40, 48, 54
Saudi Arabia, 37, 50, 91
sex, 47, 50–51; sexual assault, 26, 47, 49, 183; sexuality, 91, 166; sexually transmitted diseases, 52; sex trade, 56; *see also* homosexuality
shalwar kameez, 157
Shelley Street Mosque, 8, 25, 30, 31, 45; *see also* mosques
Shia Muslims, 9
shopping malls, 58, 129, 135, 176–179, 182, 194
shroff, 26–27
Sikhs, 5, 26, 28, 29, 160, 167
Sim, Amy, 46, 49
skateboarding 5–6, 185
Somalia, 55, 62–63, 91, 131, 191
Sorrita, Tarini, 47
South Asians, 8–9, 120–122, 137, 141, 142, 153, 180, 183, 187, 189, 191; Chungking Mansions, 22, 56–57, 102; history in Hong Kong, 23, 25–26, 28, 29, 36, 39; schooling, 128–134; South Asian Muslims, 4, 31, 35; *see also* Indians, Pakistanis
space, 5–6, 28, 45–46, 50, 52, 56–58, 64, 66, 71, 74, 77, 79, 88, 152, 155, 156, 171–190, 194; appropriated, 173, 184–190; fourth space, 173, 176; gendered, 176–180, 184–190; urban, 162, 165, 175; virtual, 180–181
Stanley Mosque, 28, 30; *see also* mosques
stereotypes, 15, 98, 139, 142–143, 156, 159
Sunni Muslims, 9

Taliban, 37
television, 110, 129, 135–138, 141, 146–147, 160, 166, 179, 194
terrorism, 3, 13, 14, 37, 38, 159
triads, 26, 194

unemployment, 9, 39, 44
Unison Hong Kong, 43, 124
United Nations High Commissioner for Refugees (UNHCR), 63
United States, *see* America
Urdu, 27, 60, 120, 129–132, 136, 179, 183
Uyghur, 99, 102, 194

Van Vliet, Willem, 173, 176, 179–180
vegetarian, 103, 104, 106, 108, 111, 146
Velayutham, Selvaraj, 153, 155–156, 166
Victoria Park, 45–46, 50, 53, 90, 108, 147, 190

Wanchai Mosque, 5–6, 9, 30, 51, 71, 74, 80, 92, 101, 148, 185
Wanchai, 4, 47, 186–188; food, 7, 102, 105, 107; and Pakistanis, 141, 182
White, Barbara Sue, 23, 26–28, 121, 160
Whitfield Barracks, 25
Wise, Amanda, 152, 189
World War II, 27–30, 160

YouTube, 46, 47

zakat, 95

www.ingramcontent.com/pod-product-compliance
Ingram Content Group UK Ltd.
Pitfield, Milton Keynes, MK11 3LW, UK
UKHW022239230426
12048UKWH00018BA/1342